Fatal ...,

Who Killed the Minister and the Choir Singer?

Gerald Tomlinson

*To Beth,
Did Willie do it?
Gerald Tomlinson
9/18/99*

Lake Hopatcong, New Jersey

Library of Congress Catalog Card Number: 98-93594

Cover by Argus Graphics

If a copy of this book is not available at your local bookstore, you may order one by sending $19.95 to Home Run Press, 19 Harbor Drive, Lake Hopatcong, NJ 07849-1332. Please add $4.00 for shipping. New Jersey residents add 6% sales tax to price of book (total $19.95+1.20+4.00= $25.15).

Also by Gerald Tomlinson

On a Field of Black
The New Jersey Book of Lists (with Ronald A. Mayer)
Murdered in Jersey
New Jersey? What Exit?

Printed in the United States of America

ISBN 0-917125-09-6

Contents

Credits

Photos

Special Collections and University Archives, Rutgers University Libraries, pages 4 (top), 23, 36, 58, 67, 75, 92, 102, 112, 125, 131, 141, 147, 152, 166, 185, 196, 203, 213, 227, 235, 246, 255, 283, 290, 301, 315, 326, 336

Gerald Tomlinson, cover; pages 4 (bottom), 82, 372, 384, 396; also, courtesy Special Collections and University Archives, Rutgers University Libraries, page 359

Daily Home News (New Brunswick, 1922), page 54

Newark Public Library, New Jersey Division, page 6

Drawings

Jason Clary, page 24

Ronald A. Mayer, page 342

Acknowledgments

This book got its start when I was researching the Hall-Mills case for *Murdered in Jersey* (Rutgers University Press, 1994). It received further impetus from a conversation with Patrick J. Owens, Historian and Curator of the ARDEC Museum at Picatinny Arsenal, who gave me a copy of Damon Runyon's *Trials and Other Tribulations*, containing the famous reporter's complete coverage of the case. Several other people made helpful contributions along the way, among them Bernard Bush, Vincent DeNike, Hugh L. Dwelley, Patricia McGarry, Dr. Richard McKeon, Rev. Stephen M. Rozzelle, George Saloom, Janet Tomlinson, Matthew Tomlinson, and August Wistner III. The detailed Source Notes and Commentary at the back of the book indicate my great debt to the journalists of the 1920s, primarily those of the *New York Times*. I spent many hours reading and photocopying the relevant *Times'* articles and editorials at the Morris County Free Library in Whippany, New Jersey, and owe a debt of gratitude to MCFL's excellent staff. The book is dedicated to my wife, Alexis, who has always loved a good mystery—but especially the fictional puzzles unraveled by Goldy Bear, Arly Hanks, Sharon McCone, Kinsey Millhone, Anna Pigeon, and Stephanie Plum.

Scene of the murders. Reverend Edward W. Hall and his choir-singer mistress, Mrs. Eleanor Mills, were shot to death on this lonely lovers' lane off De Russey's Lane in Franklin Township, New Jersey, near New Brunswick. (photo 1922)

Church of St. John the Evangelist. Reverend Hall was the rector of this Protestant Episcopal Church on George Street, near the New Jersey College for Women, now Douglass College. (photo 1998)

Choir singer Eleanor Mills. This photograph was widely circulated at the time of the murders. Mrs. Mills was younger in this picture than in 1922 and had a different hair style. Her likeness bears only a slight resemblance to the better known portrait of her on page 23. (photo pre-1922)

Reverend Edward W. Hall. In this companion photo to the one of Eleanor Mills above, the minister looks younger and less portly than he was in 1922, and he is not wearing his eyeglasses. An artist's rendition of his likely appearance at the time of his murder is shown on page 24. (photo pre-1922)

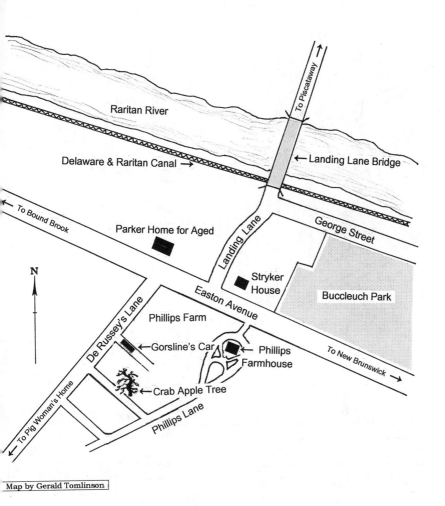

Raritan River

Delaware & Raritan Canal →

To Piscataway

← Landing Lane Bridge

To Bound Brook

Parker Home for Aged

Landing Lane

George Street

N

Stryker House

Buccleuch Park

Easton Avenue

De Russey's Lane

Phillips Farm

Gorsline's Car

Phillips Farmhouse

To New Brunswick →

To Pig Woman's Home

Crab Apple Tree

Phillips Lane

Map by Gerald Tomlinson

Scene of Hall-Mills Murders

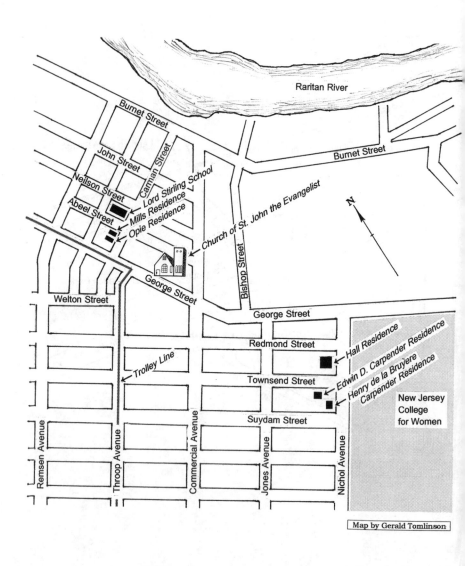

Raritan River

Burnet Street

John Street

Carman Street

Neilson Street

Lord Stirling School

Abeel Street

Mills Residence

Opie Residence

Church of St. John the Evangelist

Burnet Street

Bishop Street

N

Welton Street

George Street

George Street

Redmond Street

Hall Residence

Trolley Line

Townsend Street

Edwin D. Carpender Residence

Henry de la Bruyère Carpender Residence

Suydam Street

New Jersey College for Women

Remsen Avenue

Throop Avenue

Commercial Avenue

Jones Avenue

Nichol Avenue

Map by Gerald Tomlinson

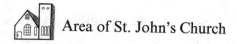 Area of St. John's Church

Preface

"This case is a cinch."

So said Ferdinand David, a detective in the Middlesex County prosecutor's office, four days after the discovery of two corpses laid out side by side not far from an unoccupied farmhouse in central New Jersey. The victims were the Reverend Edward Wheeler Hall, a prominent Episcopal minister, and Eleanor Reinhardt Mills, a choir singer in his church. Shot to death, they lay neatly dressed under a crab apple tree just off a secluded lane near New Brunswick.

Detective Ferd David, who had begun his remarks with cheery optimism, ended on a note of regret, admitting that "we have not enough evidence on which to act."[1]

He was right. There was not enough evidence to make a case against anyone. And, despite a flurry of indictments and a sensational trial four years later, there never would be enough evidence.

The Hall-Mills case, one of America's classic crimes, burst into public view in newspaper accounts beginning on Saturday, September 16, 1922. From that day forward, day after day, week after week, bold headlines told the story of an ardent, illicit relationship between the two victims, enlivened by the presence of steamy love letters and the rector's indiscreet diary. The long-standing affair, known to many who attended Reverend Hall's church in New Brunswick, was cut short on the night of September 14, 1922, by four .32-caliber bullets, one bullet aimed at the rector, three at the choir singer. About half an hour later someone slashed the woman's throat from ear to ear.

The scandalous double homicide would become, if not quite the crime of the century, as many journalists of the day supposed, quite possibly the crime of the decade, as Frederick Lewis Allen called it in *Only Yesterday,* his lively book about the Roaring Twenties.[2]

To this day the Hall-Mills murder case remains an unsolved mystery.

Yet Ferd David was probably right. A few days after he made his frank but rueful comment, the *New York Times* editorialized along the same lines: "The mystery, at least for those who view it from a distance and with no responsibility for its solution, looks like one that should have presented few difficulties and those not insuperable."[3]

Insuperable they proved to be, however, at least for the next few years. No indictments were returned in 1922. A grand jury heard testimony that year in Somerset County, where the murders had occurred, just over the county line from Middlesex. But the jury, after five days of testimony, refused to indict anyone—not the "woman in gray," nor the "bushy-haired man," nor the "Iago in the vestry," nor anyone else who had figured prominently in newspaper accounts up to that point.

No significant progress was made in 1923, or 1924, or 1925. The case disappeared from the news, apparently interred forever like the straying minister and his love-struck mistress. In New Brunswick the woman in gray, the bushy-haired man, and the Iago in the vestry, whose identities were generally known, went on with their lives as if nothing much had happened.

Then in 1926 Philip A. Payne, managing editor of the New

York *Daily Mirror,* broke a story that put Hall-Mills back on the front pages of newspapers across the United States. Amid a barrage of tabloid-driven publicity, the governor of New Jersey named a new special prosecutor for the old crime. The prosecutor was Alexander Simpson, a fiery little state senator from Hudson County.

One of the men Simpson chose to help him, detective John J. Underwood, would soon complain, justly and with a trace of bitterness, that a "proper investigation four years ago would have solved the so-called murder mystery in twenty-four hours."[4]

Detective Underwood and his Hudson County team worked diligently in 1926 to follow the trail of the Hall-Mills murders, by then camouflaged by time and protective self-interest. After much legwork, press coverage, and talk of surprise witnesses, a trio of well-to-do and already highly visible suspects, two from New Brunswick, one from Lavallette, were arrested and put on trial for murder.

They were the rector's widow, Mrs. Frances Noel Stevens Hall, and her two older brothers, the eccentric William ("Willie") Stevens, a bachelor who lived in the Hall household, and sportsman Henry Stevens, a convivial fellow who spent much of his time fishing at the Jersey shore. A fourth relative, Henry de la Bruyère Carpender, a stockbroker cousin and a neighbor of the Halls, was also charged, arrested, and jailed. He would be tried later, Simpson promised.

A sensational month-long trial featured the prosecution's star witness, Jane Gibson, a bedridden Fury known as the Pig Woman, who claimed, in vivid and ever-changing detail, to have witnessed the murders. All three defendants were found not guilty. The jury rejected Mrs. Gibson's graphic tale of what she had seen and heard on that fateful night while riding her mule Jenny. None of the prosecution's surprise witnesses amounted to much.

As the trial unfolded, more than two hundred reporters, including Damon Runyon, Dorothy Dix, Billy Sunday, and Louella Parsons, not to mention the husband and daughter of the murdered choir singer, relayed the spicy details from the white courthouse in Somerville. No other continuing story of the day came close to matching Hall-Mills in volume of coverage. Roughly twelve million words went out over the wires during the twenty-four days the court was in session.

The acquittal of all three defendants, following a long parade of witnesses, seemed to surprise no one except the special prosecutor.

It was over in time for Christmas 1926—the three Stevens family members freed, Simpson fuming at the jury of "twelve trees," the defense impassive though a bit annoyed by the tactics of the prosecution, the culprits unpunished. The indictment against Henry Carpender was *nolle prossed,* which is to say dismissed.[5]

Hall-Mills has come to be seen as the prototype of a bungled case. The investigation in 1922 was haphazard and inept, the investigation in 1926 aggressive but inconclusive. A lack of useful physical evidence led to near-total reliance on the fancied recollections of the Pig Woman. The trial, a press extravaganza, pitted Senator Simpson, a brash, shoot-from-the-hip prosecutor, against a coolly competent seven-lawyer "Million Dollar Defense" team led by Robert H. McCarter, former attorney general of New Jersey, and Clarence Case, future chief justice of the Supreme Court of New Jersey.

By 1926—indeed, by late 1922—justice never had much of a

chance. The physical evidence was irretrievably lost or com-promised, and the incentives for people to conceal information, or lie outright, grew ever greater, extending well beyond the original circle of those who knew for sure what had happened on that dark September night.

This book attempts to sort out the known facts of the case, examine the physical and testimonial evidence, and assess the truthfulness of the key witnesses. It pays special attention to the earliest clues, those uncovered in September and October 1922, before every crackpot in Christendom seemed to come forward to claim an intimate knowledge of the crime near De Russey's Lane. The book offers a reasoned solution to the long-standing Hall-Mills mystery, one that differs from the three main solutions offered so far.

The first of these prior solutions is that of Wilbur A. Mott, the special prosecutor in 1922. Mott named no names, nor did the somewhat circumspect press of that pre-tell-all era, but the three suspects he sought to indict could easily be identified by any newspaper reader who followed the case.

The second proposed solution was put forward by Alex-ander Simpson, the special prosecutor in 1926. Simpson's (and the Pig Woman's) three-Stevenses-and-a-Carpender scenario brought indictments of two of the three earlier suspects. But the trial brought no convictions.

The third solution is that of William M. Kunstler, a radical attorney, whose theory appears in his 1964 book, *The Minister and the Choir Singer.* Kunstler argues that the Ku Klux Klan did it. The KKK did plague New Jersey in the 1920s. But just as a Somerset County trial jury rejected prosecutor Simpson's scenario in 1926, so have most critics dismissed Kunstler's solution as unlikely.[6]

Several other theories of the crime have been proposed from time to time. In general, they suffer from the familiar flaw of detective fiction that author Wendy Kaminer pointed out in a recent book review; their writers tend to "discard the most plausible explanations and adopt the most improbable ones for the mysteries they encounter."[7] Nevertheless, these theories too are analyzed.

While the Hall-Mills case will never be definitively solved, the innocent and guilty alike having long since gone to their graves, the core enigma—who killed the minister and the choir singer?—seems to have a logical and not very arcane explanation, one that Jane Gibson's creative imagination managed to thwart. The Pig Woman, elevated to stardom in the absence of hard evidence, seized the initiative and derailed what would otherwise have been a weak circumstantial case.

It is unlikely there was any murderous conspiracy or brilliantly devious plan on the night of September 14, 1922. Simpson himself never thought there was, even though his rhetoric often implied it. This was not a crime dreamed up by Agatha Christie. The Hall-Mills affair was a case of infidelity, sudden vengeance, and subsequent deceit. The murders were impulsive and aberrant. Although money, status, legal expertise, and possibly bribery and intimidation played a part in the failure to gain convictions, the main cause of failure was the incompetence of the early investigation.

Despite a cast of colorful and wily characters, the story has no heroes, except in a strictly legal sense. The defendants' costly team of trial lawyers proved well worth their fees. So too did Mrs. Hall's personal attorney, Timothy N. Pfeiffer, who, in 1922 and again in 1926, protected his client and her eccentric brother with shrewd professionalism.

Many specific details of the case remain unclear. There are some loose ends. Yet in the sense that Ferd David meant his remark back at the beginning of the investigation, the basic outline of the crime, if not glaringly obvious, was almost certainly closer to the one that two county prosecutors and two special prosecutors pursued futilely with an unreliable eyewitness than it was to Kunstler's well-argued but unconvincing Ku Klux Klan solution.

1 Tableau in Lovers' Lane

Everyone who saw or heard about the two corpses under the crab apple tree was struck by the bizarre tableau. This was no caught-in-the-bedroom muddle of obscenely sprawled corpses and mussed-up clothing. No. This was a morbid exhibit contrived for effect. Such phrases as *neatly arranged, tenderly laid out,* and *strangely choreographed* appear in the published descriptions of the crime scene.[1]

The two victims were surprised at night in a lovers' lane. There is no doubt about that. But their pose—a pose created after the murders by the killer or an accomplice—was peaceful, peculiar, and puzzling. It suggested that the victims, a well-known minister and a choir singer in his church, were lovers, but it did so in an oddly formal way. The dead man's right hand cradled the woman's shoulder and neck. The woman's left hand rested on her lover's right knee.

Someone had thought to close the minister's eyes.

Both bodies lay on their backs in ankle-high grass on dry ground under a crab apple tree, their feet pointing toward the tree. Side by side in death, they were neatly dressed, as if for burial, the minister in a dark gray suit and polished though slightly scuffed black shoes, a white Panama hat with a broad black band partially covering his face. The eyeglasses he wore in life were in place, unbroken. They appeared spotted, with either fly specks or blood.

There were no signs of a struggle.[2]

The identity of the minister was never in doubt. A leather

card case on the ground between the bodies contained a driver's license, an automobile registration, and membership cards in the YMCA and Masons. A calling card, flecked with either fly droppings or blood, stood propped against his left foot. Each of these items identified the bearer as the Reverend Edward Wheeler Hall, forty-one, rector of the Protestant Episcopal Church of St. John the Evangelist in New Brunswick.[3]

A short, handsome man, though overweight and balding, he had been shot once in the head.

The choir singer wore a simple blue dress with red polka dots. Her blue velvet hat lay beside her body. She had on well-worn brown oxford shoes and stockings of black silk. A brown silk scarf, wrapped loosely around her lower neck, concealed the full extent of a ghastly wound. The scarf, soaked with blood, had a pocket that held a small lambs' wool powder puff and a handkerchief.[4]

Someone had slashed the woman's throat, "a great open gash showing on the right side under the chin," according to a front-page article in the New Brunswick *Daily Home News* that appeared on the afternoon the bodies were discovered. A reporter for the newspaper, Albert J. Cardinal, was one of the first to reach the murder scene, and, seizing the opportunity, got the scoop of a lifetime.[5]

Gruesome as the throat-slashing was, deep and ear to ear, it did not cause the woman's death. Like the minister, she had been fatally shot, evidently with a .32 caliber weapon. The killer had fired at her head not once, however, but three times. Reporter Cardinal wrote that the bullet wounds were "under the right eye, over the right temple, and over the right ear." He thought a fourth shot had struck her in the back of the head, but that proved to be an exit wound.

The throat-cutting, which occurred after the shooting, was a final touch, a statement of some sort. Its symbolic meaning, if symbolism was intended, would be a subject of speculation in the days and years ahead. The woman's eyes remained wide open, staring sightlessly at the sky.

The dead woman could not be identified as promptly as the minister. Her gold wedding band bore no engraving, and she carried no personal cards or papers. But the arrival of another reporter from the *Daily Home News,* Frank M. Deiner, ended the mystery of her identity. Deiner knew her name. She was Mrs. Eleanor Reinhardt Mills, thirty-four, a soprano in the choir of St. John's church. Eleanor, petite and attractive, was the wife of James Francis Mills, a school janitor and church sexton. She was the mother of two school-age children, Charlotte and Daniel.[6]

As a *New York Times* headline writer observed wryly in the first of countless articles on the case, the murdered rector and his choir-singer mistress "Had Long Been Friends." Indeed they had. Gossip about their ongoing affair had been common in New Brunswick for quite a while, as long as four years, some said. Now a mysterious double murder had ended their relationship.

The *Daily Home News* of September 16, 1922, reported that the two bodies were "scarcely decomposed and had hardly changed color." Another observer disagreed, saying that the bodies were "in bad shape."[7] They had lain on the grass near the crab apple tree for about thirty-six hours, and maggots filled the gaping wound in Eleanor Mills' throat.

As if the unusual arrangement of the bodies were not enough to raise eyebrows, the investigators at the scene found a collection of passionate love letters from Eleanor to the minister. Who brought these letters to the murder site would be a matter of conjecture throughout the case. There was also a question of whether the letters were stacked between the bodies, as one investigator said, or scattered about at the time the bodies were first discovered. Cardinal, who reached the scene soon after the first police officers, reported that the letters "lay about in confusion as though the bodies had been searched." No one, then or later, admitted disturbing the bodies or scattering the letters.

But who could say for sure that the corpses had not been searched, robbed, moved or otherwise interfered with even before any law enforcement official saw them? The same held true for the letters. They had lain on the ground for a full day and a half, including all of Friday night, which is generally a busy time in lovers' lanes. Later it would be suggested that the man who found the bodies, Raymond Schneider, a young ne'er-do-well, had searched them for valuables and perhaps stolen some money and a Chesterfield gold watch from the dead minister.[8]

Whatever may have transpired during those lost thirty-six hours, the love letters were still there when the first officers arrived. And more piquant than their placement was their content, which left no doubt about the nature of the Hall-Mills liaison. Scrawled in pencil on cheap, lined stationery in Mrs. Mills' childish handwriting, they breathed her love for the minister "in white hot language," as journalist Damon Runyon noted at the trial, adding that it "seemed a little hoity-toity for the wife of a church sexton and school janitor. The lady must have read some warm literature to get some of the phrases."[9]

Quotes from Eleanor Mills' letters began appearing in the

press immediately, and the entire text of the letters became public within a month. Here is a sampling:

• "I know there are girls with more shapely bodies, but I do not care what they have. I have the greatest of all blessings, a noble man, deep, true, and eternal love."

• "Never will I say you want my body rather than me—what I really am. I know that if you love me you will long and ache for my body."

• "I could fling my arms about you and pour kisses on my babykins' head and face."

• "Honey, do you suppose we could start early in the morning and not return until the following night late—say ten or eleven? Darling, do you yearn for it as I do?"

• "I am on my knees, darling, looking up at my noble man, worshipping, adoring."

• "You are a true priest—born for it. . . . I am merely your physical inspiration."

• "Oh, honey, I am fiery today. Burning, flaming love."[10]

All the elements needed for a journalistic feeding frenzy were in place. On Sunday, September 17, 1922, the *New York Times* ran the story of the murders on page one, devoting fifty-five column inches to it. The die was cast. Hall-Mills would remain a headline event for months—and then resurface as an even bigger story four years later.

2 Characters and Setting

The public interest generated by the murders of Reverend Hall and Mrs. Mills brought a legion of journalists to central New Jersey. At the beginning, in late September 1922, the press focused primarily on developments in and around New Brunswick, the county seat of Middlesex County, where the victims lived. As time passed, the focus shifted to adjoining Somerset County, where the victims died. The trial of the three defendants took place in Somerville, the county seat of Somerset County, in November and early December of 1926. It was a highly publicized event that riveted the attention of the nation.

In two separate investigations, four years apart, the Hall-Mills case brought forth a bewildering array of characters, rather like the multitude of characters in a Russian novel. And these men and women of New Jersey truly *were* characters, as more than one reporter pointed out. To help readers keep them straight, William M. Kunstler, in his book *The Minister and the Choir Singer* added a *Dramatis Personae* list at the end, consisting of one hundred and thirty-eight names.[1]

The index of *Fatal Tryst* serves the same purpose, but this chapter begins with a few thumbnail sketches to get the story started. Although the characters, even the major characters, cannot be introduced all at once, it seems worthwhile to take a preliminary look at some of the key players, and then to explore briefly the local setting in which the events unfolded.

Edward Wheeler Hall, the slain rector of the Protestant Episcopal Church of St. John the Evangelist, was a native of Brooklyn, New York. He had served as St. John's rector for thirteen years, coming there in 1909 after two years as an assistant pastor at St. Mark's Episcopal Church in Basking Ridge, New Jersey. He married Frances Noel Stevens, a well-to-do older parishioner in 1911. Photographs of Reverend Hall are rare—his widow would release none to the press after his murder—and descriptions of him vary. Journalists of the day generally portrayed him as a handsome man, and he certainly was in his youth. By the age of forty-one, however, he had put on considerable weight and had a rapidly receding hairline.[2]

Reverend Hall's slain mistress, Eleanor Reinhardt Mills, was a housewife and a choir singer at St. John's church. In 1905, when she was seventeen years old, she had married James Mills, a man then in his late twenties. Eleanor was bright and assertive, with vaulting dreams and a passionate soul. She had lived a frugal, circumscribed life with her drab husband. She was the mother of Charlotte, a sixteen-year-old high school student "of the modern type," as one reporter put it, and Daniel, who was twelve. Eleanor's affair with Reverend Hall had gone on for several years prior to the murders and had become the subject of considerable local and church gossip. Thirty-four years old when she died, the choir singer was small, slender, and pretty.

With a married woman and a married man cheating on their spouses, it would be wondrous indeed if the two prime suspects were not those selfsame spouses. And they were.

Frances Noel Stevens Hall, the widow of the slain rector was born in Aiken, South Carolina, but came to New Jersey as an infant. By 1922 she was a person of some standing in New Brunswick society, her forebears having accumulated a sizable fortune from their association with the Johnson & Johnson medical supply company. For many years before her marriage to Edward W. Hall she had lived with her mother and an older

Eleanor Reinhardt Mills. The wife of a school janitor and church sexton, she had vaulting dreams about her future life as the wife of Reverend Hall. The dreams were shattered by three .32-caliber bullets to the head. (photo pre-1922)

Edward Wheeler Hall. The rector of the Church of St. John the Evangelist, he had carried on a none-too-secret affair with Mrs. Eleanor Mills for at least four years prior to the double murder. (original sketch based on several photos)

brother in the Stevens family mansion at 23 Nichol Avenue. Mrs. Hall, an intensely private person, was thirty-seven years old when she married the then thirty-year-old rector. Their marriage was placid on the surface. When the circumstances of the double homicide cast suspicion on her, the gray-haired widow asked plaintively, "Doesn't a person's past count for anything? I have been something of a figure in this community. I have been honest and honorable. Why should I not be believed?"[3]

The husband of the slain choir singer, James Mills, was forty-five years old at the time of the murders. He worked as the acting sexton at St. John's church and as a full-time assistant janitor at the Lord Stirling School, a public elementary school. He lived within easy walking distance of both jobs. A weak-willed, hardworking man of limited intelligence, he seemed to regard his wife mainly as his housekeeper, a helpmate whose silly romantic notions and bookish inclinations distracted her from her natural role. The love letters, he suggested, were nothing but an innocent pastime of hers. For quite a while after the murders Jim Mills steadfastly, and untruthfully, claimed ignorance of the affair between his wife and the minister. "I cannot believe he [Reverend Hall] would do wrong," Jim said soon after the bodies were discovered under the crab apple tree. "He was too good a friend of mine."[4]

Two others who emerged as suspects were the brothers of Mrs. Hall. One was impulsive and eccentric, the other informal and down-to-earth.

William Stevens, always called Willie, was the younger of Mrs. Hall's two brothers. Fifty years old at the time of the murders, Willie suffered from some sort of mental disorder that kept him from holding a job or being able to manage his own

finances. His physician, Dr. Lawrence Runyon, termed him
"not absolutely normal." Willie lived with his parents, and,
after their deaths, with his sister Frances. Before and after her
marriage, he remained with her at the mansion on Nichol Avenue. An ungainly man, about five-feet-ten, dark-complex-
ioned, he wore thick-lensed eyeglasses and sported a heavy walrus mustache. Willie spent much of his time at a local firehouse, acting out his lifelong ambition to be a real fireman, but
mostly playing cards, polishing brass, and running errands.
There were striking contradictions in his character. In 1926 the
special prosecutor called him "a sort of genius in a way," and
Dr. Runyon agreed. Despite Willie's generally sunny disposi-
tion, his temper could be explosive.[5]

A devoted fisherman and retired exhibition marksman,
Henry Stevens, the older of the two Stevens brothers, was fifty-
two at the time of the crime. He owned a home in Lavallette on
the Jersey Shore, fifty miles from New Brunswick, where he
claimed to have been out fishing when the murders occurred.
Henry and his sister Frances were not especially close. He did
not attend her wedding in 1911, and after their mother's death
in 1919, he seldom visited the Halls in New Brunswick. He
became a suspect in the killings for two main reasons. First, the
purported eyewitness to the crime, Jane Gibson, declared that
she heard the woman in gray near the crab apple tree call out,
"Oh, Henry!" Second, the prosecution assumed it would take
an expert shot to place three closely spaced bullets in Mrs.
Mills' head on that dark September night.[6]

There might never have been indictments or a trial in the
Hall-Mills case if there had not been a person who claimed to
be an eyewitness. And what a person she was.

Both special prosecutors, in 1922 and 1926, relied heavily on the supposed eyewitness testimony of Jane Gibson, a quirky and often belligerent farm owner from Middlebush, near New Brunswick, who claimed she was out riding her mule Jenny on the night of the murders. While chasing after corn thieves, the fiftyish Mrs. Gibson declared, she accidentally happened upon the murders in progress. Jane Gibson, née Eisleitner, was legally Mrs. Easton since she was married to one William H. Easton of the same Middlebush address. She became known worldwide as "the Pig Woman" when journalists fastened upon the fact that she raised pigs (among other domestic animals) on her farm. The Pig Woman's story changed with nearly every telling, becoming more detailed and positive with each recitation.[7]

If the prosecution needed a strong-willed eyewitness, they also needed—given the paucity of the evidence—a devil-may-care prosecutor, and in 1926 they got him in the person of Alexander Simpson.

In 1922 a special prosecutor, Wilbur A. Mott of Essex County, an esteemed attorney nearing retirement, had been unable to obtain grand jury indictments. Four years later, after a succession of accusatory stories in the New York *Daily Mirror* led to renewed interest in the case, the governor of New Jersey named a second special prosecutor, the combative and histrionic Alexander Simpson of Hudson County, to look into the matter. Simpson, a state senator and assistant attorney general, stood just five feet tall but was every inch a fighter, a scrappy little product of Jersey City's First Ward. According to the obituary in the *New York Times*, Simpson's life was "marked with a predilection for lost legal causes," usually as a defense attorney. In the Hall-Mills case he showed he could also lose as a prosecutor.[8]

But the best prosecuting attorney in the East would have

been hard-pressed to make headway against the gilt-edged defense team hired by Mrs. Hall and her brothers. The press aptly called it the Million Dollar Defense, and the accused got the high-quality representation they paid for.

Mrs. Hall's personal attorney was Timothy Newell Pfeiffer, a graduate of Princeton University, where he starred on the football team, and Harvard Law School. Thirty-five years old at the time of the murders, Pfeiffer was serving as special deputy attorney general of New York State. Ten days after the bodies were discovered, Mrs. Hall engaged him to represent her and her brother Willie. It was a wise move. Although he was not one of the active courtroom lawyers at the trial, the tall, gaunt Pfeiffer nevertheless advised her regularly and well in 1922 and 1926. A partner for more than forty years in Milbank, Tweed, Hadley and McCloy, one of New York City's most prestigious law firms, Timothy Pfeiffer died in 1971, the last survivor of the key figures in the Hall-Mills case.[9]

Mrs. Hall's Million Dollar Defense team at the 1926 trial was led by one of New Jersey's great attorneys, Robert H. McCarter of Rumson. Sixty-three years old at the time of the trial, McCarter had once, long ago, been attorney general of New Jersey. Best known as a corporation lawyer and a founder of Newark's noted McCarter & English law firm, he occasionally defended clients in high-profile criminal cases. "Of about medium height . . . bulldoggy-built, chunky, red of jowl and bald of bean," as Damon Runyon described him, McCarter, assisted by state senator Clarence E. Case and other defense attorneys, easily demolished the flimsy case against Mrs. Hall and her two brothers.[10]

The Hall-Mills story, peopled with these and other distinctive characters, is also is a tale of two New Jersey cities, New

Brunswick and Somerville, in the Roaring Twenties. The trial, which was breathlessly reported by the so-called sob sisters of the press and more soberly reported by serious journalists, took place in Somerville, because the murders were committed just over the Middlesex County line in Franklin Township, Somerset County. But since both the victims and their alleged killers, except for Henry Stevens, lived in New Brunswick, the Middlesex County seat, that bustling city and its environs dominate the pretrial story.

Two distinct locales in and about New Brunswick figured in the drama. The first was the abandoned Phillips farm, where the murders occurred. The farm, cleared by developers almost immediately after the crime, and now studded with neat, single-family homes, lay across Easton Avenue from New Brunswick's Buccleuch Park and near the southern end of the Landing Lane Bridge. The Landing Lane Bridge, still in use, parallels the larger and newer bridge that today carries Route 18 across the Raritan River.

The second New Brunswick locale was about two miles away, well past the center of town in the opposite direction. This was where the Hall and the Mills families lived and where the Church of St. John the Evangelist stood. It was near the eastern end of George Street, in the vicinity of Douglass College, which in those days was called the New Jersey College for Women. Of the ten people sketched in this chapter, the first five—the members of the Hall and Mills families—lived in two starkly contrasting houses, one stately, the other modest, within a few blocks of each other.

An important transportation link between these two main locales in the case, the scene of the murders and the site of the church, was New Brunswick's trolley line. The trolley ran north

on Throop Avenue to George Street, northwest along George
Street to downtown New Brunswick, and then west along
Easton Avenue to Buccleuch Park. The Mills family had no
automobile, and Eleanor's journey to her fatal rendezvous
involved a ride on the trolley.

New Brunswick in the 1920s was a small, dynamic industrial
and college city of some 33,000 people. The business center of
town in those days was the corner of George and Albany
Streets. George Street, the prosperous but narrow main
thoroughfare, was lined with fashionable shops occupying the
street level of two- and three-story brick and frame buildings.
Above the stores were the offices of dentists, lawyers, account-
ants, and other professional types. Several movie theaters on
or near George Street showed the silent films of the day. On the
night of the murders, the Rivoli Theatre, at the corner of
George and Albany Streets, was showing Tom Mix in *The
Fighting Streak*, while the State Theatre on Livingston Avenue
featured *Slim Shoulders*, starring Irene Castle.[11]

At Albany and French Streets and Easton Avenue stood a
large yellow brick building, Pennsylvania Station, which served
the main line of the Pennsylvania Railroad. The high embank-
ment carrying the railroad tracks through New Brunswick
divided the city into two parts. The division was merely geo-
graphic, not along class lines, although class distinctions played
a significant role in New Brunswick society—and in the Hall-
Mills affair.

The westbound trolley line veered away from George Street
just before the Queen's campus of Rutgers College came into
view. Rutgers, the eighth oldest institution of higher learning
in the nation, had been a vital part of New Brunswick life since
1766. Although the college played no part in the Hall-Mills

case, it inherited the physical evidence many years later. The special collections at Alexander Library have several large boxes filled with exhibits from the trial, and a researcher who wants to see the Panama hat worn on the fatal night by the rector, or the silk stockings worn by the choir singer, or pages from the Pig Woman's calendar-diary can find them in one of these storage boxes.

New Brunswick's first white settlers were English, and many of the street names reflect that heritage. Dutch settlers from Albany began arriving in 1730. The Dutch Reformed Church, which took the lead in establishing Queen's College (Rutgers), became a strong presence in the community. Much more recently, Hungarians began to settle in large numbers, creating a sizable ethnic minority in the city. In the 1920s many Hungarians worked in the city's factories—Johnson & Johnson was a large employer—or ran open fruit and vegetable stands in the Hungarian section of town, near the western end of Albany and Somerset Streets.[12]

A passenger on the Easton Avenue trolley could ride as far as the near corner of Buccleuch Park. From there he or she had to proceed on foot to reach De Russey's Lane, taking a left turn onto the rural dirt road. By 1922 its days as a rustic country lane, and as a rendezvous for lovers, were severely numbered. Not long after the murders, real estate developers arrived in the area, and before the 1926 trial De Russey's Lane had become Franklin Boulevard, a paved main highway. By the time the case was finally prosecuted, the judge decided that the area around the Phillips farm had changed so drastically as to make a proposed jurors' trip to the crime scene useless.[13]

On the north side of Easton Avenue, just beyond the intersection with De Russey's Lane, stood the Francis G. Parker

Memorial Home for the Aged. This institution crops up very often in accounts of the Hall-Mills case. It was said that the minister and the choir singer sometimes claimed they were going out Easton Avenue to cheer up residents at the Parker Home when in truth they were heading that way for one of their tête-à-têtes.[14] Barbara Tough, a live-in servant in the Hall house, went to the Parker Home on the afternoon of the murders, supposedly to visit an elderly friend but perhaps, investigators suspected, to reconnoiter the lovers' meeting place for Mrs. Hall. It was from a house near the Parker Home that the phone call was made summoning police to the scene of the murders.

Both Reverend and Mrs. Hall drove automobiles. They owned two cars, a Case touring car and a Dodge sedan. Mrs. Hall at the wheel of her Dodge was a familiar figure in New Brunswick. She was an enthusiastic and confident motorist.[15] The rector could drive both automobiles, but on the night of the murders he drove neither. Instead he took the trolley to meet his lover, catching the next car after the one she was riding. Two witnesses, Mrs. Alameda Harkins and Mrs. Agnes Blust, testified that they saw Reverend Hall and Mrs. Mills hurrying separately on foot toward their mutual destination.[16]

This was a familiar route for the minister and the choir singer. From earlier assignations both knew their way to the secluded rendezvous. Others knew about their trips as well. A motorman and a conductor on the trolley said that groups of small boys would sometimes follow the minister and the choir singer, calling out to them.[17] In one of the letters found between their bodies, Mrs. Mills had written, "How friendly our Easton Avenue road seems to us."[18]

Whether the two met under the crab apple tree and stayed

there for a couple of hours, or whether they met nearby, perhaps at the deserted Phillips farmhouse, and reached the murder site later in the evening is unknown. The Phillips land, on which the tree stood and where the murders occurred, was no longer being farmed in 1922. The grounds were unkempt, the back yard strewn with rubbish. Curiously, though, the weather-beaten, two-story white frame Phillips house was fully furnished despite the fact that no one resided there, and investigators said it appeared to have been recently occupied.

The newspapers could not resist theorizing about this vacant but still used farmhouse. On September 20, 1922, a headline in the *New York Times* stated, "Former Phillips Home Believed to Have Been Trysting Place of Slain Couple." The next day the *Daily Home News* printed a photograph showing the living room of the Phillips farmhouse, dominated by what appears to be a huge plush sofa. But even given the obvious potential to titillate, this aspect of the scandal soon petered out. No one knows for sure what part, if any, the Phillips house played in the Hall-Mills love affair.[19]

The Phillips farm was apparently well known to both the rector and his wife. Early in the investigation the *New York Times* reported that "the Halls and the Stevenses and Carpenders, as related families, belonged at one time to a small gun club, which held trapshooting meets at the old Phillips farm." The same *Times* article quoted Edwin R. Carpender, a cousin of Mrs. Hall, as saying, "Before the beginning of the World War, we had a gun club and we made it a practice to go to the farm frequently with clay pigeons."[20] They could hardly have guessed it would become the minister's final destination.

Had Eleanor Mills and Edward Hall lived to return home,

they would have walked, together or separately, north on De Russey's Lane, then east on Easton Avenue to the trolley stop. They would have taken the trolley into the center of New Brunswick, back through the business district, continuing southeast along George Street. Their two-mile journey would most likely have ended at the Throop Avenue stop near the Protestant Episcopal Church of St. John the Evangelist. This handsome brick church stands today, as it did at the time, at 181-189 George Street.

In many ways the ivy-covered, nineteenth-century church at which the Reverend Hall preached is central to the Hall-Mills case. When special prosecutor Wilbur A. Mott, a resident of East Orange, took over the investigation in mid-October 1922, he was struck by the fact that nearly everyone connected with the mystery attended St. John's. A month later the *New York Times* echoed the thought, noting that "the authorities say the key to the solution is in the church."[21]

They were right, or partly right, but they could never find the key to unlock a plausible solution, one that would satisfy the press, the public, and, more importantly, a jury.

3   Mrs. Hall's Ordeal

No doubt the four people who were still living at 23 Nichol Avenue, New Brunswick, after the night of the murders had some engrossing stories to tell, but they never told them publicly, at least not fully.

The elegant two-story mansion, which occupied a large lot at the corner of Nichol Avenue and Redmond Street, belonged to Mrs. Frances Noel Stevens Hall, the widow of the Reverend Edward Wheeler Hall. In 1922 she had lived there for thirty-two years, twenty-one of them before her marriage, eleven after.[1]

As one of the two surviving spouses in the Hall-Mills affair, she was not only a grieving widow but also a suspect. She had a strong and obvious motive. The rector had been flagrantly cheating on her, and her persistent denials to the contrary, she could hardly have helped knowing it. She was a clergyman's wife betrayed, a proud woman humiliated.

Yet throughout her ordeal the sedate, gray-haired matron claimed to have been in love with her murdered husband until the day of his death, deeply in love with him, and unaware of any improprieties between "Mr. Hall," as she always called him, and the smitten choir singer.

She also claimed to have been at home when the murders were committed. She had gone out early on the morning of September 15, she said, taking her brother Willie with her. The two of them, on foot, looked in vain for her absent husband, first at the Church of St. John the Evangelist, then outside the darkened home of James and Eleanor Mills.[2]

Frances Noel Stevens Hall. The wife of the straying rector of St. John's, she was a murder suspect from the moment the bodies were discovered. But few who knew the decorous Mrs. Hall could imagine her as a killer. (photo 1926)

Frances Hall said she thought that robbery explained the slayings. The minister had been carrying fifty dollars or so, and it was gone. He had been wearing an antique gold watch, and it too was gone. As for the eleven love letters at the crime scene, she assumed they were forgeries. They could be nothing else. When it became increasingly obvious that robbery would not explain the crime that had taken Mr. Hall's life (the widow's remarks often failed to acknowledge that anyone else had been killed), she declared the whole thing unfathomable. Later she and her relatives would float a blackmail theory.

A week after the bodies were discovered, Frances Hall released a prepared statement to the press, describing her actions from Wednesday, September 13 (the day before the murders) through Saturday, September 16 (the day the corpses turned up). Her statement told a story of ordinary pursuits on Wednesday and Thursday, followed by increasing concern about the minister's whereabouts on Friday and early Saturday.[3]

This statement, which accounted for her actions on each of the four days, formed the outline of her alibi. It never changed in any fundamental way, although critical details were added later, and at the trial a few adjustments were made to bring her story into line with the then-known facts.

On Wednesday, September 13, the Halls, Edward and Frances, had gone on a picnic to Lake Hopatcong. This was an annual outing to honor two industrious women of the St. John's congregation, one of whom, not surprisingly, was Eleanor Mills. Eleanor's contributions to the choir and the ministry could hardly be doubted.

The other woman honored that day was Mrs. Addison Clark, of 134 Redmond Street, New Brunswick, a somewhat puzzling figure in the Hall-Mills case. Minnie Clark, rather tall, a bit stout, with a determined countenance, was active in St. John's Sunday School. Both women were in their mid-thirties, and both, though married, vied more or less openly for the attention of Reverend Hall. Sometimes the rivalry was almost schoolgirlish, as when they tried to see who would be the one to place flowers on the rector's desk in his church study.

The antagonism between Eleanor and Minnie did not surface at the picnic, but it was there. And it was nothing new. A passage in one of the undated letters found under the crab apple tree told of Eleanor's annoyance over Minnie's flowers. Mrs. Mills wrote: "She [Minnie Clark] provokes me so at times, and tonight, if her flowers are still there [Eleanor having lost that morning's run for the roses], I'll put them in the kitchen. Not that I am jealous of Minnie. Why, darling, there isn't anything to be jealous of. . . . Oh, well, poor Minnie! She is easily contented with crumbs, isn't she, dear?"[4]

If the picnic at Lake Hopatcong was one of Minnie's crumbs, it was also a crumb for the rector's mother, Mrs. Fanny B. Hall. The elder Mrs. Hall was a passenger in the Case touring car that carried the picnic party north for the day. Fanny Hall was not well-to-do, nor had she benefited much from her son's fortunate marriage. She lived in a single rented room in a boarding house, The Bayard, across from the courthouse in New Brunswick.[5]

The picnic at the lake was uneventful, according to Frances Hall, and the party returned to New Brunswick at about nine o'clock in the evening. But something did happen on the trip, something that may have played a part in the tragedy about to unfold.

Although Mrs. Hall gave it no thought, and it sounds trivial enough, Reverend Hall tore his trousers as he was climbing over a barbed wire fence near the lake. Frances immediately mended them for him. This wifely act of sewing up the rip in her husband's pants irritated Eleanor Mills, who saw it as an indication of her own status as an outsider. She longed to do such things for him herself.

The next day, her last day on earth, Eleanor sat down in her home on Carman Street to write a love letter to her "babykins." Like the other letters it was undated, unsigned, unaddressed, and unmailed. It referred to her love for the rector—and to the picnic the day before: "Do I love you too much? I know that now I could leave, yes, even your physical presence, and go into a convent. You are always in my mind and heart, but there I wouldn't see anyone touch you, call you 'Dear,' rub your tired body, sew your torn trousers. . .Yesterday [at Lake Hopatcong] I was happy, in a way, in the boat and in the water; but on the way home I was thinking hard. . .Oh, my darling babykins, what a muddle we are in! But I will be content. I will."[6]

Of all the love letters written by Eleanor Mills that came to light, this one has special importance because of the timing—it was written on the day she died—and because of its unknown readership. Eleanor probably took it to the rector's study in the church, to the secret hiding place for letters that he and she used for their correspondence. But, if so, how did it end up among the letters that were found under the crab apple tree? Did the minister carry it there, and, if so, why? Had someone else seen it, read it, perhaps even made off with it, and, if so, did Hall know that this had happened?

It may be, of course, that Eleanor carried this final letter with her to her rendezvous with the rector. But since she had not expected an imminent meeting with him, it seems more likely that sometime during the day she put the letter in the usual hiding place at St. John's. If so, someone other than the rector may have removed it—and may have used it, perhaps along with other unearthed letters, to help convince Frances Hall of the perilous state of her marriage. Or it may have been used by someone active in the church to emphasize the disgrace being visited upon St. John's by the rector's adulterous behavior. Or it may be, as the defense lawyers would contend, that the letters were never out of the hands of the minister and the choir singer until they were found scattered between their bodies.

Poor Mrs. Hall. Throughout this whole ordeal, she gave every appearance of being a refined, forbearing woman, the long-suffering wife of a minister. How had her life come to such a pass? Murder in a lovers' lane. Screaming headlines. Public scandal. Stoic though she was, or perhaps a fatalist, these must have been oppressive burdens for her to bear. A faithful wife, a forgiving wife, an honest and honorable woman, as she called herself—and then, suddenly, four pistol shots and disaster.

Frances Noel Stevens was born in Aiken, South Carolina, on January 13, 1874. Her parents were Francis Kirby Stevens and Mary Noel Carpender Stevens. She was the baby of the family. Two brothers, the unexceptional, outgoing Henry and the "not absolutely normal" William, preceded her into the world.[7] When Frances was about a month old, the Stevenses moved to New Brunswick. Her father died soon thereafter.

Mrs. Hall had several distinguished forbears, including John Neilson, born at Raritan Landing near New Brunswick in 1745. Neilson served as a member of the Continental Congress, a colonel of militia in the Revolutionary War, and a trustee of

Rutgers College for more than fifty years. Another ancestor, Charles J. Carpender, established, with Jacob J. Janeway, a successful wallpaper manufacturing company in New Brunswick. Eventually, the firm moved to a larger factory, selling its original four-story building on Neilson Street near the railroad tracks to Robert Wood Johnson. The old Janeway & Carpender factory became the first headquarters of Johnson & Johnson, the fast-growing surgical supply firm.[8]

Frances Stevens, heir to some of the profits realized by Johnson & Johnson, was well-to-do but not flashy or snobbish about it. Even when she was young, she "wore reserve and conservatism like a double petticoat."[9] Her looks were against her from the start. She would become wealthier as time went on, but prettier, never. At Mrs. Hall's first interview after the murders a reporter described her as having "a long, narrow face, a firm, tight-lipped mouth, a suggestion of hair on the upper lip, a broad chin. On her right temple, at the fringe of her hair, is a tiny, crescent-shaped scar. Although her hair has turned gray, her eyebrows, unusually prominent, remain black."[10]

On July 20, 1911, at the age of thirty-seven, she married for the first and only time. Her husband, the Reverend Edward Wheeler Hall, had been installed two years earlier as rector of the Protestant Episcopal Church of St. John the Evangelist, four blocks away from the Nichol Avenue home where Frances lived with her mother and her brother William. The marriage took place in the grandly spired Christ Church, at the corner of Church and Neilson Streets in downtown New Brunswick. Her mother gave her away.

The maid of honor was Sally Peters, a girlhood friend. Miss Peters, who never married, gained attention in New York City as an active suffragette, filling her days with social and political pursuits. She wrote vehement letters to the *Times,* one of them complaining about "dead animals which are allowed to lie about the streets for days at a time."[11] A woman of wealth and leisure, she resided in a fashionable section of Manhattan.

Immediately following the discovery of Reverend Hall's body Sally Peters hastened to join her lifelong friend in New Brunswick as a live-in confidante and spokesperson.

Frances Hall, a wintry gray matron with pince-nez, declined to be visibly embarrassed by the circumstances of Mr. Hall's demise. An unbending Victorian in an age of flappers, she did not believe for a moment (or so she said) that her husband of eleven years had been unfaithful. The love letters could not be genuine. She refused to look closely at them.

Indeed, her happiness was evident for all to see, she declared. She could point to the September 13 Lake Hopatcong trip as proof that she remained till the very end on good terms not only with her husband but also with her unacknowledged rivals, Eleanor Mills and Minnie Clark.

Frances Hall's prepared statement to the press concluded with these words: "Mr. Hall had no private enemies. [Naturally, there was much speculation about the significance, if any, of the word *private;* friends said it was simply an unfortunate use of the adjective.] I can form no conjecture as to the motive of the deed or the perpetrators. Our life together had been absolutely happy and sympathetic. My confidence in him is boundless and unshaken."[12]

So, apparently, was the confidence of the Episcopal clergy. Letters expressing condolence for the widow and an abiding trust in the slain clergyman poured in from Episcopal ministers around the country. On the Sunday after the discovery of the bodies, the Right Reverend Albion B. Knight of Trenton, Protestant Episcopal Bishop of New Jersey, delivered a sermon to the slain rector's congregation. In it he mentioned a recent visit to the Hall residence. "A more ideally Christian home I have never seen," he said. "From my knowledge of Hall, I could not bring myself to believe that there was anything unusual in the fact that he happened to be with one of his parishioners when the shooting occurred."[13]

A few weeks later another Episcopal bishop turned his attension to defending Mrs. Hall against "the irresponsible statemeats and cruelly unjust insinuations against Mrs. E. W. Hall which are being published. . . ." He was Paul Matthew, Bishop of New Jersey. In a long letter sent to the *New York Times* on November 6, he concluded, "I feel that the newspapers are quite right in publishing facts, but they ought to know their facts; and in this case, perhaps more widely published than any case in recent years, I feel that time and time again a cruel and bitter wrong has been committed against a high-minded Christian woman and one altogether innocent. I wish to enter an indiaant protest against it."[14]

The *Times* responded in an equally long editorial, pointing out that when the newspapers reported "accusations and imptetanies," they were not making them up but, rather, reporting statements made publicly "by the prosecuting officials of New Jersey and by the men and women . . . they have interrogated in their search for evidence." In other words, "Whether false or correct, these accusations and imputations were facts in themselves. . . ."[15]

New Brunswick's *Daily Home News* also responded to Bishop Matthew' protest, attacking from a different angle: "The good Episcopal Bishop who today gives Mrs. Hall so complimentary a notice in a New York newspaper will find many to endorse his views. But how about the hasty and precipitate vote of confidence on Rector Hall voted by this Bishop and his clerical followers on the occasion of the funeral of the fallen rector?"[16]

Bishops Knight and Matthews, like Mrs. Hall, were evidently in deep denial. The rector of St. John's had been less than a model husband, as scores of people in New Brunswick could attest. Many in his congregation had come to believe that their spiritual leader lacked the rectitude expected of a servant of God. He was openly cheating on his wife, and if Mrs. Hall had not yet learned of his adultery, it was only because of her strict adherence to the rule of See No Evil, Hear No Evil, Speak No Evil.

Not long before the trial in 1926, an unnamed acquaintance of Frances Hall said, "If you knew Mrs. Hall as well as I do, it would not seem at all peculiar that, whether or not there was gossip outside, none of it reached her ears. Her dignity and reserve make it obvious to her friends that she would be the last person to whom anyone would have mentioned anything of the sort."[17]

Maybe so. Maybe not. Early in the investigation, Mrs. Elsie P. Barnhardt of Paterson, a sister of Eleanor Mills, testified that in a conversation two months before the murders Frances Hall had admonished the choir singer, "Mrs. Mills, you are making my life very unhappy."[18]

4 Babykins and Wonder Heart

Edward Wheeler Hall was born in Brooklyn, New York, in 1881. As a boy he entered the choir school of Grace Church at Broadway and Eleventh Street Manhattan, where in 1895 he was named the "best and brightest" in a class of twenty-two. He attended Brooklyn Polytechnic Institute, graduating in 1898, and won a scholarship to Hobart College in Geneva, New York, but did not graduate. Opting for the ministry, he entered General Theological Seminary in Manhattan, and was ordained a minister at New York's Grace Church, in whose school he had once excelled as a student.

After a stint as curate of Grace Church's eastside chapel, he accepted an assignment in 1907 as assistant pastor at St. Mark's Episcopal Church in Basking Ridge, New Jersey, a mission chapel of St. Bernard's Episcopal Church in Bernardsville. A genial, urbane young preacher, he was well-liked by his parishioners at St. Mark's, evidently a minister with a bright future. On July 15, 1909, he was installed as rector of the Protestant Episcopal Church of St. John the Evangelist in New Brunswick, replacing Reverend W. Dutton Dale.[1]

Frances Noel Stevens had been attending Christ Church in downtown New Brunswick, an old and fashionable Episcopal church. But even before Reverend Hall arrived in town she had sometimes taught Sunday school at St. John's, which had started as a mission chapel of Christ Church. With the arrival of St. John's new minister, Frances seems to have switched her allegiance to his nearby house of worship on George Street. Like many of the women in Hall's flock, Miss Stevens was attracted to the personable young bachelor. Not much is known about their courtship. After Frances and Edward were married, they settled down to a life that for the minister remained filled with church activities.

The marriage was a curious mismatch, not only in age—Frances was seven years older than Edward—but also in personality. Frances was reticent, determinedly private; Edward was gregarious. Frances was ill at ease in social situations and seemed standoffish to many people; Edward was genial and well-liked. Another difference, one that may have mattered more than the others to the rector, since he was reputed to be a bit of a fortune hunter, was the difference in their bank accounts. Frances already had money and would inherit much more. Edward was not well-off financially.[2] After his death, Mrs. Hall estimated Edward's estate at twenty thousand dollars—and some of that was Carpender money. Before their marriage he boarded in a modest Victorian home at 161 George Street.[3]

Mrs. Hall's wealth came from two main sources, both connected to the Carpender family and both acquired subsequent to her marriage. When Aunt Lucy Helena (Carpender) Hart, the widow of Professor Charles E. Hart of Rutgers, died, she left Frances a bequest said to have been seven hundred thousand dollars. When Frances's mother, Mary Noel (Carpender) Stevens died in 1919, she left a fortune of perhaps two million dollars to be divided among her three children: Henry, William, and Frances.

These figures may be inflated. Mrs. Hall pooh-poohed the estimates of the size of her fortune when they appeared in the press. Still, even before her two large legacies, Frances Noel Stevens was a glittering catch, in wealth if not in beauty, for the popular young minister at St. John's.

A cynic might have predicted trouble ahead for the couple. While hardly a Rudolph Valentino look-alike at five-feet-six inches and two hundred pounds, the thirty-something rector radiated confidence and good cheer. Women were attracted to him. Although he was no longer a bachelor, neither was he a father, tied down with a bouncing baby on his knee. He and Frances remained childless.

Mrs. Hall avoided most of the churchly routine at St. John's. It appeared to some parishioners that Eleanor Mills and Minnie Clark performed many of the duties expected of a minister's wife. A statement released to the press through a family friend about two months after the murders described the situation this way: "Mrs. Hall is not an active church worker. She was not a member nor actively associated with any of the church organizations or societies. She considers it a mistake for a minister's wife to become too closely involved in the actual work of the church."[4]

In July 1922, two months before the murders, Reverend Hall accompanied some of the married women of his congregation on a week-long summer outing at Point Pleasant on the Jersey shore. The married men of St. John's had been there the week before. At the women's camp, the rector occupied a small tent apart from the women. Eleanor Mills was one of the women at the camp. According to an unnamed woman who attended the outing, Reverend Hall offered to drive home one of the other women who wished to leave early. Mrs. Mills was so upset at this that she "ran into her tent, threw herself down on the cot, and sobbed hysterically. They said she cried, 'When he goes away, one half of me goes with him.'"[5]

No specific improprieties were noted between her and the

rector, although one woman congregant did comment darkly, "Things have been scandalous down there."[6] Mrs. Hall drove to Point Pleasant several times during the week but did not stay at the camp.

The rector said that his purpose in staying overnight was to protect the women. Rumors that were later circulated but never confirmed had it that he carried a .32 caliber pistol with him on the outing.[7] Presumably, there were campers who saw the weapon, if in fact there was a weapon, but all of them were loyal members of his flock. After the murders, when detectives began to probe the relationships among church members, most of St. John's congregants, men and women alike, seemed to clam up like bivalves.

One Point Pleasant incident did come to light, not because of the candor of the congregants but because of the indiscretion of the lovers. When the church camp broke up on Saturday, Mrs. Hall drove down from New Brunswick in her Dodge sedan to pick up her husband. He climbed into the car, and Frances started to drive away. Eleanor Mills, seeing what was happening, ran toward the car and stopped it. In a huff she asked the minister if he intended to leave her behind. Reverend Hall, trying to smooth things over, invited Eleanor to accompany him and Mrs. Hall on the trip back to New Brunswick, which she did.[8]

Some of the other women at camp were put off by this incident—most of them had to return home by train. Still, no one bothered to mention it to the authorities until a passage in one of the rector's letters to Eleanor led investigators to question them about it.

Reverend Hall, it turned out, had promised to keep a kind of love diary for Eleanor (and she for him) when, at the end of

July, the minister and his wife left for their annual three-week vacation at Islesford, Maine, on Little Cranberry Isle near Bar Harbor. They stayed at Islesford's Woodlawn House, a large frame building with shady lawns, and a sunny beach, but spent much of their time hiking and boating between the islands in the region.

The rector and Eleanor intended to exchange their love diaries later, when the Halls returned from Islesford. Evidently they did, but Eleanor's diary never came to light. The lovers also agreed to send each other frequent letters. A few of the letters Edward and Eleanor exchanged during this time were church-related and businesslike. Others were personal and emotionally charged. The rector picked up Eleanor's more intimate letters surreptitiously at the post office in Seal Harbor on Mt. Desert Island, taking either the daily mail boat there or Captain Burt Spurling's small ferry, the *Restless.*[9] Several of Reverend Hall's amorous outpourings, on the other hand, went directly (and it would seem indiscreetly) to the Mills' home at 49 Carman Street, New Brunswick.

In time the rector's diary and letters were stashed in a crocheted sewing bag of Eleanor's that hung behind the living room door in the Mills' flat, where sixteen-year-old Charlotte Mills found them after her mother's death.[10]

The letters from the rector were signed D.T.L., standing for the German words *dein treuer Lieber,* meaning "Your True Love." Their content left no doubt (except perhaps in Mrs. Hall's shuttered mind) that the minister was fervently in love with the choir singer. Here are a few excerpts from the rector's letters:

• "Dearest, will these days ever pass? Each one seems weeks long. Oh, how I long to be with you again. Clasp you to me.

Kiss you all over. Talk-talk-talk to you and just look at you and dream wonders."

• "I want to fondle and caress you, oh, so much. I want to hold you close [in] my arms and know you are safe and happy and warm. Dearest, we were made for each other's arms—that is our heaven."

• "My own dear wonder heart . . . It seems as though we have together open[ed] the doors of a wonderful world . . . intangible and yet eternal it is! <u>We know</u> it and it is ours <u>forever</u>."

• "But to see you anyway, and to hold you, crush you and pour my burning kisses on your dear body and to look deep deep into those wonderful eyes of love! . . . <u>I love you</u> more than words can tell and my every prayer is for the divinest blessings for you."

• "Dearest, love me hard, hard, harder than ever, for your babykins is longing for his mother."

• "How fierce [I am loving you]—and, oh, so deeply and truly—a long strong burning kiss on your lips—liquid fire into your very soul."[11]

The rector knew that the Point Pleasant incident still bothered Eleanor. In one of his letters to her he tried to mollify his miffed "wonder heart." He wrote: "Her [Mrs. Hall's] remarks at Point Pleasant were foolish and entirely uncalled for. I don't blame you for being hurt—you know how I feel. . . . Dearest, don't let it trouble you. I didn't show her your letter to me—but you were wise to send it to Islesford—for she might have commented if no letter came from you. But she didn't ask to see it—just said, 'Is there any news from Eleanor?'"[12]

That is a rather peculiar message. Hall seemed to believe his wife was acting harshly toward Eleanor by not seeming to be pleased when she was obliged to chauffeur the choir singer back to New Brunswick. Like a few other encounters between Frances and Eleanor, it suggests that both women may have been resigned, in quite different ways, to an uneasy acceptance of the status quo.

Exactly how much anyone knew about the affair prior to the murders is conjectural. The press routinely suggested that the love affair between the minister and the choir singer was common knowledge among St. John's congregation for quite some time before the fatal night. Apparently, the impending breakup between the Reverend and Mrs. Hall—for that too was routinely assumed—became increasingly anticipated in July, August, and early September. Although the affair had gone on since at least 1919, its intensity seems to have escalated in the late summer of 1922.[13]

After the murders, one of the first people to speak about the dissension among members of St. John's choir was Alvah Jordan, the paid choir leader and soloist. Mrs. Jordan noted that the choir of Reverend Hall's church had become a hotbed of trouble, saying that Eleanor Mills had pushed herself forward for some time. There was a faction, Mrs. Jordan suggested, that resented Eleanor's increasing influence over the rector and the conduct of church affairs.[14]

Alvah Jordan said she herself had nothing against the rector. She described him as a devout and friendly man who was always trying to keep peace in the choir, usually without much success. The rector attended choir rehearsals on Friday nights and tried to keep everyone happy. When the choir broke up, Mrs. Jordan noted, Eleanor Mills generally stayed behind and went with the clergyman to his study behind the altar. No one considered this unusual or suspicious, she said.

Most people connected with the choir, or with the church in general, were less frank than Mrs. Jordan. A *New York Times* article of November 9, 1922, indicated the frustration that beset the authorities from the outset. Investigators said they had questioned about a dozen witnesses who showed great reluctance to give them any information at all about the crime or about relations between Reverend Hall and Mrs. Mills. The detectives interviewed these witnesses on the basis of information obtained from other persons. What they got from each of them was "an obviously deceitful denial of knowing anything about the case."[15]

A person less reluctant to talk was Mrs. Mills' sister, Elsie Barnhardt. She told reporters about an auto trip in early September to The Evergreens, an Episcopal home for the aged in Bound Brook. According to Mrs. Barnhardt, who had heard the story from Eleanor, Mrs. Hall offered a toast as they sped along: "Here's to our sweethearts and wives. May our sweethearts be our wives and our wives our sweethearts." That was wishful thinking on Frances's part, and Eleanor (according to the story she told Elsie) parried it with a toast of her own: "May our sweethearts and wives never meet." Mrs. Hall, Eleanor observed, was not amused.[16]

Elsie Barnhardt, as an outsider, felt free to tell such tales. But when a member of the church choir, C. Russell Gildersleeve, told a much more innocuous story, he quickly corrected himself, repudiating his statement as soon as the press reported it. What Gildersleeve had seen—and then was rash enough to talk about—was not exactly wild sex in the sacristy. He had observed the rector and the choir singer walking "arm in arm" in front of the Rivoli Theatre on Broadway near Fiftieth Street in New York City about a year before the murders.

Although this looked like a fairly trivial incident—one he would testify to under oath at the trial four years later—Gildersleeve fired off a hasty disclaimer to the press as soon as the grand jury refused to issue indictments in 1922. He wrote: "The statements attributed to me [at the grand jury hearing]... were almost, if not wholly, inaccurate. My testimony was direct, relatively unimportant, and not that as reported by the newspapers."[17]

Investigators felt from the beginning that there was fear-inspiring pressure, or perhaps it was only influence, emanating from 23 Nichol Avenue. Barely submerged turmoil dwelt within the ivied walls of St. John the Evangelist. The *Newark Evening News* reported that some of the congregants took "unseasonable vacations."[18] Still, most of the congregation must have been as bewildered about the murder of their rector and choir singer as Mrs. Hall claimed to be. Not all of them, however. Information was unquestionably being withheld by some. As for the rest, no matter how mute they remained, they were caught up in the excitement of the mystery.

A few weeks after the crime, several of the choir's hymnals were found to have one page missing, torn out by a person or persons unknown. The page contained Reverend Hall's and Eleanor Mills' favorite hymn: "Peace, Perfect Peace."[19]

Willie Stevens leading firemen's parade. This photograph of a younger Willie Stevens, as a volunteer firefighter, appeared in the New Brunswick *Daily Home News* on September 22, 1922. (photo pre-1922)

5 Willie the Fireman

The death of Frances Hall's mother in 1919 left three people (not counting the two live-in servants) still residing at the big house on Nichol Avenue. They were the Reverend Edward W. Hall, his wife Frances, and her older brother William. Nearly everyone who knew William Carpender Stevens called him "Willie." The press, reporting on the murders, pictured him as eccentric, childlike, and something of a town character.[1]

Willie Stevens, childlike though he might be, was no youngster. Fifty years old in 1922, a good-natured bachelor, he had lived with his parents and his sister since infancy. A communicant of Christ Episcopal Church, New Brunswick, he did not switch his allegiance from the downtown church after his sister's marriage to the rector of St. John's.

He had never held a job.[2] Outside the mansion, he busied himself by hanging around Engine Company No. 3 on Dennis Street, wearing a fire helmet, playing cards, polishing the brass, and running errands for the firemen.[3] Willie would dearly have loved to be a real fireman. Knowing this, the men at the firehouse humored him to some extent, even letting him wear a full uniform on special occasions. A file photograph in the *Daily Home News* of September 22, 1922, shows the dressed-up Willie, several years younger and a bit awkward, carrying a flag at the head of group of uniformed men in a firemen's parade. Since the Stevens family released no photographs to the press for some time after the murders, the *Daily Home News* made do with such earlier shots.[4]

Journalists never tired of describing Willie's appearance. At the time of the trial Damon Runyon pictured him as "a heavyset man with thick, bushy hair, which stands up on his head straight and stiff like quills upon a fretful porcupine... It gives Willie a startled appearance, which is increased by a pair of thick, black, arched eyebrows and wide open, staring eyes.

"He wears spectacles with heavy lenses. A heavy, dark mustache, shaped like bicycle bars, sags over his mouth. He has no great amount of chin. He has a thick neck, heavily ridged in back. Take him all in all, Willie has a rather genial appearance." Runyon thought he looked like "a successful delicatessen dealer."[5]

Successful, no. Not Willie. In fact, there was something about Willie that was clearly awry. Back in those days reporters did almost no psychologizing and were content merely to include the bushy-haired bachelor's behavior as colorful filler in their stories about the slayings. They were amused when Willie buried his face in his hat so that news photographers could not take his picture. "Please chase them away," he protested. It all seemed like a good show.[6]

Police investigators took Willie more seriously and tried hard to get him to talk. A few days after the bodies were found, Middlesex assistant prosecutor John E. Toolan, Somerset detective George D. Totten, and others grilled Frances's bachelor brother for about two hours. They were surprised by his guarded manner. The normally voluble Willie Stevens responded to each question briefly and cautiously, in a way that led the probers to conclude he was "acting under instructions." The fire buff had a set story, and he never deviated from it, then or later.[7]

Three weeks after the murders the governor of New Jersey,

Edward I. Edwards complained about the lack of arrests in the case. Stirred to action, or so it appeared, Somerset authorities whisked Willie away from his home—"kidnapped" him, his attorney claimed—and took him to the Somerset County Courthouse, where they questioned him for about seven hours. According to Willie, they swore at him and called him a liar. "Everything else having failed," his irate counsel complained, "they are going out with battleaxes." The battleaxes failed, too. Willie stuck to his story.[8]

No matter how clever he was at repeating a story line, Willie Stevens suffered from some kind of mental disorder. He was not merely eccentric like one of those dotty English lords. He was mentally impaired, abnormal in a way that left him incompetent in certain respects but self-sufficient in others. Although he was kept on a strict allowance to curb his spending, he went off every summer by himself to vacation at Bay Head on the Jersey shore. In the winter he traveled, also on his own, to St. Petersburg, Florida. Willie, whether at home or away, had many acquaintances but no close friends.

He never caused any trouble in New Brunswick. On the contrary, he was well thought of, if sometimes patronized. Occasionally, he did get overenthusiastic about firefighting. One day he set a small fire on the front lawn of his home at 23 Nichol Avenue. Responding as a good fireman should, he donned his helmet and put out the blaze with a bucket of water.[9]

Willie's mental state had always been a source of concern to his family. When Frances's mother died, leaving a large sum of money to her three children, two of them, Frances Hall and Henry Stevens, were named executors. They placed Willie's share of the fortune in trust for him, to be administered by

William Carpender (Willie) Stevens. One of Frances Hall's two brothers, bachelor Willie lived with Mrs. Hall and the rector at the family mansion. Mentally impaired yet "a sort of genius," Willie loved firefighting. (photo 1926)

Joseph H. Porter, a New Brunswick banker. Willie, by then in his late forties, received a modest monthly allowance.

Small as the allowance was for a person of his substantial means—a mere forty dollars a week—Willie spent it with happy abandon. He bought steaks and chicken for the firemen, candy for the neighborhood children, and once, in a burst of patriotism, a seventy-dollar American flag for the firehouse.[10] He also purchased the black-and-white bunting with which the building was draped when a member of the company died.[11]

The firemen's stories about Willie showed him as a person with wide-ranging interests and remarkable powers of recall. One day "a salesman of shaving materials dropped in at the enginehouse. Finding that Willie had visited St. Augustine, Florida, he mentioned an old Spanish chapel there. Willie described it and gave its history, replete with dates, and greatly impressed the caller."[12] Another visitor mentioned a kind of insect that he said was common in the countryside. "You mean they used to be," Willie replied. "That type of insect has been extinct in this country for forty years." And he was right. He could also rattle off the Latin names of familiar flowers.[13]

When Willie was not engaged at the firehouse, he roamed through the Hungarian section of the city. Hungarians were a sizable ethnic minority in New Brunswick, many of them working in the busy New Brunswick factories. At one time more than two thirds of the Johnson & Johnson work force consisted of Hungarians, and the company was jokingly called "Hungarian University."[14] Willie felt at home among the Hungarians, who enjoyed his company and did not make fun of his eccentricities. He ran errands, carried messages to earn extra cash, or leaned back and relaxed on front porches, talking to those who knew him. During his winters in Florida he sometimes sent boxes of fruit to the Hungarian children of the town.[15]

Willie's room in the Hall mansion was on the second floor, near the rector's study. When not at the firehouse or in the Hungarian section, he spent much of his time in his room, smoking his pipe and reading books, some of them quite erudite. At the time of the trial he was deep into a book on metallurgy. According to Ethel Stevens, brother Henry's wife, Willie explained from his jail cell, "This is the bread and butter of my literary repast."[16]

In a desk drawer in his room Willie kept a .32 caliber Iver-Johnson revolver, a firearm that aroused the interest of investigators. According to the *New York Times,* "Mr. and Mrs. Hall had decided several years ago that a person of Willie's excitable temperament should not have a weapon. Not wanting to appear to 'baby' him, they decided to render the pistol [the Iver-Johnson revolver] useless by filing off its firing pin, and this the rector did. Willie did not discover the trick until the weapon was taken from his desk after the crime."[17]

What aroused greater interest on the part of investigators than the disabled weapon was Willie's apparent knowledge, on Friday, September 15, of the yet-to-be-discovered crime off De Russey's Lane. That afternoon, less than twenty-four hours after the murders, he told Captain Michael Regan at Engine Company No. 3, "Something big is going to pop. You'll hear about it later."[18]

Reporters were as fascinated by Willie's statement at the firehouse as were the police investigators. When they asked Mrs. Hall's attorney, W. Edwin Florance, about it, the lawyer replied with a smile: "Did Willie say that? Well, if you knew Willie as I [do], you wouldn't be surprised at anything he said. Willie is not to be taken seriously."[19]

So Willie was "not to be taken seriously." That became the refrain of the family, and later of its team of lawyers, as evidence accrued of a possible link between the Stevenses and the murders.

When Willie was asked if he had accompanied Frances when she went out to look for her missing husband in the early morning after the murders, he replied obliquely, "I am tied by my sister's honor, and that of my family."[20]

Early on Saturday, September 16, a couple of hours before the bodies of the rector and his mistress were found, Willie Stevens was back at Engine Company No. 3 with another curious remark. "I've had trouble at the house," he told Captain Regan. (Later reports changed this personal admission to "There's been trouble at the house"; the distinction in wording may be worth noting.) Willie added: "If I seem cross today, don't pay any attention to me."[21]

A second witness who believed that Willie Stevens knew something important about the murders was George Kuhn, a cigar-store owner at 355½ George Street, New Brunswick. During funeral services for Eleanor Mills, Willie came into Kuhn's cigar store. When the owner expressed his hope that "they get the guilty parties and punish them," Willie looked aghast. His eyes bulging, he placed his hand over his heart and said, "My heart is almost coming through my clothes, George. I don't know how I can stand it."

A moment later, he leaned over the counter and said, "George, I want you to do me a favor. Lots of people come in here and talk about this thing. I want you to deny any rumors you hear about the Hall-Stevens-Carpender family having anything to do with these murders."

When Kuhn said he would not agree to do it, Willie turned

and left, "looking rather dazed."[22]

On September 26, W. Edwin Florance, former mayor of New Brunswick and former state senator, yielded his place as Mrs. Hall's personal attorney to a young out-of-town lawyer with more experience in criminal cases. The man who replaced him was Timothy Newell Pfeiffer, a lean, serious man with impressive credentials and a brilliant future, who had an office at 120 Broadway, Manhattan.[23]

As personal attorney for Mrs. Hall and Willie Stevens in 1922 and 1926, Pfeiffer spent a great deal of time in New Brunswick, orchestrating the public appearances and public utterances of Frances and Willie. Although the police generally treated Mrs. Hall and her eccentric brother with deference, both were under suspicion from the outset. Pfeiffer's challenge was to make these two prime suspects, each with an alibi supported only by the other, into objects of sympathy.

One of Pfeiffer's first moves, or so it now seems, was to have Willie Stevens establish himself firmly in the public mind as a harmless chucklehead. Willie made a good beginning. On September 28, two days after Pfeiffer's appointment, the fifty-year-old fire buff confronted the press and involved himself in "a humorous interlude to a grim case," as a reporter for the *New York Times* put it. As Willie emerged from the Middlesex County prosecutor's office, he paused on his way to the Hall family car to address a group of reporters:

"I want you fellows to understand," he said, "that I don't want to be referred to as 'Willie' any more. You must address me as 'William' or 'Mr. Stevens.' I'm not a half wit, as you have been saying, and I'm not a sissy. If you don't believe me, I'll show you this—"

Whereupon he pulled from his hip pocket "as manly looking

and evil smelling a briar pipe as one would want to see."[24]

Willie, the simpleton. He would continue to divert journalists with his bulging eyes, bushy hair, and walrus mustache, but henceforth it would be at a safe distance. While Timothy Pfeiffer occasionally allowed the reticent Mrs. Hall to talk to reporters—which she did with considerable poise and benefit to her cause—he kept the talkative Willie under wraps. No interviews, no photographs.

Frances Hall made one of her statements to the press in late October, 1922. It was a carefully crafted document, released to counteract the sensational charges then being leveled against her by Mrs. Jane Gibson, the Pig Woman. An interview followed, though not with Mrs. Hall herself, but with Timothy Pfeiffer. When asked about Willie's possible involvement in the murders, the attorney answered, "Willie is of the type who could not hold anything back successfully, even if he wanted to, especially if he had seen a crime committed. The other members of the family tell me that Willie has a perfect horror of death or of dead people."[25]

Not everyone saw it the way the family did. Julius Bolyog, a retired New Brunswick gas station owner who claimed to have been an acquaintance of Willie's, insisted that Willie Stevens hated Reverend Hall. Bolyog, however, made his statement forty-eight years after the murders, believing he was about to die. Nevertheless, he passed two lie detector tests administered by the New Jersey State Police at the request of George Saloom, a New Brunswick police officer to whom the ex-gas-station owner made his revelations. In his statement Bolyog confirmed what Captain Regan had said at the time, that Willie considered his monthly allowance so meager as to be insulting. He held Hall accountable for his chronically empty pockets. The rector was apparently blameless on this charge, because it was the trustee, not the minister, who determined the amount of the allowance. Willie despised the rector nonetheless, and on several occasions spoke about "taking care of the bum." Bolyog thought Willie was serious when he talked about getting help from two local hoodlums.[26]

When Timothy Pfeiffer suggested that Willie "had a horror of blood," an unnamed investigator countered by quoting a statement Willie had supposedly made to the authorities. Under questioning, Willie admitted that "his great ambition in life was to witness a surgical operation in a hospital."[27]

He may well have said that, but his most obvious everyday interests were hanging around the firehouse, visiting the Hungarian section of the city, and reading in his room. He also liked to run errands. More than one person in New Brunswick told investigators that Willie sometimes carried notes or letters from Reverend Hall to Eleanor Mills at her Carman Street home. He denied it. If he did act as a go-between for the lovers, it seems a safe bet that he remained in the dark about his role, that he knew nothing of the content of the messages.[28]

6 Carman Street

"Peace, Perfect Peace" was the hymn Eleanor Mills loved best and often sang with the choir at St. John's. But there was precious little peace for her at home in the four-room Mills apartment, which occupied the second floor and the attic of a narrow frame house at 49 Carman Street, around the corner from the rector's church.

James Mills, forty-five years old, was janitor at the nearby Lord Stirling School and acting sexton at the Church of St. John the Evangelist. His home reflected his humble status in life. Jim knew that his wife Eleanor, eleven years his junior, was unhappy in the marriage. They often argued, and she was no longer sleeping with him. For the past two years she had shared an attic bedroom with their sixteen-year-old daughter Charlotte, a high school senior. As much as Eleanor and Charlotte might joke with each other and call one another "kid," the tension in the household was always there.[1]

Jim and Eleanor Mills—like Edward and Frances Hall—were not well matched. Jim, meek and hardworking, a shoemaker in his earlier years, never earned more than thirty-six dollars a week. He had neither money nor ambition. A reporter for the *New York Times* portrayed him as "a thin, emaciated, drooping man, with a perpetually apologetic expression on his face."[2] The judgment seemed universal. At the time of the trial Damon Runyon saw him "as a veritable little mouse of a man . . . [with] a peaked face, and sad eyes, and stooped shoulders . . . a man as you might imagine to be a henpecked husband at home, a man bullied by his children and by all the world."[3] Jim Mills' brother Henry said people had called him "Simple Jim" when they were boys.[4] A reporter who interviewed Jim Mills after the murders found him "as colorless as a catfish," a judgment with which Eleanor, had she been alive, would have readily agreed.[5]

Eleanor Reinhardt, one of ten children in a working-class family, married James Mills in 1905 when she was seventeen years old. Whatever attraction he held for her then, and it may have been little more than a chance to escape from her crowded household, it had long since vanished by 1922. Bright, vivacious, and purposeful, Eleanor at thirty-four was a choir singer and sometime soloist at St. John's.

The choir was the richest part of her life. As a homemaker she felt cramped and limited in her frugal Carman Street flat. She wanted much more. In one of her letters to the rector she wrote, "Honey, there isn't a house large enough for me. My dreams are as big as the earth. ... I know I'm a crazy cat, but I can't be different."[6]

Her crazy-cat dreams may have led her into an earlier love affair. According to one newspaper account, Charlotte claimed that her mother and Ralph V. Gorsline, a vestryman and choir member at St. John's, had been lovers about eight years earlier.[7] If true, this would make Gorsline's subsequent actions more understandable, for the slippery Mr. Gorsline was to play an important role in the De Russey's Lane drama. But how Charlotte could have learned about such a liaison—it seems doubtful that her mother would have told her—makes the claim questionable.

There is no doubt at all, however, about Eleanor Mills' passionate and ongoing affair with Reverend Hall.

If the morose sexton of St. John's and the restless choir singer had little in common, the same could hardly be said of

Mills' home at 49 Carman Street. Janitor Jim, choir singer Eleanor, daughter Charlotte, and son Daniel lived on the second floor of this house around the corner from St. John's Church. (photo 1920s)

Eleanor and the rector. They seemed to be made for each other. Mrs. Mills, with her oval face and fine figure, her true and lovely soprano voice, her devotion to the church, and her avid interest in reading, must have struck the minister as an earthbound angel. She was everything his wife was not. Just over five feet tall, weighing one hundred and eighteen pounds, she radiated a youthful flame that made Frances Hall's settled conservatism seem all the more dreary by comparison. It highlighted the fourteen-year age difference between the rector's wife and his mistress.

Reverend Hall's letters to Eleanor made it clear which of the two he preferred. "You are all the wonder of life for me," he wrote in one of his many letters to Eleanor.[8]

She was no longer all the wonder of life for Jim Mills, though. Despite his mild manner toward others, Jim often quarreled bitterly with his wife. Millie Opie, a dressmaker who lived at 51 Carman Street, next door to the Mills' home, heard many of these arguments. She knew Eleanor well. Just recently Millie had modeled the gay polka-dot dress that Eleanor had sewn for herself, the dress in which she died.

Millie Opie recalled one exchange between the husband and wife that had occurred about six months prior to the murders. As Jim was returning home from work, Eleanor was leaving.

"Where are you going?" Jim asked. "Over to that church again, I suppose."

"Yes," Eleanor replied. "I'm going over to the church."

Obviously annoyed, her husband said, "You do more for the church and Mr. Hall than you do for me."

To which she responded, "Well, why shouldn't I? I care more for Mr. Hall's little finger than I do for your whole body."[9]

Jim turned away.

Eleanor's harsh comment was one she used on other occasions, to other people.[10] She was not shy about making known her regard for the minister and her scorn for her husband. When Jim raised his voice to her in their apartment, Miss Opie told reporters, Eleanor would drown out his voice by raising her own and repeating over and over, "Blah-blah-blah-blah-blah." Or else she would sing loudly until Jim gave up his protests.[11]

Millie Opie concluded that Eleanor ran the Mills household and did as she pleased. Although Jim would deny it over and over in the days ahead, he had surely known about his wife's love affair for quite some time. She had made little effort to hide it; indeed, she sometimes seemed to flaunt it. Lacking the money for a divorce or the drive for a separation—"If I do put her out, I'd have to support her anyway, and there would be no one here to do the housework," Jim whined to Charlotte—he simply accepted her infidelity.[12] But after the murders, he could not bring himself to admit to such craven conduct.

Jim Mills never denied knowing that his wife made a practice of writing love letters—or what appeared to be love letters. The day after the bodies were discovered he told the press, "She was fond of reading books of romance. She very often copied passages from these books that struck her fancy. She used to carry them in her brown scarf, and one day I demanded that she show them to me. They were harmless things, so I forgot about them. I am certain that the letters were never mailed. They probably were in her scarf when she left here Thursday evening."[13]

At the trial, on cross-examination, Jim added a couple of details to his account. The letters his wife wrote were addressed to "Dear" and "Honey," he said, and "she would keep [them] for a while and then take them and burn them."[14]

On the day of the crime, Jim went across Abeel Street to work as usual at the Lord Stirling School. How Eleanor spent her time that morning is unknown, but it seems likely she spent some of it writing and perhaps delivering to the "post office" at the church her Lake Hopatcong letter ("Oh, my darling baby-kins, what a muddle we are in!"). In Jim's pretrial testimony he stated that both he and Eleanor were home for lunch, which he called "dinner," at about noon.

Sometime around three o'clock in the afternoon Millie Opie took a phone call from Reverend Hall. Since Millie's home had a telephone and the Mills' apartment did not, the dressmaker often received incoming calls for Jim and Eleanor. The rector wanted to speak to Mrs. Mills. Miss Opie shouted this message out her window—the two houses were so close together that such communication was easy—but Mrs. Mills did not respond. Later she told Millie she had been taking a nap.[15]

Over at 23 Nichol Avenue, Mrs. Frances Hall received a phone call from Mrs. Mills on that same Thursday afternoon, or so she testified at the trial. She could not remember the exact time, she said, but recalled Eleanor saying "there is something about the doctor's bill that I do not understand."[16]

Mrs. Mills was referring to the surgeon's fee for an operation she had undergone in January 1922. A malfunctioning right kidney had been causing her excruciating pain, and Dr. Arthur L. Smith removed the offending organ at Middlesex General Hospital. His bill was two hundred dollars, a budget-busting amount for the Mills family. St. John's, through its compassionate rector, was gradually paying off the bill, since Jim Mills clearly could not afford to pay it.[17]

Now in September Eleanor Mills was inquiring vaguely about Dr. Smith's bill. This purported mid-afternoon phone call is curious on several counts. One is that Millie Opie had not yet relayed Reverend Hall's message to Eleanor, so the choir singer could not have been returning his call. Another is that "the doctor's bill" sounds like a transparent excuse for a phone call, since the doctor's bill was months old and the minister and the choir singer, quite apart from their semisecret affair, saw each other nearly every day. Still another is that Eleanor's call, arriving at an indeterminate time in the afternoon, gave Mrs. Hall this doctor's-bill story, which, so far as is otherwise known, reached the Hall household only in an evening phone call. This later phone conversation, crucial to the case, was from Eleanor to the rector. It was a call whose contents (including a planned meeting between her husband and Eleanor) Mrs. Hall swore she knew nothing about.[18]

Jim Mills saw Reverend Hall once more before the minister's fatal encounter near De Russey's Lane. After finishing his day's work at the Lord Stirling School, he went to the church, arriving at about a quarter to six. He began cleaning up some shavings in front of the outside vestibule to the Sunday school, where carpenters had been working that day. Within a few minutes, the rector appeared, examined the work that had been done, and went into the church, staying for about ten minutes. When he came outside, Jim remarked that some paint would be needed, and Hall said he would order it. Then the rector left for home in his Dodge sedan. The sexton left on foot about ten minutes later.

When Jim got home, Eleanor, Charlotte, and Daniel were there. They had supper together, after which Eleanor and Charlotte sat and talked for a while on the front stoop. Although Charlotte and her mother confided in one another to some extent, it is unclear how much the daughter knew about her mother's love affair. Miss Opie thought it was plenty, but Charlotte's trial testimony added little to what others already knew. The pert Charlotte, who prided herself on being a flapper, quickly gained dominance of the household after Eleanor's death. Like her mother, she had the compliant Jim "buffaloed," as his more forceful brother Henry remarked. "Have you seen Charlotte?" Henry Mills asked reporters. "Well, there's your heredity for you. She's her mother all over again."[19]

On the stoop that evening Eleanor told Charlotte she had clipped an article from the New York *World* that dealt with the question of divorce. The article particularly interested her because it concerned Dr. Percy Stickney Grant, the celebrated but controversial rector of the Episcopal Church of the Ascension in New York City. Wanting Reverend Hall to see it, and not expecting a tryst with the minister that night, she took the clipping to the church to put on his desk in the study. She left Charlotte on the front stoop and returned home fifteen minutes later.

On her way back from the church Eleanor met Millie Opie, who was waiting for a trolley. Miss Opie remembered to mention the rector's phone call that afternoon. Eleanor hurried back to 49 Carman Street, bounded upstairs to get a nickel, and told Charlotte she was going around the corner to phone Reverend Hall. That was the last her daughter ever saw of her. Charlotte left the house before Mrs. Mills returned from making her phone call.

Out on the rear stoop, meanwhile, Jim had started working on some window boxes he was making for Mrs. Hall.

At 7:30 p.m. Eleanor, having returned home once again, started down the back stairs. She told Jim she was going out.

"Where are you going?" he asked.

She replied, "Follow me and find out."

Jim refused to rise to the bait. "I didn't say anything back," he explained laconically at the pretrial hearing. "I just passed it off like it was a joke."[20]

It was the last time he saw his high-spirited wife—alive or dead, as it happened, because, like Mrs. Hall, he never looked at the corpse of his spouse.

While Mrs. Mills was riding the trolley to the last stop at Buccleuch Park and walking toward her final destination under a crab apple tree, Jim was laboring on his window boxes. He worked until approximately 9:45 p.m.—well past dark, which he was able to do since he had moved inside to work—after which he adjourned to the front stoop. He sat there until "pretty near eleven o'clock."[21]

The whereabouts of his wife did not concern him at the time. She was usually home by ten o'clock, but not always. Sometimes she stayed away all night, but Jim generally knew—or thought he knew—where she was. On this night of impending murder, however, even his children returned late. Charlotte had gone to visit one of her many aunts, and Daniel was at a friend's house on George Street. They were away from home from about 7:15 p.m. until between 10:00 and 10:30.[22]

At approximately eleven o'clock that night Jim walked to Nettie Blitz's nearby grocery store, where he bought a glass of soda water. He may have asked the proprietor whether his wife had made a phone call from there earlier in the evening. Apparently he told detective Ellis H. Parker in January 1923 that he had asked the question, but by the time of the trial, nearly four years later, he had no recollection of it. In any event, after finishing his soda, he went to the church, closed the windows, locked up, and went home to bed. He left a light on in the kitchen.

At about 2:00 a.m. he awoke and noticed that the light in the kitchen was still burning. Checking the attic bedroom, he saw that Charlotte was asleep but Eleanor was nowhere to be seen. He got dressed and walked once again to St. John's, where he turned on the lights and looked around. His wife was subject to fainting spells, he told investigators, and he thought she might have passed out in the church. Finding no one there, he closed up, returned to his apartment, and went to bed.[23]

Next morning he got up as usual at a quarter to six. Eleanor still had not come home. Jim made breakfast for Charlotte, Daniel, and himself. This was not an uncommon event, but Eleanor's unexplained absence was. According to Charlotte, Jim said during breakfast, "Damn her. She went away with him after all. She has given him the love she wouldn't give me."[24]

In a disgruntled mood he crossed the street to start his workday at the Lord Stirling School. At about 8:30 a.m. he left the school and turned the corner to go to St. John's, where he opened the windows, as he always did on warm days. While in the rector's study, he noticed the clipping about divorce on the rector's desk. No sooner had he glanced at the headline than Mrs. Hall came in and greeted him. As Jim remembered the conversation:

"Good morning, Mr. Mills."

"Good morning, Mrs. Hall."

"Did you have any sickness in your house last night?"

"No."

"Mr. Hall did not come home all night."

"My wife did not come home all night." Then, as Jim would testify at the trial, "something cropped up" in his mind, and he added, "Do you think they eloped?"

Mrs. Hall's response would haunt her in the coming days
and bedevil her lawyers throughout the case. She said, "God
knows. I think they are dead and can't come home."[25]

James (Jim) Mills. Jim Mills was an assistant school janitor and the church
sexton at St. John's. He meekly accepted his wife's infidelity and regarded her
married lover, Reverend Edward W. Hall, as a good friend. (photo 1926)

7 The Woman in Gray

On the afternoon of the murders, while Jim Mills was doing his janitorial chores at the Lord Stirling School and Eleanor Mills was napping in her attic bedroom, Mrs. Frances Noel Stevens Hall was working in her kitchen at 23 Nichol Avenue, making preserves, canning pears, making pickles, or trying out a new recipe for chili sauce or tomato catsup—accounts of her activities that afternoon vary.[1]

Reverend Hall drove to Berdines Corners to address a PTA meeting, and then, after returning home briefly, left to take some flowers to a sick parishioner at St. Peter's General Hospital in New Brunswick. He went to Berdines Corners by himself but took his ten-year-old niece, Frances Voorhees, with him to the hospital, along with another little girl, Barbara Webb, who, like young Frances, had come to spend the day with the Halls.[2]

With Mrs. Hall at work in the kitchen—according to her account of the day's activities—Mrs. Minnie Clark arrived at 23 Nichol Avenue with Miss Marion Stokes in tow. Marion, a recent Sunday school graduate, had brought a camera with her. The object of the visit, which Minnie Clark had cleared earlier with Mrs. Hall, was to take some photographs of Marion in her graduation dress in the Halls' photogenic garden. This task accomplished, Minnie Clark and Marion left the house at about 4:30 p.m. or a quarter to five.[3]

Minnie Clark, who lived close by at 134 Redmond Street, had gone with the Halls the day before on their trip to Lake Hopatcong. A tireless volunteer worker at St. John's, Mrs. Clark was well known to Reverend and Mrs. Hall and had been entrusted with one of the five keys to the church. On the face of it there was nothing suspicious about her being at the Halls' home that afternoon. If no collection of love letters had been found at the scene of the murders, her brief visit to the Nichol Street mansion would have aroused little interest among investigators.

But the salient fact, in view of Eleanor's eleven letters to the rector, is that Minnie *was* there. And since she was a friend of Frances Hall and a rival (in some sense anyway) of Eleanor Mills, and since she had a key to the church, it struck investigators as conceivable that she had found a hidden batch of Eleanor's letters, or at least the latest of the letters, in the lovers' post office at the church and was delivering to Mrs. Hall this concrete evidence of the rector's affair with the choir singer. Such an incident fit the prosecution's theory of what had led to the killings, although Marion Stokes, a prosecution witness, said that she personally saw no letters pass between Minnie Clark and Frances Hall.[4]

Mrs. Hall flatly denied to reporters that Minnie brought her any letters that day.[5] What Minnie Clark said on the subject is hard to determine. A reluctant witness, she succeeded remarkably well in avoiding the glare of publicity. More than a month after the murders, her husband, Addison E. Clark, a stonemason, confirmed Minnie's visit to the Hall home on the afternoon of the murders to take some photographs of Miss Stokes, but he said nothing one way or the other about the letters. At the same time, Mrs. Clark wrote a note to the New Brunswick *Daily Home News* to point out the inaccuracy of some of the statements being made about her in the press, but she too said nothing about the letters.[6]

How the crime-scene love letters came to light, who read

them, and how they came to be between the two bodies are questions without clear-cut answers. The letters were meant to be found. There can be little doubt about that. Whoever arranged the corpses and smoothed out the victims' clothing, thus producing the macabre tableau that mesmerized the nation, must have known that the letters (scattered or stacked) were a central part of the staging. In what the *Times* suggested might be an "act of moral sentimentality," the killer, quite apart from the damning letters, left a potent visual message about the lovers' relationship.[7]

It would be helpful to be able to track the letters from the time Eleanor wrote them to the time the killer or killers left them under the crab apple tree, but it cannot be done. In any event, it is probably more important to know, as the murderer or murderers did know, that such letters existed and that they proved beyond any reasonable doubt the choir singer's love for the rector and, by inference, his love for her.

The letters, and the relationship they illustrated, supplied a persuasive motive for the murders. No wonder detective Ferd David thought the case was "a cinch." With a motive of jealousy, there were only a very few credible suspects—and jealousy seemed almost explicit in the crime. It was not a case of a robbery gone wrong or blackmail thwarted. It was a crime of resentment and revenge.

But the case still had to be proved, a process that required investigative skill well beyond that of David and his colleagues. One thing the detectives tried to do was break the alibi of one or the other of the obvious suspects. They got nowhere in their set-tos with James Mills, whose puttering-around-the-house alibi—bolstered by candid and believable witnesses, including Mrs. Elizabeth Kelly, who lived in the downstairs apartment—

stood up to intense questioning. The prosecutors would have been delighted to charge poor, passive Jim with the crime. Unlike the rector's widow, he had little status in the community. No band of friends stood ready to rush to his defense. But unhappily for this easy solution to the mystery, Jim Mills' tale of making window boxes held up.

That left Mrs. Hall. As the other aggrieved spouse, she could hardly be ignored as the possible killer. Her motive was as strong as Jim's—indeed stronger, because Jim Mills (no matter what he said) had glumly accepted the fact of being cuckolded, while Mrs. Hall, a proud pillar of the community, insisted to the end that everything was fine with her eleven-year marriage. "I lived for him and he lived for me," she said.

Was she lying? Probably, but how could it be proved? In public she continued to act like the rector's devoted wife. She never lost her calm detachment. Either she knew as little about the Edward-Eleanor love affair as she claimed to know, or else, as the detectives and prosecutors seemed to suspect, she was well aware of it but refused to acknowledge her distress beyond the confines of 23 Nichol Avenue.[8]

Despite Mrs. Hall's money and social standing, and her reputation as a woman of absolute rectitude, there were a couple of developments that made her look like a plausible suspect.

The first was a phone call to the Hall home at about 7:00 p.m., three hours and twenty minutes before the murders. Four prosecutors—two county prosecutors and two special prosecutors—all believed that this phone call set in motion the events leading to the murders near De Russey's Lane. The call was from Eleanor Mills.

Mrs. Hall picked up the downstairs receiver. Louise Geist, the Halls' parlor maid, picked up the upstairs receiver.

Questions about exactly what was said on the phone that night—and who heard the words that would pass between the lovers—swirled around the case for the next four years. Unfortunately for the prosecutors, the only living persons who may have known the answers (though both denied they did) were Mrs. Hall and Louise Geist, a jaunty young servant who cast herself from the beginning as an ally of the widow. Eleanor Mills and Reverend Hall carried the knowledge of the conversation to their graves.

Mrs. Hall claimed she was out on the piazza when the telephone rang that night. She went into the house on the second ring and took the receiver off the hook. Upon learning from Louise Geist that the rector would answer the phone upstairs, she replaced the receiver. "I did not hear a thing," Mrs. Hall testified.[9]

Louise Geist, for her part, recognized the voice on the other end of the line as that of Mrs. Mills but heard only a fragment of what was said. According to her testimony, Reverend Hall said, "Yes, yes, yes. That is too bad. I was going down to the church a little later. Cannot we make arrangements for later, say, about quarter after eight."[10]

Louise Geist unexpectedly bolstered her mistress's story of having heard nothing by testifying that "Mrs. Hall placed back the receiver, turned around, and walked out." The prosecutor at the trial, Alexander Simpson, acted startled by this apparently gratuitous slap at his theory of the evening's events. Louise Geist had never indicated up to that very moment that Mrs. Hall could not have heard the conversation. Simpson, stung, gazed steadily at the witness, and she stared back at him, defiantly.[11]

The special prosecutor had good reason to be annoyed. At

the pretrial hearing, Louise Geist (by then Mrs. Arthur S. Riehl) had not excluded the possibility of Mrs. Hall having listened to the conversation between her husband and Eleanor. In fact, she had seemed to suggest that it might have happened.

Q—What did you see Mrs. Hall do with the telephone downstairs? . . .

A—. . . I went to the top of the stairs . . . Just then Mr. Hall called from the bathroom, and she [Mrs. Hall] said, 'Oh, he is up there; it is all right.'

Q—Did you go to get him then?

A—No, I saw that she had the receiver.

Q—How long did she have the receiver up to her ear?

A—She took it off and was just like this (illustrating) when I called to her.

Q—When you were watching her she had it up to her ear?

A—Yes.[12]

Mrs. Riehl did not go beyond that observation at the pretrial hearing. She did not say that Mrs. Hall actually *had* listened to the conversation. At the trial itself, Simpson's attempts to show that she *could* have listened in on the dialogue between Edward and Eleanor gained no ground.

It may be that Simpson and the earlier prosecutors were making too much of the specific content of this phone call. After all, the rector and the choir singer trekked regularly to their rendezvous out beyond the Parker Home. At least two and probably more of the St. John's congregants knew the courting habits of the lovers. If Reverend Hall was on his way to meet Eleanor—and Mrs. Hall admitted that she believed he was (the matter of the surgeon's bill and all)—there might have been no great mystery as to where their meeting was likely to take place.

Hall mansion at 23 Nichol Avenue. Frances Stevens and her brother William lived here for twenty-one years prior to her marriage to Edward W. Hall in 1911. The mansion is now the home of the Dean of Douglass College. (photo 1998)

Lord Stirling School with former Mills home in background. Jim Mills had only to cross Abeel Street (where cars are parked) to reach the public school (fronting on Carman Street) where he worked as a janitor. (photo 1997)

A more important incident than the 7:00 p.m. phone call from Eleanor Mills was the nocturnal walk Mrs. Hall claimed to have taken with Willie Stevens in the early morning hours of Friday, September 15.

The details of this walk came to light almost immediately, but they were not volunteered by Mrs. Hall or her brother Willie. At around noon on Sunday, the day after the bodies were discovered, Somerset County prosecutor Azariah K. Beekman and detective George D. Totten questioned Mrs. Hall about her movements on the night of the murders. She seems to have maintained, or at least strongly implied, that she and Willie had been at home the whole time. Her lack of candor in this regard can only be surmised, however, because no one in the county prosecutor's office took notes. Beekman died before Mrs. Hall was indicted, and special prosecutor Alexander Simpson had to rely on Totten's memory. At the preliminary hearing, the questioning of Totten, a Somerset County detective for twenty-eight years, went like this:

Q—Did you [Totten] have any conversation with Mrs. Hall with reference to September 14?

A—Yes.

Q—Did she state what time it was during the evening that Dr. Hall went out?

A—Yes.

Q—Did she say at what time she went to bed?

A—Yes.

Q—Did she say anything about being out of the house before you asked her about it?

A—No.

Q—How did this come up?

A—After prosecutor Beekman finished talking to her, I said,

"Pardon me, Mrs. Hall, but I have information that somebody, either another person or yourself, entered the rear of the house at 2:30 o'clock Friday morning after Dr. Hall disappeared. She hesitated for a moment or two and then said: "Well, that's right."

Q—Then she had said nothing before that time.

A—No.[13]

Perhaps Totten could have led Mrs. Hall into an outright lie. Perhaps he could have induced her to say she had not gone out at all that evening, then confronted her with the information about a witness having spotted her (or at least having seen "a woman in gray") entering the Hall gate on the Redmond Street side. If so, he missed his opportunity.

The witness, William Phillips, a tall, burly night watchman at the New Jersey College for Women, was sitting that night on the side porch of Cooper Hall, facing Redmond Street, across from the side entrance to the Hall mansion.[14] Sometime between 2:30 and 2:45 a.m. he heard a dog barking and saw a woman hurry up Redmond Street, enter through the gate on the Redmond Street side of the Hall mansion, and skitter into the entrance of the house used by the servants.[15] Phillips said he jumped from the porch and walked in the direction of the woman, but before he reached her she disappeared into the mansion through the entrance used by the servants. The watchman was positive the woman was alone. He could see she was of medium height and wore a gray polo coat, but he could not identify her for sure as Mrs. Hall.[16]

Phillips failed to mention that on his walk toward the mansion he had a run-in with the dog he had heard barking. This dog, which belonged to Alan H. Bennett, a neighbor of the Halls, had also come to investigate. According to Bennett's trial testimony, the dog pinned Phillips against the Halls' four-foot-high iron fence and had to be called off. Bennett himself arrived too late to see anything of the hurrying woman.[17]

The rector's widow, reacting to the night watchman's reported sighting, acknowledged being the woman in gray, but she said her coat was "khaki-colored." Her story differed in other, more significant respects from the one told by Phillips. She insisted that she had left the house at approximately 2:30 a.m. (not entered it at that hour), accompanied by her brother Willie. They walked first to the church on George Street and then to the Mills residence at Carman and Abeel. Learning nothing at either place about the missing rector's whereabouts, they returned home at about 3:30 a.m.[18]

The reason for the walk, Mrs. Hall said, was a growing concern about her husband's absence. When he left home at 7:30 p.m., she assumed he was going to the church and, from her purported afternoon telephone conversation with Eleanor, she knew that the reason for his departure involved Mrs. Mills' doctor bill. Thus the visit to the closed church and then to the darkened Mills' residence.

She claimed throughout the case that she went both places with Willie and returned home with him. She could not explain why the night watchman for the college had seen—and insisted he had seen clearly—only the figure of a woman entering (not leaving) at about 2:30 a.m. through the side gate of the Hall house.[19]

William Phillips might not have come forward as readily as he did if he had realized how hard Mrs. Hall's defense team would try to discredit his testimony. He reported voluntarily what he had seen. He had no incentive to lie. Yet the reaction of the Hall-Stevens camp to his story, according to an article in the *New York Times,* was "an immediate attack on the character of Phillips. It was shown that he had entered into a conspiracy to rob the Rockefeller Institute in New York City, of which he was a watchman, and had turned informer, causing the arrest of his confederates. At their trial, he was committed to the Tombs for perjury by Judge Wadhams, but was never tried or convicted."[20] This episode had nothing at all to do with what he observed on the morning of September 15, 1922, but it made him an evildoer in the eyes of the Hall-Stevens supporters.

By the time of the trial, four years later, William Phillips had changed jobs. A night watchman no more, he had become a truck driver, and his long-term memory had somehow been eradicated. Either that or he had gained a heightened sense of realism. He could remember very little of what he had told Beekman, Totten, and others who interrogated him in 1922. Indeed, his testimony was of so little help to the prosecution that the attorneys for the defense saw no need to cross-examine him.[21]

8   Collecting Evidence

It was quiet at St. John's Church on George Street on the morning of Saturday, September 16, the second day after the murders. But out on the Phillips farm, confusion was about to make its masterpiece. A young man and his girlfriend, taking a walk down lovers' lane, noticed two people lying motionless in the grass. The strolling couple may or may not have been the first to see them, but they were the first to do anything about it.

At first the young couple thought the two people were alive, but as the girl moved closer, she saw the true state of affairs. "The people ain't breathing," she yelled to her companion.[1] Whereupon the pair dashed away from the scene to a house near the Parker Home on Easton Avenue. This house, about six hundred feet from the crab apple tree, belonged to Edward H. Stryker, whose niece, Mrs. Grace Edwards, was there that morning. At 10:30 a.m. Mrs. Edwards telephoned the New Brunswick police station, thereby setting in motion the murder investigation.[2]

Ordinarily, passersby who report a crime contribute little to the investigation or the ongoing story. Their names make the early news accounts and then fade away, at least until the time of the trial. But in this case, the young couple, Raymond Schneider and Pearl Bahmer, who told police they had been picking mushrooms, gained a measure of unwanted and persistent notoriety. In a short while, each of them would suffer in different ways from their unintentional and peripheral involvement in one of the most widely reported crimes in American history.[3]

The first law enforcement officer dispatched to the scene was patrolman Edward T. Garrigan of the New Brunswick Police Department. It seems prophetic of the whole investigation that to get there Garrigan had to hitch a ride. Near the Pennsylvania Railroad station in downtown New Brunswick he hailed an automobile driven by George Cathers, a car dealer, and asked him to drive him to Easton Avenue and De Russey's Lane. Cathers said okay, and the two of them took off to find Schneider and Bahmer.[4]

On the way, patrolman Garrigan spotted another New Brunswick police officer, James Curran, and invited him to come along. Curran jumped in. A few minutes later the two policemen found Raymond Schneider and Pearl Bahmer waiting nervously for them near the two corpses. While studying the neatly arranged bodies, the officers apparently did nothing to secure the area. Nor did they see the need to leave the physical evidence untouched for the county detectives who would be investigating the crime.[5]

After a short stay at the crime scene, officer Curran left to telephone headquarters with the news of the discovery.

Garrigan took a closer look at the victims. He saw a cut on the woman's throat and noticed that the ugly wound was covered with maggots. Someone had wrapped a scarf around the woman's neck, partially concealing the wound. Garrigan also saw a leather card case on the ground between the two bodies and a calling card leaning against the sole of the minister's left shoe. The calling card and a driver's license—which the officer apparently removed from the card case—carried the name of Edward W. Hall. Officer Curran too had seen the name on the calling card.[6]

Curran's phone call reached Lieutenant Thomas F. Dwyer, the officer on duty at New Brunswick police headquarters. Lieutenant Dwyer phoned Somerville, the county seat of Somerset County, to let the authorities there know about the pair of dead bodies lying in their jurisdiction. Learning of the slayings, three Somerset investigators headed for the scene, twelve miles away. They were sheriff Bogart T. Conkling, detective George D. Totten, and county physician William H. Long. The three were accompanied by Raritan police chief Joseph Navatto, who went along because of his fluency in Italian. The neighborhood around the Phillips farm had recently seen an influx of Italian residents.

Alerted at about 11:00 a.m., the four men left promptly but misinterpreted the directions they received. Consequently, they sped off on the wrong road and arrived at the crime scene at about 11:45, much later than the distance warranted.[7]

By then several things had happened. For one, Albert J. Cardinal, a reporter for the New Brunswick *Daily Home News,* had arrived and begun nosing around. With a journalist at the site, the word was out and would spread fast. Knowing this, patrolman Garrigan might well have thought to preserve whatever order he could. But no. He struck up a friendly conversation with Cardinal, who expressed interest in the calling card at the foot of the dead man and asked if he could pick it up and examine it. Garrigan said, sure, why not? When Cardinal replaced the card—judging by later testimony—he propped it not against the sole of the rector's shoe but against some nearby blades of grass.[8]

Also found at the crime scene, near the bodies, was a Peters .32 caliber cartridge case and "a piece of steel, about two feet long, fashioned like a footrest from the running board of an automobile." The .32 caliber cartridge case was almost certainly connected to the crime, but the large piece of metal could never be tied in. Very likely it was there before the murders occurred.[9] Two more .32 caliber cartridge cases turned up later.

Officer James Curran, returning to the scene after making his phone call, caught sight of a New Brunswick-bound car on Easton Avenue driven by Dr. E. Leon Loblein, a local veterinarian, and flagged it down. As luck would have it, Dr. Loblein knew the rector of St. John's and offered to take a look at the body. When patrolman Garrigan lifted the Panama hat from the male victim's face, Dr. Loblein nodded. It was Reverend Hall all right, he said. Dr. Loblein could not identify the woman.[10]

By the time the four tardy investigators from Somerset County drove up, the crime scene was already contaminated, and not just by the eagerness of the *Daily Home News*'s Albert J. Cardinal. The Phillips farm lay only a mile or so outside of busy downtown New Brunswick, and word of the scandalous discovery spread through the city like fulminations against sin at a tent revival. While Conkling, Totten, and Dr. Long were still en route, trying to find the Phillips farm, a growing number of spectators, first a trickle, then a tide, began to arrive, milling about at the scene, gawking at the bodies (which were never photographed by the police or anyone else), trampling down the surrounding grass, possibly disturbing or even making off with evidence, and stripping the bark from the crab apple tree for souvenirs.

How much effort, if any, was made to prevent or limit these depredations is unclear. When the Somerset authorities finally arrived, the once quiet, grassy site off De Russey's Lane resembled a street fair. And it got steadily worse. Detective George

Totten, though he could not or did not shoo away the onlookers, took detailed notes about what he saw under the crab apple tree. He was an experienced investigator, twenty-eight years on the job, and his notes gave a reasonably complete description of the position and appearance of the bodies.[11] It was well they did, because Garrigan, Conkling, and Dr. Long would all prove to be careless, inconsistent, and unreliable in what they observed and reported.

In the midst of the willy-nilly search for clues, Edwin R. Carpender, one of the widow's several first cousins, drove up in his mother's green Mercer touring car, accompanied by W. Edwin Florance, a former state senator and now Mrs. Hall's personal attorney. They both identified the male victim as the Reverend Edward Wheeler Hall. Having done their duty, they drove off, visibly shaken.[12]

Of the first five people who arrived at the crab apple tree after the two youthful strollers sounded the alarm, only Cardinal and Totten seem to have gotten the facts about the victims' appearance essentially right, although the bodies were more decomposed than Cardinal reported. Totten, despite his adequate verbal description of the scene, came up short on other aspects of his work. So many curious spectators continued to roam the area, so much basic investigation was left undone, so hasty and premature was the removal of the victims' bodies, it seems fair to say that, barring a confession or an eyewitness to the murders, the prosecution lost its case before the first newspaper accounts of the murders reached the reading public.

To add to the problems, the bodies of the minister and his mistress lay in Franklin Township, Somerset County, about three hundred and fifty feet beyond the Middlesex County line.

Ferdinand A. David.
A Middlesex County
detective for many
years, Ferd David
investigated the
Hall-Mills murders
in 1922 and again
in 1926. (photo 1926)

**Reverend Hall's calling
card.** This is the card that
was allegedly propped
against the murdered
rector's left shoe. A type-
written caption below the
two photos reads: "Photo-
graphic copy of visiting
card of Rev. Edward W.
Hall, found at scene of
Hall-Mills murder, on
Sept. 16, 1922." (date
of photos 1926; date of
caption unknown)

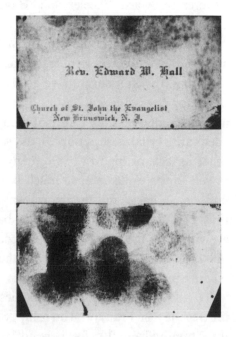

Rev. Edward W. Hall

Church of St. John the Evangelist
New Brunswick, N. J.

From first to last there were persons involved in the case who believed the rector and the choir singer were slain in New Brunswick and then transported across the county line. Had that theory been generally accepted, the main investigators would have been detectives in the prosecutor's office of Middlesex County, headed by district attorney Joseph E. Stricker. This might have been a less than desirable development, because as early as Monday, September 18, Stricker was quoted as saying that the murder was a baffling one "and may never be solved." In the event indictments were obtained, the case would have been tried at the Middlesex County courthouse in New Brunswick.[13]

The question of jurisdiction was a significant matter. Because of the costs likely to be involved, as well as the dilemma presented by a probable suspect or suspects of high social standing, neither county really wanted the case. Only after Horace B. Holaday, a scientist at New Brunswick's E. R. Squibb & Sons laboratories, analyzed one hundred and fifty-two pounds of soil upon which the bodies lay, and opined that the victims had been killed at that spot, did the reluctant Somerset County authorities, headed by district attorney Azariah Beekman, accept the fact that New Brunswick's most notorious crime, intrinsically a Middlesex County double homicide, fell within the jurisdiction of Somerset County.[14]

The early inquiry, including the critical forensic work, was muddied by this jurisdictional debate. A headline in the *Daily Home News* of September 18, 1922, stated, "Authorities of Two Counties, Together with the State Police, On Trail in Double Murder Case," but in fact the cooperation was tentative and often unsatisfactory. The state police, founded just a year earlier, played an insignificant role in the 1922 inquiry.[15]

By the time Holaday reported his findings, more than a month after the murders, investigators from both counties had lost valuable time, the victims were in their graves, and arguments about who would foot the bill for this *cause célèbre* were ongoing and heated. These arguments boiled up again in 1926, even more furiously, when the costs of putting on the supposed "trial of the century" sent Somerset County taxpayers and editorial writers into a righteous crusade for frugality.[16]

Meanwhile, the investigation went on, even though much of the physical evidence had been mishandled, ignored, or carried off. Nothing demonstrates the near-comical nature of the procedure better than the occasional news updates concerning the state of the crime scene. Souvenir hunting had begun in earnest even before the first detectives reached the crab apple tree, and it never abated. Nor was it restrained by order of the authorities, or by ridicule in the press, or by common sense.

A month after the murders the *New York Times* reported more than three hundred cars parked along Easton Avenue near De Russey's Lane on a Sunday afternoon. A special police officer was detailed to keep traffic moving. The *Times* noted: "Fakers from New Brunswick flocked to the scene with balloons, popcorn, peanuts and soft drinks, so that the scene resembled a circus lot more than a farm. The curiosity seekers took everything they could get their hands on as souvenirs, and denuded the murder tree of its branches and leaves."[17]

Two weeks later the frenzy continued. "Thousands of sightseers . . . drove out to the scene of the crime at the Phillips farm. The crab apple tree was no longer to be seen, having been destroyed by souvenir hunters who first stripped it of its leaves, then its branches and finally cut away the whole tree trunk. Nevertheless, the sightseers were able to buy post card photographs of the original scene which an enterprising photographer had prepared. They sold like hot cakes."[18]

At about this time, James F. Mason, the Essex County detective working for special prosecutor Wilbur A. Mott, who had been appointed in late October, was directing the making of his own maps and photographs of the crime scene. A well-dressed woman got in the way of the cameraman, and Mason asked her to step aside.

"Are you newspaper photographers?" she asked.

"No," Mason replied. "We're officials."

"Well," the woman said, "it's too late now for pictures. The ———— [family name deleted by *Times* editor] said they could get away with anything in this town except murder. It looks as if they . . . got away with that this time."[19]

Two months after the discovery of the bodies the owner of the Phillips farmhouse leased it to Henry Masterson, a local carpenter, who planned "to convert it into a 'museum' with a 25-cent charge for admission" and to serve soda water, sandwiches, and other refreshments. His museum would have to do without the insinuatingly photographed horsehaired sofa, however. The sofa, once the centerpiece of the main floor of the house, had reportedly been sold, along with an old-fashioned piano, to a New York museum for $250.[20]

There seemed to be no end to sightseers' interest in the place where Reverend Hall and Mrs. Mills had met their fate. Two days after the report of Masterson's projected museum, the weekend visitors, many of whom, as always, were from out of state, were at it again. "The crab apple tree being no more, some brought shovels and dug up portions of dirt from the spot where the bodies were found. This became so popular that the proprietor of the show bought paper bags which he resold at a big profit to those who needed a receptacle for their souvenirs."[21]

And so it went. None of it, not the inept collection nor the casual destruction of evidence, augured well for building a conclusive case against anybody.

Three weeks after the 1922 grand jury had refused to issue indictments, Sir Basil Thompson, former head of Scotland Yard, spoke to four hundred people at Roosevelt Junior High School in New Brunswick. Sir Basil declined to speculate on the identity of the killer or killers in the Hall-Mills murders, but he did note "a parallel case which occurred in England some months ago" in which "every scrap of evidence available at the scene of the crime" had been collected and analyzed. "The police in this instance," he said, "roped off the ground, no one was permitted near, and, as in all such cases, a most complete autopsy was made. The criminal was captured and within two months he had been convicted and hanged."[22]

9 A Crackerjack Idea!

It would be unfair to hold detectives of the early 1920s to the standards of present-day crime scene investigators. The impressive strides in forensic science since the Hall-Mills case demand a far more thorough and precise collection of physical evidence than was dreamed of, or needed by, George D. Totten, Bogart Conkling, Ferd David, and their contemporaries. Still, a few irreducible standards existed then as now. And it was widely recognized at the time of the Hall-Mills investigation that the officers at the scene handled their duties with remarkable ineptness.

After the Somerset County grand jury refused to return indictments in late November 1922, an editorial in the *New York Times* expressed this dim view of the inquiry:

"Work was begun on the case in an amateurish way. Time was given for the removal of evidence from the scene of the crime. . . . Medical officers looked at the bodies to be able to depose that a murder had been committed, but there was no autopsy, an omission that deplorably impeded the investigation. . . . So ineffective was the work of the authorities that reports of secret influence to shield persons involved in the crime were bruited about. . . . [An early and ill-advised arrest] was so stupid that it was decided to assign a special prosecutor to the case."[1]

That is the editorial voice of the august *Times,* America's newspaper of record, not the outburst of a tabloid journalist.

One of the standard textbooks for students of criminal justice is *Techniques of Crime Scene Investigation,* by Barry A.J. Fisher, of the Los Angeles County Sheriff's Department, and others. Although the text is modern, its fundamental principles have been applicable ever since the Sûreté began chasing criminals in nineteenth-century Paris. The authors state: "The ability to recognize, collect, and use evidence in criminal investigations determines to a large degree the success of the officers as investigators. . . . To a great extent, the very success of the investigation and, perhaps, the chance for a successful prosecution, hinge upon the actions and steps taken by the first officer to arrive at the crime scene. . . . Errors committed in the protection and examination of the crime scene can never be rectified."[2]

A common complaint about the early stages of the Hall-Mills investigation was that the authorities seemed almost unconcerned about solving the crime. After failing to shake James Mills' alibi, they appeared hesitant to interrogate in any serious and sustained way Mrs. Hall and her wealthy and socially prominent relatives. When Governor Edward I. Edwards, having learned of the apparent foot-dragging, dispatched three state troopers to New Brunswick to assist the reluctant locals, the *New York Times* noted that this action "stimulated the county authorities to more activity than they had shown at any time during the two weeks since the discovery of the bodies."[3]

Since there was a dispute from the very beginning over whether the victims had walked to the spot where they were murdered or had been driven there after their deaths, you might expect the detectives to pay close attention to the condition of the victims' shoes. But no. It was officially stated that the first investigators to arrive at the scene took "no particular notice of the shoes worn by the victims." Moreover, "whatever dust there was on the shoes was removed when the clothing was later wrapped in bundles." But another report had it that the rector's shoes bore traces of red clay, similar to the clay on the Phillips farm, suggesting that he had walked in the vicinity before the murders.[4]

No one at the scene, or afterwards, found either the weapon that fired the fatal shots or the weapon that slashed Eleanor Mills' throat. The official search was perfunctory at best. In early October, two weeks after the discovery of the bodies, a newspaper reporter asked Azariah Beekman, the Somerset County prosecutor, whether the two wells on the Phillips farm had been searched for weapons. "No," said Beekman, "but, by gum, that's a crackerjack idea! I never thought of that before!" Beekman ordered the search but found nothing.[5]

While the local authorities continued to bumble, Timothy N. Pfeiffer brought in a private investigator of his own to look into the case on behalf of Mrs. Hall. He was Felix B. De Martini, a Brooklyn detective who had served with the New York City Police Department before going into business for himself. About forty years old, De Martini was a mild-looking man with curly black hair, a Roman nose, and a dark complexion. He wore black-rimmed glasses. De Martini and his several side-kicks shadowed Jim Mills for quite some time, apparently without result, but paid no attention at all to Jane Gibson and her supposed eyewitness account of events under the crab apple tree, never bothering to interview her.[6]

De Martini was on the case from early October 1922 until March 1923 and billed Pfeiffer for more than five thousand dollars. What this money bought is unclear. Certainly, De Martini did not unmask the killer or killers, nor did he turn up any physical evidence to add to (or call into question) the items being assembled by the investigating officials. He received little publicity in 1922, but in 1926 Alexander Simpson saw him as a slippery, unprincipled rascal, the chief intimidator and briber on the Hall-Stevens team. The special prosecutor was never able to make the charge seem as convincing as he evidently thought it was.[7]

Given the millions of words journalists produced about the Hall-Mills case, you might think that most of the basic questions about physical evidence would long since have been answered. They have not been. Trying to pin down the discovery, description, and travel of any of the various handkerchiefs in the case, to take one example, is like trying to bottle the morning mist. Totten's trial testimony in connection with two handkerchiefs found at the scene—one with the monogrammed letter *H*—was so vague and muddled as to be useless, "an absolute failure of identification," as defense attorney Clarence E. Case pointed out. Here is a sample of Totten's curious responses: "Q: Did you put the handkerchiefs in the safe? A: There were fifteen items of exhibits."[8]

The tortuous and multiforked trail of handkerchiefs in the Hall-Mills case ultimately led nowhere.

Near the end of October, more than five weeks after the slayings, Governor Edwards appointed a special prosecutor, Wilbur A. Mott of Essex County, to attempt to sort out the clutter. Mott learned to his surprise that the authorities of Somerset and Middlesex Counties had not yet made a thorough search of the Phillips property. Nor had they tried, from first to last, to keep sightseers from stomping across the grass, gathering souvenirs, and carrying off or destroying whatever evidence might exist.

It finally occurred to someone among the investigators that there might be incriminating fingerprints on objects found at the crime scene. This inspiration led investigators to look for fingerprints on the cuffs of the shirt Reverend Hall was wearing. Although they promptly claimed to have found a few, they managed to restrain their enthusiasm. As the *New York Times* acknowledged, chances for success were slim:

"Eight weeks have passed since the bodies were discovered, and many officials and detectives have handled the clergyman's shirt, as well as the letters found with the bodies and other exhibits. The fingerprints may be found to be only those of the various investigators."[9]

Two days later a retired New York City police lieutenant and fingerprint expert, Grant Williams, scoffed at the report of fingerprint evidence having been found on the rector's clothing. "If they wanted fingerprints," he said, "they should have attempted to obtain them from Mr. Hall's card."[10]

This bit of advice must have struck one or more of the detectives as a crackerjack idea too. When the case came to trial four years later, lo and behold, the strongest—and yet in some ways the most questionable—item of physical evidence was the rector's calling card, the one originally propped against his left foot. Although Reverend Hall had other calling cards in his card case, the one the killer chose to display allegedly bore the fingerprint of Willie Stevens. At first blush this exhibit would seem to be conclusive and damning. It was not.[11] The card had all too many times been passed from person to person, from hand to hand, and carried from place to place. It was unquestionably contaminated.[12]

One of the basic requirements for handling physical evidence is maintaining an unbroken chain of custody. This chain shows "who had contact with the evidence, at what time, under what circumstances, and what, if any, changes were made in the evidence."[13] Obviously, tampering with the evidence could occur

Eleanor Mills' bloodstained dress. Somerset County detective Joe Hanlon holds up the dress the choir singer was wearing when someone shot her three times and then cut her throat. (photo 1926)

(although, of course, it might not) if there was a break in the chain of custody. Such a break could be fatal to the prosecution. Given such a break—the pun is unavoidable—any good defense attorney would argue that tampering had in fact taken place.

Recall, if you will, patrolman Garrigan, who was one of the first officers on the scene, letting the *Daily Home News* reporter Cardinal pick up the minister's calling card and examine it. The possibility that the killer's fingerprints might be on that card (a very real possibility) seems not to have occurred to Garrigan. The casual handling of the card did not end with these two men. As Rex Stout, the mystery writer and creator of Nero Wolfe, commented in his review of William M. Kunstler's *The Minister and the Choir Singer:*

"The wanderings of that card during the four years that elapsed before the trial were typical of the whole tragicomic performance. It was taken to the office of the Somerset prosecutor; then, in the summer of 1926, to the office of a fingerprint expert in Newark; then on a ride in a taxicab where it was handed over to the editor of the [New York *Daily] Mirror;* then, somewhat later, to Middletown, N.Y., to another fingerprint expert; and then—no one knew just when—back to the prosecutor's office in Somerville."[14]

This itinerary sounds peculiar enough, but the calling card was an iffy piece of evidence even before its meandering journey. It had been exposed to the elements for thirty-six hours before anyone in law enforcement saw it. Then, after it had been handled by Cardinal, Somerset County Sheriff Bogart Conkling placed the card in a brown paper package. Nor did he use fresh brown paper, but instead brown paper picked up from the ground in the neighborhood, brown paper that might itself have been evidence. To compound this gaffe, Conkling put the calling card in the package with other items—among them the love letters from Eleanor Mills and the .32 caliber cartridge case found near the bodies.[15]

In 1926 special prosecutor Simpson introduced the calling card as Exhibit S-17. It was a move Rex Stout considered "ludicrous and appalling." But under the circumstances it made sense. The special prosecutor could hardly ignore the card. He was not sitting atop a mountain of physical evidence. Under better circumstances Exhibit S-17 would have been a strong evidential link between Willie Stevens and the crime. Unhappily for Simpson, the haphazard treatment and poorly documented travels of the calling card made it suspect, a tempting target for the defense to discredit and the jury to disregard.

The Million Dollar Defense team, while surely holding Stout's jaundiced view of the fingerprint exhibit, nonetheless spent a great deal of time and money, and called several expert witnesses, to make sure the jury would reject the contention that Willie Stevens had handled the minister's calling card on that fatal night under the crab apple tree. The defense attorneys hinted darkly of forgery and fraud.[16]

A dearth of usable physical evidence left Simpson without much of a case. There were the love letters, to be sure, but they merely proved the fact of an intimate relationship between "babykins" and his "wonder heart." Jealousy as a possible motive was already as obvious as stripes on a zebra. The affair was known to many people in New Brunswick. Quite incredibly, though, the racy letters failed to prove the likelihood of infidelity to either the phlegmatic James Mills (although he was clearly and, later, admittedly lying) or the patrician Frances Hall (who steadfastly pronounced her dead husband as faithful as a lap dog, although not in those words).

What the prosecution needed and lacked was the murder weapon, or a bloody knife or razor or garden shears or sharp ax, or anything else that would tie the crime inextricably to a particular suspect or suspects. The investigators had plenty of suspicions, but no tangible proof except for that disputed fingerprint smudge on the rector's flyspecked calling card. Simpson, assigned to bring the culprits to justice and dedicated (so it appeared) to humbling the mighty, decided he had little choice but to play the fingerprint card.

Scientific crime detection was in its infancy, or perhaps its early childhood, at the start of the 1920s. Fingerprinting was gradually replacing the old Bertillon method of identification, a nineteenth-century French system based on a set of physical measurements of people. Not that fingerprinting was brand new. The plot of Mark Twain's *Pudd'nhead Wilson,* published in 1894, revolves around fingerprint identification, and readers of the novel may remember that one of the reasons the people of Dawson's Landing persist in calling lawyer David Wilson "Pudd'nhead" is because of his interest in the new crime-fighting technique. They consider him a bit daft.[17]

Acceptance of the new method of whorls, loops, and arches was slow, and in 1922 fingerprint identification still had many skeptics, particularly outside of the police departments of major cities. By the mid-1920s, however, the Bureau of Investigation (later the FBI) under its young director, J. Edgar Hoover, was putting its support solidly behind the procedure. At the time of the Hall-Mills trial the Bureau's files contained more than a million sets of fingerprints. Local law enforcement officials, following the federal Bureau's lead, had by then begun to learn about the advantages and techniques of fingerprinting.[18]

Satisfactory fingerprint evidence would have been rather avant-garde in a trial in central New Jersey in 1926 and probably quite persuasive. Such evidence may have existed in abundance at the crime scene. But the paltry and tainted evidence that Simpson had, the deficiencies of which were not primarily his fault, failed to impress the trial jury.

In a satiric essay about the case, Alexander Woollcott, a well-known journalist of the day, focused on what went wrong in September and October of 1922. He wrote:

"You may labor under the naive delusion that if you, yourself, are ever discovered some morning with a knife in your back, a vast, inexorable machinery will automatically start tracking your murderer down. But that machinery will prove more dependable if you can manage to be killed in a metropolitan area, and preferably at a good address. Out on the outskirts of New Brunswick, the limited resources of the local constabulary were further strained by the capricious circumstance that the bodies were found on the borderline between two counties, and in each the prosecuting authority was guided by a thrifty hope that the costly job would be handled by the other. The Hall-Mills murderer (or murderers) would probably have long since paid the penalty if the bodies had been found under a bush in Central Park instead of under a tree in De Russey's Lane."[19]

10   Burial Now, Autopsy Later

Prompt and competent autopsies of the victims' bodies might have yielded some useful information. But in a startling oversight, or a lapse of common sense, or a concern for the sensibilities of the survivors, or a nefarious plot, no one bothered to order or perform autopsies on the bodies of the rector and the choir singer. The Somerset County physician, Dr. William H. Long, who was present at the crime scene with sheriff Conkling and detective Totten, made only a cursory examination of the corpses. He neither suggested nor asked about autopsies.

Dr. Long saw nothing wrong with his inaction, saying it was self-evident that Hall had been murdered, and that was all there was to it.[1] Detective Totten remembered that Dr. Long had surprised him at the crime scene by turning to him and warning, "Don't know too much," or maybe it was, "Don't talk too much."[2] Another version of the story had Totten pointing to the deep cut on Mrs. Mills' neck and Dr. Long responding, "Don't talk too loud about that."[3] Whatever the words, the doctor could see nothing amiss in what he'd said, explaining he merely meant that in a big case like this it would be wise to avoid speculating in public.

At Dr. Long's direction, the bodies of the two victims were trundled off to a Somerset funeral home. "Better get them out of here in a hurry," he told the undertaker who had been summoned to the scene. "They've been dead at least thirty-six hours."[4] When the undertaker, Samuel T. Sutphen, got back to his funeral home in Somerville and began to remove the minister's coat, a .32 caliber bullet fell to the floor. He turned this piece of evidence over to the authorities.

At about six in the evening on the day the bodies were discovered, Dr. Long informed Sutphen in person that, at the request of the Hall-Stevens family, a New Brunswick undertaker, John V. Hubbard, would be coming to pick up Edward W. Hall's body and take it to his establishment in New Brunswick. Hubbard arrived shortly thereafter and removed the body in his hearse.

With Hall's body on its way back to New Brunswick, Dr. Long, possibly without Sutphen's knowledge, managed to squeeze in one more controversial act. Acting on his own, or so he said, he made an incision in Mrs. Mills' abdomen, "from the navel to the privates," examined her uterus, and then closed the incision with a suture. He found no sign of pregnancy. When questioned later about this procedure, Dr. Long searched for an answer but could offer no plausible reason for doing what he had done.[5]

The next day, at the request of Jim and Charlotte Mills, Hubbard sent a hearse to pick up the body of Eleanor Mills.

Dr. William H. Long was an experienced physician, in practice since 1906. After his actions (and nonactions) were discovered as a result of genuine autopsies, he maintained with some vehemence that no one had asked him to do autopsies—or, for that matter, to do the examination for pregnancy. It was not up to him, he said, to decide on an autopsy in a murder case. It was up to Azariah Beekman, the Somerset County prosecutor, and Beekman had made no such request.

Nevertheless, until September 29, 1922, Dr. Long had seemed quite willing, even eager, to imply to the press and public that he *had* performed autopsies. Along the way he made a number of inaccurate statements about the condition of the victims' bodies. Two days into the investigation he still did not know the number of bullet holes in Mrs. Mills' head. But then, a couple of days later, he told the *Daily Home News* he was positive that only one bullet had struck her.[6] He did not know for sure whether Mrs. Mills' throat had been cut, only that it had been "haggled or tampered with."[7] He gave conflicting statements about how many times the rector had been shot. His official report, issued several days after the discovery of the corpses, did nothing to clarify his findings.

Dr. Long's bumbling is hard to fathom. Had he done nothing more than read New Brunswick's daily newspaper on the day the bodies were discovered, he could have commented with more accuracy on their condition. As it was, his remarks made him look foolish.

If Dr. Long, as Somerset County physician, could provide no help to investigators, perhaps the new undertaker, John V. Hubbard, could. In addition to operating a funeral home at 96 Bayard Street, New Brunswick, Hubbard also served as Middlesex County coroner. Now that both bodies were at his funeral home, there was a second chance for autopsies to be done, and the question naturally arose as to whether Hubbard had performed them. At the pretrial hearing in 1926 the exchange went like this:

Q—You [Hubbard] were the coroner weren't you, over in Middlesex?

A—Yes.

Q—And you knew this had been a murder, didn't you?

A—Well, it was supposed to be.

Q—What did you think when you saw a woman with her throat cut and three bullet holes in her head?

A—I supposed it was.

Q—And you were coroner. Did you do anything to see that there was an autopsy on this body up to the time it was buried? **A**—No, sir.[8]

While John V. Hubbard, like Dr. Long, sidestepped doing an autopsy, a Middlesex County doctor got into the act. He was Dr. Edwin I. Cronk of New Brunswick, the city physician and health officer. As luck would have it, while the two bodies were being prepared for burial, Dr. Cronk walked into Hubbard's funeral home. He arrived a few moments after Mrs. Hall's lawyer, W. Edwin Florance, had phoned to ask for an official identification of the rector's body. Mrs. Hall did not want to view the body herself.

Since Dr. Cronk had known both the rector and Mrs. Mills, he was pressed into service, with attorney Florance's approval, and asked to make the identifications.

What Dr. Cronk saw in the embalming room made him wonder what in the world Dr. Long had been thinking when he examined the bodies and commented on their condition. Clearly, the choir singer had been shot three times, not once. The three bullet holes in her head were unmistakable. How could Dr. Long have missed them? Clearly, too, there was only one exit wound, which meant that two bullets were still in her skull. Since Dr. Cronk knew this for a fact, you might think he would try to call a halt to the embalming and suggest an autopsy. But no. Without objection he let coroner-undertaker Hubbard continue to prepare both bodies for burial.[9]

Still, what Dr. Cronk had seen—the divergence between his knowledge and Dr. Long's statements—would soon become known to investigators and the public.

Unfortunately for his own reputation, Dr. Cronk went one step further. The same question crossed his mind that had crossed Dr. Long's, and he found it impossible to resist the temptation posed by the sight of Eleanor Mills' sutured abdomen. Without authorization, or any known reason for doing so, Dr. Cronk removed the suture to take a look, to see if she was "in a certain condition."[10] She was not.

Like Dr. Long, Dr. Cronk could never explain his action in a satisfactory way. His defense (when a true autopsy revealed what had happened) invoked the principle of "concealed evidence." He seems to have thought a "concealed" fetus would have evidential value while, by some unfathomable logic, two concealed bullets would not.[11]

On Monday, September 18, two days after the discovery of the victims' bodies, funeral services were held for the Reverend Edward Wheeler Hall at his church on George Street. They were conducted by Bishop Albion B. Knight of Trenton, assisted by twenty-eight clergymen, all of whom signed resolutions expressing confidence in Hall's character. No mention was made of the cause of the forty-one-year-old rector's sudden passing. After the service, an automobile cortege consisting of a hearse and three limousines carrying family members left New Brunswick, crossed over to Brooklyn on the Staten Island Ferry, and proceeded to Green-Wood Cemetery, where the body was interred.[12]

Funeral services for Eleanor Reinhardt Mills were held the next morning in the chapel of the Hubbard Funeral Home in New Brunswick. Mrs. Mills' sixteen-year-old daughter Charlotte made the arrangements, choosing, as a distraught teenager might, a six-hundred-dollar solid mahogany coffin, even though her janitor father had never in his life earned more than two thousand dollars a year. Few people attended the service. Floral arrangements were sparse, but a wreath from Mrs. Frances

James Mills at his wife's gravesite. Jim Mills kneeling in Van Liew Cemetery, North Brunswick, at the spot where Eleanor's body has been exhumed. A second autopsy, ordered by Simpson, confirmed the results of the first. (photo 1926)

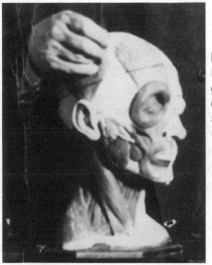

Explaining the autopsy results Dr. Otto H. Schultze used this grisly bust to trace the path of each of the three bullets that struck Eleanor Mills in the head. (photo 1926)

Stevens Hall rested on the closed coffin. Charlotte made a scene when she was prevented from raising the lid to see her mother one last time. After a short service Eleanor Mills, her crazy-cat dreams unrealized, was buried in Van Liew Cemetery, North Brunswick.[13]

She did not stay quietly buried for long, nor did her lover. A cry went up from the press and public as to why the two murder victims had been so hastily consigned to their graves. There were some who took Dr. Long at his word that autopsies had been performed and believed that nothing could be learned by exhuming the bodies. But with Dr. Cronk fueling the skepticism, it became increasingly plain that Dr. Long's flawed and superficial examinations did not qualify as the kind of post mortems needed in a homicide case.

On September 27, nearly two weeks after the murders, prosecutors Azariah Beekman of Somerset County and Joseph E. Stricker of Middlesex County announced that "new" autopsies would be performed to settle questions raised by the differing observations of Dr. Long and Dr. Cronk. The bodies would be, and were, disinterred. Doctors representing each of the two counties, Dr. Runkle E. Hegeman of Somerville and Dr. A. L. Smith of New Brunswick, examined anew the remains of Eleanor Mills.[14]

The *New York Times* reported on the results: "One of the bullets entered the woman's forehead about two inches above the nose, another ploughed through the right cheek, and the third pierced the right temple. Her jugular vein, the cartoid artery, and the esophagus were severed by a knife or razor, which made a 'necklace incision' across the throat. The bullets found in the head were from a .32 caliber automatic pistol, such as would fit the three empty shells found with the bodies."[15]

Mrs. Mills' slashed throat caused much comment in the press and much speculation among investigators. Its viciousness argued that here, if ever, was a crime of jealousy, revenge, bitter retribution. When it was learned that the upper part of Eleanor's windpipe, her larynx, and her tongue had been cut out, it seemed clear to many that the killer's real target was not just Eleanor Mills but all that Eleanor represented. Lust and betrayal had been avenged by death and mutilation.[16]

The autopsy on the body of Mrs. Mills also revealed, less horrifically, a few scratches or abrasions on her right arm, extending from the wrist to the shoulder. As to whether these wounds might have been caused by the clawing of fingernails, Drs. Hegeman and Smith said that decomposition made it impossible for them to say. A slight puncture wound on her upper lip was never conclusively explained.[17]

Dr. Long now admitted that his autopsy of the choir singer had been inadequate. But he refused to acknowledge having missed the glaring fact that Mrs. Mills' neck had been cut so severely that her head was almost severed from her body. In exculpation Dr. Long pointed to the words of his official report: "The anterior surface of the neck is badly decomposed, probably due to external violence."[18] It looked as if he had been heeding his own advice to detective Totten at the crime scene: "Don't know too much."

Next, the authorities focused on the Reverend Edward Wheeler Hall. Because his body was interred in Brooklyn, they had to go through some red tape to get permission to proceed. On October 5, 1922, the remains of the amorous rector were removed from the Stevens family vault in Brooklyn's Green-Wood Cemetery. Dr. Hegeman and Dr. Smith once again went about their task, this time accompanied by a small army of official onlookers, including Dr. Long and Dr. Cronk and undertaker-coroner Hubbard, the three of whom must have been a mite embarrassed by the proceedings and apprehensive about what would be discovered.

"We found nothing particularly new," Dr. Hegeman reported. The minister "was killed by a [single] bullet that entered his head near the right temple and came out at the back of the neck on the left side. The point of exit was three and a half inches lower than the entrance. The bullet went through the brain and was apparently of .32 caliber."[19]

The examining doctors found abrasions on the back of Hall's hands and on his left wrist. These could have been sustained in a struggle—"Hall Put up a Fight, Autopsy Indicates," headlined the *New York Times*. But, in fact, the abrasions were more likely to have been caused by his body falling backward to the ground after he was struck by the fatal bullet.[20] Neither autopsy suggested a "furious attack" preceding the murders, as the press had reported in the first few days after the bodies were discovered.[21]

An important question the autopsies addressed was the distance from which the fatal shots were fired. An early news report declared that powder burns were visible on Mrs. Mills face,[22] suggesting pointblank range, but later accounts did not repeat the claim. By the time the bodies were exhumed in late September and early October 1922 and autopsies performed, the examining doctors said that decomposition made it impossible for them to detect powder marks. Their statement was challenged four years later, however, when a second autopsy was performed on each body. The man who did the 1926 autopsies, Dr. Otto H. Schultze, the New York County Medical Examiner, announced that there were no embedded powder grains, no powder burns on either body, and never had been.[23]

In 1922 the doctors estimated that the assailant was less than three feet from Reverend Hall when the fatal shot was fired.[24] Dr. Schultze, who appeared as an expert witness at the trial in 1926, testified that the distance could have been as little as six inches.[25] No investigator, no doctor, no journalist ever put the distance at more than three feet. It took prosecutor Simpson to suggest, out of the blue, a likely distance of six feet in one of his several ill-advised questions at the trial.[26]

The actual distance of the four shots, according to those doctors who did the autopsies and were presumed to know, was between six inches and three feet. Although the night was pitch black at the time the shots were fired, the killer or killers presumably carried flashlights. Given those conditions, one has to wonder whether it took a skilled marksman to fire the fatal bullets. It seems entirely possible that a pistol-packing novice could have committed the crime.

11   Bizarre Interlude

No account of the Hall-Mills case would be complete without a look at the peculiar sequence of events that occurred in early October 1922, when a young New Brunswick man, innocent as a newborn pup, was arrested and charged with the double murder. In retrospect, the events of these few days seem inane, if not insane. A cynic would say they cast doubt on the seriousness of purpose of the authorities. More charitably, and perhaps more accurately, they appear to confirm the chaotic and by then half-desperate nature of the stalled investigation.

The episode involved the two young people who had discovered the bodies: Raymond Schneider and Pearl Bahmer. As many people speculated at the time, these two were probably not picking mushrooms that morning near the crab apple tree.   Raymond Schneider, a twenty-three-year-old married roustabout, was sexually involved with fifteen-year-old Pearl Bahmer. So too, according to wayward Pearl, was her father, Nicholas, who owned a saloon and poolroom, Nick's, on Neilson Street in New Brunswick. This being Prohibition, Nick's occupation was listed in the 1921-22 city directory as "confectioner."[1] In fact, Nick was a barkeep with a personal fondness for his illegal hooch.

Schneider and his teenage girlfriend were questioned at length about their Saturday morning find. Since the minister's pockets contained only sixty-one cents, and since a valuable gold watch in a hunting case was missing, and since Raymond and Pearl lacked any kind of clout in the community, they were not treated with deference. Both went a bit squirrelly under the harsh interrogation.

Pearl accused her father of incest, and he was arrested and jailed.[2] The intense questioning also brought out the story of her involvement with Raymond Schneider, putting Schneider in a dicey spot and landing Pearl herself in Newark's House of the Good Shepherd as "incorrigible."[3] The young couple's good-citizen action of reporting the murders had put them both in trouble. For Schneider—and for an unsuspecting friend of his—it would get a lot worse.

Investigators thought it was a good bet that Schneider had taken most of Reverend Hall's money. No one knew how much that was, but he was known to carry quite a bit of cash. Mrs. Hall's guess was fifty dollars or so. They also assumed that the young ne'er-do-well had made off with the minister's watch. In an odd non sequitur, Azariah Beekman, the Somerset County prosecutor, remarked that if the watch were found, "You'll discover who committed the murder."[4]

The watch was never found. Nor was the missing cash ever accounted for. But the harder Middlesex authorities pressed Raymond Schneider, the more he began to tell them about Pearl and Nicholas Bahmer and about his—and their—activities on the night of the crime. It was an intriguing tale, part of which could be corroborated, but the centerpiece of which, the bombshell, was an obvious, easily disproved lie.

According to Schneider's statement, made in the presence of Middlesex County detective Ferd David, Middlesex deputy sheriff Frank Kirby, and New Jersey state trooper Henry L. Dickman, the Hall-Mills killer was Clifford R. Hayes, a twenty-one-year-old friend of Schneider. The murders were a case of mistaken identity, Schneider said. Disoriented in the dark of the moon, Hayes thought he was shooting Nicholas

Bahmer and Nick's daughter Pearl, having caught them out beyond Buccleuch Park in an incestuous embrace.[5]

But why would Hayes do the shooting? It was Schneider, after all, who loved Pearl and despised her abusive father. It was Schneider, like Reverend Hall, who occasionally sent love letters to his youthful mistress. One of Schneider's letters read in part: "My Girl: You are the only one I care about in this world. Nothing will make me go back to my wife. If you are going to be my girl you can't go out with other fellows. I don't want you to go with anyone but me."[6]

Presumably that prohibition against other fellows included Pearl's father. But Nick continued to molest his teenage daughter, or so she claimed, and Nick had the same objection to his rivals that Schneider did. They were poaching on his parental rights. Pearl, vowing that she would "jump into the river and never come up," told reporters, "Father never wanted me to go out with a single fellow. I never knew a girl who had to go out with her own father."[7]

Such was the sordid background for the Bahmer-Schneider episode in the Hall-Mills investigation. It began outside the Rivoli Theatre on George Street at 10:35 p.m. on the night of the murders (a few minutes after the slayings had occurred, in fact, but no one yet knew that for sure). Raymond Schneider, Clifford Hayes, and sixteen-year-old Leon Kaufmann—whom Ray failed to mention in his sworn statement—caught sight of Pearl and her father walking north on George Street. Pearl later said that Nick was walking off a bender.[8]

Astonishingly enough, Nick Bahmer and Clifford Hayes were both carrying firearms that night. Bahmer toted a .45 caliber pistol, while Hayes packed a gun that fired only blank cartridges. Nick may have needed protection in his line of work, but Clifford Hayes dismissed the weapon he carried as "a foolish and a boyish" Fourth of July purchase.

At George Street and Seminary Place, across from the Johnson & Johnson factory, there was a brief, inconclusive confrontation between the Bahmers and their pursuers. No dialogue from this encounter was preserved for posterity. Nobody pulled a gun.[9]

Evidently, Schneider and Hayes did go on to Buccleuch Park, where they stayed until about midnight, but after the altercation near the banks of the Raritan they were no longer pursuing saloon-keeper Nick and his wayward daughter. Nonetheless, it was this late-night journey to the general area of the murders that supplied the core of truth at the heart of Raymond Schneider's lie. In Schneider's defense, it should be said that he had been questioned more or less continuously for thirty hours, and may have reached the end of his rope. In any case, he broke down and provided Ferd David, Frank Kirby, and Henry Dickman with a fanciful story of what had happened out beyond the Parker Home.

The way Raymond Schneider told it, he and Clifford Hayes "followed Mr. Bahmer and his daughter Pearl up George Street, to Hamilton, then to College Avenue, up College to McCauley's Lane and thence to Easton Avenue, where we lost track of them. Hayes and I went through De Russey's gulley and when about three quarters of the way up we came across a man and a woman. Hayes said to me, 'There they are' and pulled a gun from his pocket and fired three or four times."[10]

The time was approximately 1:30 a.m., he said. The three detectives should have winced at that. By then the Reverend Edward W. Hall and the choir singer Eleanor Mills had been dead for more than three hours.

Although Schneider's statement left nearly every question about the crime and the crime scene unanswered, Somerset County prosecutor Azariah Beekman pronounced himself satisfied. On the basis of Schneider's dubious confession, Beekman had a charge of murder lodged against Clifford Hayes, and the young man was whisked off to the county jail in Somerville, where he was held without bail for the grand jury.[11]

Reporters expressed disgust at this turn of events, pointing out the discrepancies and omissions in the young man's story. One asked Beekman whether he thought Schneider was telling the truth.

"Truth?" Beekman replied testily. "We are not trying to determine the truth of his statement. I don't have to do that. All I have to do is look for a reasonable basis for prosecution."[12]

When asked if he had such a basis, Beekman snapped, "Yes, I do." Could the state obtain a conviction on the basis of the confession? "Sure, we can."[13]

Hardly anyone believed him. Hayes vigorously denied the murder charges, saying of Schneider, "He's a nut." Hayes' brother thought Raymond was being made "the goat." Their friends and neighbors announced "Hayes Tag Day," on which all New Brunswick residents were urged to wear a badge with Hayes' name on one side and a quotation from John Ruskin on the other: "The truth in one's heart does not fear the lie on the other's tongue."[14]

John E. Toolan, assistant prosecutor of Middlesex County, made it clear that he doubted Hayes' guilt. He told reporters, "This murder has not been cleared up; we have not quit our efforts to learn whether the families of Mr. Hall and Mrs. Mills know more than thus far they have seen fit to tell us."[15] Jim Mills expressed his belief that Hayes was innocent. Having already been subjected to many hours of interrogation himself, he observed, "I know how long periods of questioning can break a man down."[16] The widow of the slain rector offered no comment.[17]

Resentment against the treatment of Hayes built rapidly in New Brunswick. A particular object of scorn was deputy sheriff Frank Kirby, who townspeople believed was mainly responsible for getting Schneider to confess. The Sixth Ward council had offered a thousand-dollar reward to the person solving the crime, which Kirby hoped to receive.

The folks in the Sixth Ward, as in the rest of New Brunswick, didn't buy Hayes' confession. They rose up against it. On a street outside the Pennsylvania Station, deputy sheriff Kirby found the members of the Sixth Ward committee who were in charge of disbursing the reward. Instead of his thousand dollars, he got shouts of "frame-up" and a barrage of epithets. He tried to talk calmly to the upset citizens. He started to walk toward the police station. The group of angry citizens grew larger. After three blocks, his anxiety began to increase. He was being jostled, and the crowd, ever growing, became uglier.

Kirby broke and ran. Individuals in the mob, finding a pile of loose paving stones, began launching them at the fleeing officer. He raced past a stack of bricks. Several mob members paused to add bricks to their arsenal. Miraculously, all the thrown missiles missed, and Kirby stumbled back into the train station, out of breath and thoroughly rattled. He took refuge in the baggage room, where railroad employees helped to keep the mob at bay. Someone phoned the police. Soon eight uniformed officers arrived and escorted Kirby back to the station house, four blocks away.[18]

The unpopularity of Hayes' arrest continued to grow even after the cornering and put-down of Frank Kirby. Except for Azariah Beekman, nobody was ready to proclaim the investigation over. Newspapers outside of Somerset County were contemptuous of the actions taken and the statements made. An editorial in the *Trenton Times* put it this way:

"Whatever the motive behind the strange antics of the prosecuting officials in the New Brunswick murder case, they certainly are bringing the good name of New Jersey into disrepute all over the country. It will indeed be a sorry day if the latest arrest is merely a political gesture.

"But is it all politics, or social influence, or is it something more sinister? If Governor Edwards is honestly in earnest about clearing up the foul stench, he might with propriety send the Attorney General into Middlesex County."[19]

No one in Middlesex County seemed all that pleased with Beekman's stance either. The *Daily Home News,* a surprisingly outspoken newspaper considering the faint-heartedness of the Middlesex County prosecutor's office, also took Beekman to task:

"A prosecutor is far more than a prosecuting machine. He is a public servant, charged with the duty of seeing that real justice is effected, not merely with conducting prosecutions. Even if the defendant is acquitted, serious damage is done to him by the charge that hangs over him, and the prosecutor owes it to be himself at least reasonably satisfied of the truth of a charge before taking it to court."[20]

One law-enforcement officer in Somerset County who distrusted the truth of Schneider's statement from the beginning was detective George D. Totten. Much as he would have liked to see the case cleared, he could not accept the prosecutor's conclusions. At 7:00 p.m. on Wednesday, October 11, Totten visited Ray Schneider in his cell at the Somerville jail. They talked and smoked for more than three hours, sometimes with warden James Major in the cell, sometimes just the two of them.

After a while Totten asked to have the lights turned out, thinking the psychological effect of talking in the dark might make a difference. It did. By ten-thirty Schneider admitted that his signed statement was untrue. As far as he knew, Schneider now confided, Hayes had nothing whatever to do with the murders. He hoped his friend wouldn't hold the false accusation against him, he said.

Charges against Hayes were dropped, and the young man was released from custody.[21]

Schneider, contrite and apologetic, remained in legal hot water, but the authorities could never prove he had disturbed anything at the murder scene or made off with Reverend Hall's money and watch, or, more seriously, with the murder weapon or the throat-slashing implement. He was charged with perjury for his false accusation of Hayes, and sentenced to two years in the state reformatory at Rahway.[22]   Incest charges against Nicholas Bahmer were dropped.[23]   Nick's daughter Pearl remained at the Home of the Good Shepherd as an incorrigible.[24]

This unhappy episode had two significant effects on the Hall-Mills investigation. First, it convinced Governor Edwards that a special prosecutor was needed, and on October 23 he appointed Wilbur A. Mott of Essex County to that position.[25] Second, it convinced an eyewitness to the murder (or so she claimed to be anyway) to renew her efforts to bring her story to the attention of detectives on the case. Her success in that endeavor changed the direction of the investigation, finally and disastrously.[26]

George D. Totten. An experienced Somerset County detective, he was in charge of the initial 1922 Hall-Mills investigation. In 1926 Totten joined the staff of the New York *Daily Mirror*. (photo 1926)

12 The Witness from Hell

No one played a more central role in the Hall-Mills saga than Mrs. Jane Gibson, the Pig Woman. A purported eyewitness to the murders, she became, as she confidently predicted she would, "the Babe Ruth of the trial."[1] Yet for the first month after the murders, her identity and her story were unknown to the public. They may even have been unknown to the police, although that remains a matter of speculation. Mrs. Gibson claimed she tried again and again to tell detectives what she had seen and heard out by the crab apple tree, but that prior to the Clifford Hayes fiasco no one seemed to care.

Such a lack of interest would be odd, because if the early investigators were in need of anything, it was a credible eyewitness. The difficulty with the Pig Woman, first and last, was her credibility. She was intelligent, glib, but not wholly believable. When she first appeared as a mysterious presence at the Somerset County Courthouse, evidently to take a close look at Mrs. Hall in a gray coat, the press identified her as "a Hungarian woman."[2] By that time Mrs. Gibson was telling investigators a strange but compelling tale of having been in De Russey's Lane on that fateful night. To the detectives, at least at first, her story must have sounded like that of a typical publicity-seeking crank. But if what she said was true, her tale might counter to some extent the woeful lack of physical evidence.

Mrs. Gibson told a detailed story of having seen—yes, actually having *seen*—the crime in progress. What detective could avoid being drawn in, especially when stuck with a crime scene as contaminated as the Phillips farm and a murder weapon or weapons that appeared to have vanished?

In late September and early October 1922 the county prosecutors of Middlesex and Somerset were in the middle of a muddle. They had a double homicide on their hands, trumpeted to
a national audience through fervid and none too friendly press
coverage, and, on the face of it, not a prayer of getting an indictment against the killer or killers. Whether through design
or incompetence, they, their staffs, or both had made it all but
impossible to prosecute anyone in the case. It was a state of affairs that daily cast a harsh spotlight on law enforcement and
the criminal justice system in New Jersey.[3]

Joseph E. Stricker, fifty-two, prosecutor of Middlesex County, played a prominent part in the case at the beginning. His
role as prospective prosecutor ended after it was established
that the crime had been committed in Franklin Township, Somerset County, but his office continued to be involved in the
investigation. The day after the bodies were discovered, Stricker could not resist making his absurd pronouncement about the
case being so baffling that it might never be solved. This abrupt
washing-of-hands lost most of its significance, though not its
peculiarity, when the case landed in the lap of his counterpart,
Azariah Beekman of Somerset County.

Like the pessimistic Stricker, investigators in the Middlesex
County prosecutor's office, among them Ferd David and Frank
Kirby, contributed little to the sum of knowledge about the
double homicide. David, according to special prosecutor Simpson in 1926, in the presence of newspaper reporters, rubbed the
reverend's eyeglasses with his thumb, saying, "These are not finger marks; these are blood spots."[4] Kirby, for his part, was the
interrogator who helped pressure Raymond Schneider into
falsely accusing his friend, Clifford Hayes, of the murders. The

citizens of New Brunswick chased Frank Kirby down the street with flying stones and bricks, whereas Ferd David suffered most of his indignities later on the witness stand.

Four years after these unhappy events, just as the belated trial of the supposed culprits was about to begin, Joseph E. Stricker died suddenly at a hospital in Long Branch after undergoing an operation for acute appendicitis. A highly successful lawyer before and after his service as public prosecutor, he left behind a widow and a five-year-old daughter, an equivocal record in the Hall-Mills case, and a magnificent home, Rosewood, at Deal, on the Jersey shore. Shortly before he expired, the former prosecutor was reported to have murmured, "Ambition! Ambition! What does it amount to?"[5]

Azariah Beekman might have asked the same question. Faced with a scandal involving some of the first families of New Brunswick, he seemed lethargic and disinclined to get to the bottom of things. Indeed, if Beekman had any real desire to collar the culprit or culprits, he kept it well concealed. Immediately after the murders, when Dr. John T. Leahy, senior coroner of Somerset County, urged him to hold an inquest or to authorize an autopsy, Beekman replied: "Don't hold an autopsy; it might mix matters."[6] When William Fitzpatrick, a Middlesex County detective, found fingerprints on the calling card propped up near Reverend Hall's body, Beekman ordered him, according to a later report, not to photograph the prints.[7]

As the investigation entered its second month, Governor Edward I. Edwards was becoming impatient with the failure of local authorities to deal successfully with the *cause célèbre* that had been thrust upon them. Mrs. Jane Gibson, still nameless in the newspapers, had made a statement to the authorities, reportedly on Monday, October 16, one month to the day after bodies were found. Journalists passed along what they were able to find out about her story. Evidently, she had seen the rector and the choir singer near the crab apple tree that night "and also saw their two assailants." *The New York Times* headline read:

SAW COUPLE MURDER
HALL AND MRS. MILLS,
WOMAN NOW SWEARS.[8]

In Somerville there was talk of indictments, of imminent arrests, but still nothing happened. Then on October 23, 1922, the State of New Jersey took over the case. Attorney General Thomas F. McCran appointed Wilbur A. Mott of East Orange, former prosecutor of Essex County, as a special deputy attorney general, giving him complete charge of the investigation. Mott, a portly, stoop-shouldered native of Vermont, was sixty-two years old and highly regarded. A founding member of the law firm of Mott & Bernheim, he had an office in the Prudential Insurance Building in Newark. Mott, attempting to succeed where Stricker and Beekman had failed, moved quickly to assimilate the available information about the case. One of his first acts was to name James F. Mason, an experienced Essex County detective, as his chief investigator.

On the day Mott and Mason arrived in Somerville, they lifted the veil of anonymity from the woman who would become the state's key witness. She was Mrs. Jane Gibson, the soon-to-be-famous Pig Woman, a leathery, energetic woman of fifty-two, who ever afterwards occupied a place at or near the center of action. A local farmer who lived about a mile from the Phillips farm, she owned forty-eight pigs—thus her sobriquet—and several other animals, including chickens. She grew corn on twenty-three of her sixty-one acres.

Mrs. Gibson's first starring role was in the state's 1922 investigation and grand jury presentation. Her second was in the Simpson investigation and trial of 1926. In the first go-round, her testimony, which consumed almost two hours, was almost all the state could offer the Somerset County grand jury. Mott and Mason tried to assemble other evidence against the "bushy-haired man" and the "woman in gray" who Mrs. Gibson maintained she had seen kill Reverend Hall and Eleanor Mills, but the prosecution team ended up with little more than her unsupported word. It was not enough. The grand jury refused to hand up indictments.

Mrs. Jane Gibson was a strange and picturesque character, starting with her name. As the wife of William H. Easton, a New Brunswick toolmaker, she was technically Mrs. Easton—in fact, Mrs. Mary Jane Easton[9]—although at first she vigorously denied her married state to reporters (which meant little, since at one time or another she denied virtually everything about her life, even disavowing the truth of her De Russey's Lane tale, saying that she was never out of her house on the night of the murders).[10]

Why did she call herself Gibson? Her first answer was that she had been married to a clergyman named Gibson, who had died seventeen years earlier. When that explanation proved to be a lie, she offered a second answer.[11] Her new explanation was that the farm she owned in Middlebush, near New Brunswick, had previously been owned by the Gibson family and was known as the Gibson farm. She figured it was less confusing to people if she called herself Mrs. Gibson, and so she did. So too did the investigators, the attorneys, the press, and just about everyone else.

Jane Gibson, the Pig Woman. Mrs. Gibson, the owner of a small farm, was an intelligent, articulate woman who claimed to be an eyewitness. She gave a detailed, if fanciful, description of the crime in progress. (photo 1920s)

What, then, had Mrs. Gibson seen and heard on the night of September 14, 1922? Good question. It depends on the date she was telling her story, for her account became more specific and complete, and many of the details changed as time passed.

In her Hamilton Avenue home, converted from a barn, Mrs. Gibson kept a desk calendar on which she made daily diary entries. On the calendar page dated September 14, the day of the murders, she had jotted down: "Mama [Salome Cerenner, Jane Gibson's mother] got here 11am had dinner followed thief lost him—open wagon lost moc[casin] Farmer fired 4 shots."[12]

Three days later, on the page dated September 17, the day after the bodies were discovered, she updated her earlier entry: "Must have been what I heard and saw on the 14th."[13]

William M. Kunstler, in *The Minister and the Choir Singer,* suggests that these entries contradict parts of the Pig Woman's testimony, which, of course, they do. But an outspoken critic of his, J. L. Bernstein of Paterson, wrote a letter in response to Rex Stout's review of Kunstler's book, pointing out that "If anything, it [the calendar-diary] shows that the principal witness for the state, Mrs. Jane Gibson, the 'pig woman,' was in the vicinity of the crime at the time she says she was."[14]

And so it does. Yet, on balance, the diary-calendar seems far more damaging to the prosecution than to the defense. It strongly suggests that Mrs. Gibson knew almost nothing about the specific details of the murders. Small wonder, then, that Alexander Simpson did not introduce it as evidence in 1926, but instead scoured the New Brunswick countryside for a witness or witnesses who would, in some other way, confirm Mrs. Gibson's presence on that fatal night in De Russey's Lane. The absence of the diary-calendar from the trial also led the defense into a futile attempt (mainly through the faulty recollection of a neighbor, Nellie Lo Russell) to prove that Mrs. Gibson spent the entire evening at home.[15]

Evidently, the Pig Woman *was* somewhere near the scene of the murders at the time they occurred. The real question is, what did she see and hear while she was there? Her reference to the farmer firing four shots and her tentative "must have been" phraseology of September 17 lend little credence to the vivid and explicit narrative she would weave for investigators, attorneys, and journalists a month later.

Mrs. Gibson, after having been interviewed by investigators for more than a week, first told her story to the press on October 25. Its content followed the same general lines reported during the preceding few days, mostly while she was still anonymous, but she added a number of narrative details.

It seems that some of her neighbors, "foreigners," she assumed, had been stealing corn and chickens from her farm. On the night of September 14 one of her five dogs began scratching at the door. She looked out and saw a man "slinking across the cornfield." (She later amended this to say she was outside in the cornfield when the dog started to bark.) Thinking he might be one of the corn-stealers, she went to the barn, put a saddle and a bridle on one of her five mules—Jenny, by name—and started out to catch the fellow, who by then had gotten quite a head start. Her first account seemed to have the man on foot, but in later versions he was driving a horse and an open wagon.

Noticing him going "down toward De Russey's Lane" she took off after him, telling herself that sooner or later she would have to "empty a shotgun" into one of these thieving foreigners. She carried no shotgun on this occasion, though, or any other weapon. Mrs. Gibson soon lost sight of her quarry, but, unwilling to give up the chase, she opted to take "a roundabout course so as to come out on the little lane that runs in from De Russey's Lane, past the old Phillips farmhouse."

From a distance she heard voices. As she got closer, she crouched down on Jenny's neck so as to be as inconspicuous as possible. No problem on that score, she thought. It was so dark she doubted that anyone could see her on the mule. She estimated the time at between 9:30 and 10:00 p.m. when she finally rode close enough to the four persons to be aware that they were quarreling. Engrossed in their dispute, they failed to notice her approach, continuing to yell angrily at each other.

Mrs. Gibson concluded her narrative as follows:

"I saw that there were two men and two women.

"After they had been quarrelling for some time, all four of them began to fight. It didn't all happen in a minute. But suddenly there were shots, four of them. I saw a man fall and then I saw a woman fall.

"Jenny became frightened at the shots and turned around and ran. We went home as fast as we could and I did not go back to the scene until long afterward, after I had told my story to the authorities."[16]

Although special prosecutor Mott must have been delighted to have an eyewitness to the murders, he was clearly dubious about the value of Mrs. Gibson's story. He noted a lack of positiveness in her identification, a lack that is understandable given the dark, moonless night and her lack of a flashlight.[17]

But the Pig Woman was nothing if not resourceful, and overnight, quite literally, she came up with a way to make the crime scene as bright as noonday. Questioned the next day about how she had managed to see the faces of the assailants on a dark and moonless night, as she claimed she had, she explained that just as the two walked from Easton Avenue into

De Russey's Lane, heading toward the place where they expected to find the lovers, the headlights of an automobile picked them up, accentuating their features against the dark background "as plainly," according to the *New York Times* correspondent, "as a performer on the stage is shown up by a spotlight."[18] The woman wore a gray polo coat. The man had bushy hair and Negroid features.[19]

"It was only an accident," the *Times* writer continued, either disingenuously or tongue-in-cheek, "that an automobile happened to come along at this particular moment . . . and throw a light on the scene for Mrs. Gibson."[20]

Well, why not? Mrs. Gibson continued to supply details, or alter details, as needed to build an airtight case against . . . whom? Primarily against the rector's widow, Mrs. Hall, it seemed. Just as William Phillips, the night watchman at the New Jersey College for Women, had seen a woman in gray earlier that evening hurrying back to the Hall residence at about 2:30 a.m., so had Mrs. Gibson seen a woman in gray at 10:00 p.m. or thereabouts, hastening toward the scene of the crime. And unlike Phillips, Mrs. Gibson could make a positive identification—although, as Mott must have known, she had been unable to do so earlier at the staged meeting in the Somerset County Courthouse. The woman in gray, the Pig Woman now said, was none other than that honest and honorable woman, that pillar of New Brunswick society, Mrs. Frances Noel Stevens Hall.

The real problem for the Pig Woman lay in the identification not of Mrs. Hall but of her male partner in crime, the "bushy-haired man." From the beginning, she insisted she had heard the woman in gray scream, "Oh, Henry!" after the first shot was fired. Mrs. Gibson must have wished many times thereafter that she could change that anguished cry to "Oh, Willie!" It would have simplified things immensely.

But the die was cast. It was too late—and Mrs. Gibson's "Oh, Henry" was a calamitous snag for the prosecution. Willie Stevens, after all, was the one who had accompanied Mrs. Hall on her reported nocturnal trek to search for the missing rector. He was indisputably a "bushy-haired man" with what could be considered Negroid features. Indeed, Willie fit perfectly the physical description of the man the Pig Woman claimed she had seen in the glare of those fortuitous headlights.

Yet if there were only four people at the scene, as she had also insisted from the outset—the two victims, Mrs. Hall, and the bushy-haired man—then that man, the presumed assailant, had to be named Henry. The others were named Edward, Eleanor, and Frances. Henry was the fourth person under the crab apple tree. He had to be.

But Henry Who?

For Mrs. Gibson, necessity was the mother of prevarication. Ever resourceful, she could surely dream up some way to accommodate the required Henry. Mrs. Gibson knew she was being taken seriously by Wilbur A. Mott and James F. Mason, the big-city prosecutor and the reputedly able detective. They said as much in print. "I think her story stands up," Mott insisted, and Mason echoed that he believed it "will stand the strictest examination."[21]

Some of the journalists had a different opinion, but Mrs. Gibson was not daunted by them or by the burgeoning contradictions in her story. Admitting that she had lied on occasion, she said, "The story I told the authorities and the story I told to reporters are two different things. And when I get on the stand [at the closed grand jury hearing in 1922] I will give you a better story than you have had yet."[22]

Perhaps she did, but the grand jury was having none of it. There is a saying that a good prosecutor can indict a ham sandwich. Wilbur A. Mott, the old pro from Essex County, was a good prosecutor. But on November 28, 1922, the ham sandwiches, despite the Pig Woman's story, went home scot free.[23]

NOVEMBER 9, 1922.

PROSECUTOR MOTT READY TO ACCUSE HALL-MILLS SLAYER

To Confer With Justice Parker Today About Indicting Woman and Two Men.

CALLS EVIDENCE COMPLETE

Authorities Believe Identification of Man With "Woman in Gray" Is Positive.

SECOND MAN IAGO OF CASE

Believed to Have Driven Others to Phillips Farm and to Have Waited Until After Murder.

NOVEMBER 29, 1922.

HALL-MILLS JURY REFUSES TO INDICT IN MURDER MYSTERY

Does Not Call Rector's Widow, Who Keeps All-Day Vigil in Court House.

FUTURE OF CASE IS IN DOUBT

Foreman Gibb Says That Action by Present or Subsequent Jury Is Not Precluded.

"IN SUSPENDED ANIMATION"

Prosecutor Mott Thus Describes His Own Status and That of the Investigation.

Headlines from two of the sixty-two front-page articles about the Hall-Mills case that appeared in the *New York Times* from September through December 1922

13 Two Henrys

In mid-December 1922 Justice Charles W. Parker of the New Jersey Supreme Court made a special trip to Somerville to discharge in person the Somerset County grand jury that had refused to issue indictments in the Hall-Mills case. He wanted to commend the jury members for their conscientiousness and sound judgment in resisting the public clamor for action. Parker's move was unusual, for grand juries in New Jersey were ordinarily dismissed by a local judge of the Court of Common Pleas.[1]

Justice Parker, a native of Newark and a graduate of Princeton University, had a reputation as a tough but fair judge. When he praised the grand jury in 1922, he could have had no inkling that four years later he would be back again, the presiding judge in Somerville at the trial of Mrs. Hall and her two brothers for the murder of Eleanor Mills. Justice Parker emerged from the 1926 trial as one of the few people whose reputations were enhanced rather than sullied through association with the notorious case.[2]

When the grand jury in 1922 rejected Mrs. Gibson's long-winded tale of what she had seen and heard, it did so even though she had added a belated recollection of having made a second trip to De Russey's Lane that night, very late, about one o'clock in the morning. Once again mounted on her mule Jenny, she clip-clopped down De Russey's Lane until she reached a spot several yards from the scene of the murders. She tied Jenny to a tree stump and "walked carefully behind the sumac bushes and the field of goldenrod between the tree and De Russey's Lane, until she came close enough to identify a woman kneeling by the rector's body as the same woman in the gray coat she had seen before."[3] The moon had risen, she said (as it had, in fact, according to a Princeton astronomer),[4] and she could see with great clarity the poignant scene being enacted under the crab apple tree. It was a fulsome outpouring of grief, the woman in gray weeping and sobbing in despair.[5] The man with the bushy hair was nowhere in sight.

Why had Mrs. Gibson returned the mile or so to the Phillips farm? Was it curiosity about the shootings? In part it was, she said, but mainly she hoped to recover one of her moccasins, which she discovered three hours later she had lost somewhere along the way.

Wilbur A. Mott always had a few problems with Mrs. Gibson's story, despite his public statements to the contrary. Lacking physical evidence to present to a grand jury, he was shackled—as Alexander Simpson would be four years later—to his star witness's widely reported "Oh, Henry!" quotation. If Mrs. Gibson was telling the truth, and Mott's strategy assumed she was, then the actual killer, the bushy-haired man with the gun, was Henry Somebody.

This "Henry" complication in the Hall-Mills case had important consequences. Mott in 1922 and Simpson in 1926 were forced to skirt the most obvious and likely solution to the murders in order to accommodate a perpetrator named Henry. It led both of them into absurdities that went a long way toward destroying their attempts to see justice done. On the other hand, it could be argued that if Mrs. Gibson had not come forward at all, there would never have been a publicized official version of the crime. Without an eyewitness, none of the four prosecutors—Stricker, Beekman, Mott, or Simpson—could have presented enough evidence to obtain an indictment, let alone a conviction, against the killer or killers. Like Ferd David, they might all have felt the case was a cinch (Mott at one point called it "very complex but not a mystery"), yet they would have been unable to prosecute with any hope of success.[6]

The Pig Woman's "Oh, Henry!" demanded a flesh-and-blood Henry, and the one who first came to investigators' minds was Henry Stevens, Mrs. Hall's older brother. Henry Stevens, a retired exhibition marksman for the Remington Arms Company, owned a home in Lavallette on the Jersey shore. He was fifty-two years old at the time of the murders, a man with thick, dark hair (not quite bushy), outsized ears, spectacles, and a full, neatly trimmed mustache, "a nice fellow [wrote Damon Runyon at the trial], fond of fishing and hunting, and a companionable sort on such expeditions when companionship is something of an essential."[7]

When investigators, with James F. Mason in charge, turned their attention to Henry Stevens in late October, they immediately ran into "a copper-riveted alibi for his movements at the time the murder was committed."[8] He claimed he was fishing along the beach in front of his home on Thursday night, September 14. He said that many of his neighbors in Lavallette could corroborate the fact. He related at length his fishing activities that evening, including the fact that he had caught three bluefish by sundown and that Arthur Applegate, a town councilman, landed a six-pound bluefish shortly afterwards. Henry, with others present, weighed Applegate's sizable bluefish, using a pocket scale he always carried in his fishing jacket.[9]

Henry Stevens claimed to have been seen by many people that night, and he gave the names of ten of them who would remember him. Reporters dutifully called each one, and all ten

Henry Hewgill Stevens. The oldest of the three Stevenses, Henry was a retired exhibition marksman who lived--and fished--at Lavallette on the Jersey shore. Alexander Simpson was determined to implicate him in the crime. (photo 1926)

declared that, yes, to their personal knowledge he had been fishing near his home in Lavallette at the time he claimed. According to Henry's story, he went to bed at about eleven o'clock, fifty miles away from where the murders had been already been committed.

As if ten persuasive witnesses weren't enough, Henry Stevens also produced a diary in which he had written for September 14: "3 blues Art. 1 blue 6 lbs at Max's in aft 1 blue 4 lbs"[10]

Nonetheless, the state police assigned two detectives to work undercover in Lavallette to see what they could learn about Henry Stevens: his reputation, his movements, and his alibi. Posing as cigar salesmen, they learned very little, except that it is difficult to remain undercover for very long in a town of 175 people. The folks in Lavallette, more amused than annoyed by the fake cigar peddlers, revealed nothing that cast doubt on Henry Stevens' alibi.

Except for the fact that his name was Henry, it made little sense to try to place him under the crab apple tree with Mrs. Hall, the rector, and the choir singer. Henry Stevens lived more than an hour's drive from New Brunswick, which meant that Mrs. Hall would have had to place a hurry-up phone call to him sometime after 7:00 p.m. on the 14th, an event that no one on either end of the phone line could recall having happened and that investigators could never prove. Henry would then have had to jump in his Ford and dash off to join his sister.

And for what? To confront his compromised brother-in-law with some steamy-letter proof of the rascal's infidelity to Frances? Why did she need the far-off Henry for that purpose? If all she wanted was a witness or a male escort, Willie, who lived in the same house with her, would serve as well.

Then, too, Frances and Henry were no longer close. They

had visited one another only sporadically in the eleven years since her marriage to Edward W. Hall. It was rumored that Henry disapproved of the union, although he denied it. He admitted to not having attended their wedding, but insisted that the press of business made it inconvenient, if not impossible, for him to go.[11] It strains credulity to suppose that more than a decade later he would drop everything to hurry off for the purpose of helping Frances confront her husband and his mistress in a distant lovers' lane.

Mrs. Hall's personal attorney, Timothy N. Pfeiffer, occasionally made candid and incisive comments to the press, and in late October he made one concerning the Pig Woman's "Henry." Upon learning that Mrs. Gibson had quoted the woman in gray as saying, "Oh, Henry!" after the first shot was fired, he remarked, "Well, if she did make that statement, it would be of great benefit to Mrs. Hall's side of the case."[12] Precisely—and prophetically.

None of the investigators seriously suggested that the Hall-Mills murders were planned—at least not in the way they were carried out. Had the slayings been the result of a prearranged scheme, had there been a Stevens family decision to kill Edward W. Hall and Eleanor Mills—a case could be made that Henry Stevens might have motored over to New Brunswick to join in the grim enterprise. No such claim was ever made. The assumption of Ferd David, George Totten, Azariah Beekman, and others who were connected with the case in 1922 was that the confrontation itself was intentional. The shooting, however, was sudden and unexpected—not quite accidental, perhaps, but not carefully thought out, either. Some believed Hall's death might have resulted from a struggle over the gun.[13]

Faced with ten resolute witnesses and a diary, detective

Mason pronounced Henry Stevens' alibi airtight, as did prosecutor Mott. They decided that no case could be made against the convivial sportsman from Lavallette. Scratch one Henry from the short list of suspects.

How short was the list? Well, there seemed to be only one other feasible Henry. He was Henry de la Bruyère Carpender, a cousin of Frances Hall and her next-door neighbor. Except for the misfortune of his first name, Henry Carpender was a less likely suspect than Henry Stevens. Forty years old at the time of the murders, he was a floor member of the New York Stock Exchange firm of McCleve & Co., 67 Exchange Place. He commuted each day by train from New Brunswick to lower Manhattan. A handsome man with a receding hairline, Henry Carpender kept his remaining hair cut short. Bushy-haired he wasn't, although it was noted among investigators, grasping for straws, that short hair in November didn't necessarily mean short hair two months before.[14]

Henry de la Bruyère Carpender, whose family background was as impressive as his Wall Street bearing and his Gallic name, had an alibi. Unaccountably, the special prosecutor seemed not to realize this inconvenient fact until almost the onset of the grand jury hearing.

On the night of the murders, as it happened, Henry Carpender and his wife, Mary Neilson Carpender, had been dinner guests in Highland Park at the home of Mr. and Mrs. J. Kearny Rice, Jr. The Rices readily corroborated their friends' story. The Carpenders, they said, had arrived at the Rices' home across the Raritan River at approximately seven o'clock on the night of the murders and had left at ten-thirty. Their hour of departure cut it a bit close, of course, if the Pig Woman's timetable was slightly off. Mason and Mott concluded that Henry

Carpender's presence in De Russey's Lane at the time of the crime, though unlikely, was not impossible.[15]

Detective Ferd David took Mrs. Gibson to New Brunswick's Penn Station on the morning of Wednesday, November 8, and "remained in hiding while Mrs. Gibson stood at a vantage point where she could see commuters leaving their automobiles and entering the station." She was to jot down the license number of the car from which the bushy-haired man emerged, if he did. Mrs. Gibson watched as a dozen or so commuters entered the station, and then, lo and behold, she recognized the man she had seen with the woman in gray in the glare of those adventitious headlights. As instructed, she wrote down the license number of his car.

The car belonged to Henry de la Bruyère Carpender. The prosecution now had its Henry.[16] True, he was far from being bushy-haired. True, his features looked more WASPish than Negroid. And, true, he had no believable motive for murdering the minister and the choir singer. Indeed, logic would suggest that the urbane Henry Carpender would have been about as likely to shoot his cousin's lecherous husband as a parish priest would be to commit a drive-by shooting.

Carpender's name was not bruited about in the newspapers of the day, but the various descriptions of him—a New Brunswick resident, a New York commuter, a man of high character, a man not previously suspected, a man with the same given name as the one Mrs. Gibson heard at the scene of the crime—all made it clear who he was. Readers who followed the case knew beyond any doubt that special prosecutor Mott would be seeking an indictment for murder against Henry Carpender.

Buried in the accounts of Carpender's credentials for being the killer (he was reputed to own a pistol, for example, and to be a crack shot, "having practically [grown] up with firearms"), was an offhand statement he made to a reporter. Mrs. Gibson and the special prosecutor should have noted this remark for future reference, but they either missed it or ignored it. When told of the "Oh, Henry!" exclamation reported by Mrs. Gibson, Henry Carpender said, "If anybody were to call me Henry, my relatives and friends would not know that I was meant. I am always called Harry."[17]

How Mrs. Gibson made her successful identification of Henry Carpender at the train station is unknown. She was a shrewd, enterprising woman who followed the case closely. It is easy to speculate how she might have learned of Mrs. Hall's next-door cousin Henry and decided he looked like the right man, maybe the only man, to match her quotation. The grand jury didn't buy the Pig Woman's train-station identification of the lady-in-gray's partner, and it may be that Wilbur A. Mott didn't buy it either. As the date of the grand jury hearing approached, the special prosecutor began to caution reporters that indictments were by no means certain.[18]

On the same day the authorities fingered Henry Carpender, they let it be known that Henry Stevens and Willie Stevens had been eliminated from any suspicion of involvement in the murders.[19] The decision regarding Henry Stevens is understandable, given his vocal army of Lavallette supporters. But it is hard to avoid the conclusion that Willie Stevens, with his bushy hair, his allegedly Negroid features, his sometimes impulsive and unpredictable behavior, and his well-documented late-night jaunt with his sister Frances, was being passed over as a suspect primarily, if not solely, because he had the wrong first name.

Jane Gibson's phantasmagorical story had taken on an aura

of accepted truth, at least among those responsible for finding and prosecuting the perpetrators.

Henry de la Bruyère Carpender. A New York City stockbroker, a cousin and neighbor of Mrs. Hall, he was the "Henry" the Pig Woman first identified as being at the crime scene. (photo 1926)

14   Iago in the Vestry

Of all the characters in the Hall-Mills saga, none is more enigmatic than Ralph V. Gorsline, a choir singer and vestryman at
the Protestant Episcopal Church of St. John the Evangelist. A
tall, thin man with a narrow face, his skin "drawn as tightly
over the bones as the head of a drum," Gorsline often made a
favorable first impression on people, especially women. He was
a man of considerable ability, an industrial engineer and an assistant plant manager at Reckitts, a manufacturing company in
New Brunswick that produced bluing, a laundry bleach. Married to the former Helen Brower, he had a nine-year-old daughter, Jean.[1]

The president of Reckitts Blue Company, William G. Bearman, served as secretary of the St. John's vestry. Bearman's
wife, Anna, who was a first cousin of Mrs. Hall, appeared as a
witness at the trial in 1926, since a few days after the murders,
Anna K. Bearman, at Mrs. Hall's request, had sent a brown
summer coat and a brown scarf belonging to the widow to Philadelphia to be dyed black for mourning. This act led Alexander
Simpson to suspect that the dyed coat was the famous gray polo
coat, hastily shipped out of town to alter its appearance and
perhaps eliminate bloodstains. It seems plainly not to have
been the same coat, however, and Mrs. Bearman's straight-
forward testimony did nothing to further the prosecution's
case.[2]

Ralph V. Gorsline's testimony, by contrast, never came
across to anyone as straightforward. For all his know-how and
charm, the gaunt vestryman seemed to possess as shaky a grasp

on the truth as the Pig Woman. How much he actually knew about the goings-on in De Russey's Lane on the night of September 14, 1922, could never be determined. It is a virtual certainty that he knew more than he let on. At the time of the trial, Damon Runyon said the prosecutor was convinced that Gorsline "could tell plenty about the murder of the parson and his sweetheart, the choir singer, if he would open his wide, loose-lipped mouth . . . and talk freely."[3] But everything that came out of that loose-lipped mouth, from first to last, was as unreliable as a politician's promise.

If one were given the job of casting director for a morality play about the Hall-Mills case, with characters like Faith, Anger, and Good Deeds, this lanky choir singer and vestryman would be an excellent choice for the part of Hypocrisy.

His claim on that role began as soon as the news of Reverend Hall's death reached the St. John's congregation. On Saturday night, the same day the bodies were discovered, the vestry of the church held a meeting and adopted a resolution of confidence in their slain rector. The resolution was introduced by Henry L. Bartholomew, Jr., and seconded by Ralph V. Gorsline. It was Gorsline who spoke to reporters later. "We have explicit faith in our dead rector," he told them. "I have eaten and lived with him. I was intimately associated with him in church work. There never lived a finer man."[4]

Gorsline and Hall had certain characteristics in common. Like the rector, Gorsline had earned a reputation around New Brunswick as a womanizer.[5] He owned a dark green Apperson, a sporty seven-passenger touring car. A classic car of the 1920s, it was more costly and distinctive than the Halls' Dodge and about on a par with their Case. The girls around town loved it. One of them, Catherine Rastall, a pretty stenographer for a New Brunswick lumber company, had ridden in it more than once prior to the night of the murders. Miss Rastall, like Eleanor Mills and Ralph V. Gorsline, sang in the choir at St. John's.

The Apperson was easy to spot, and to Gorsline's enduring dismay, one or more persons saw him driving it in the neighborhood of the Phillips farm on the fatal night. Not only that, but a "woman parishioner of the church" was seen in the car with him, the implication being that she too had been recognized.[6] Although investigators learned of this sighting right away and never had the slightest doubt about its accuracy, Ralph V. Gorsline denied and continued to deny that he was anywhere near the scene of the crime that night.

Investigators kept after him, probing, mocking, insinuating, and in time he admitted that, yes, he had been squiring a young woman in his car that evening; to wit, Catherine Rastall. But he had not, absolutely not, driven her out to De Russey's Lane. No, sir. He had not dreamed of entering that dark pathway of local lechery. The story he told, which Miss Rastall confirmed item by item, was a transparent lie—the authorities knew the two of them had been there—yet it was a story they both stuck to for four years.[7]

According to him, he had been hanging around the YMCA on George Street, watching some men play billiards until about 10:00 p.m. Upon leaving the Y, he sauntered out to his automobile, which was parked across the street. Whom should he see advancing toward him on foot but the lovely Miss Rastall? She had just come from a movie at the State Theatre on Livingston Avenue and was on her way home. Gorsline offered to drive her, which she agreed to, and which he did, straight to the house at 13 Senior Street, near Rutgers College, where she lived with her parents. That was their joint story. No detours.

Detective Mason discounted most of this story as fictitious, but he still couldn't figure out exactly what was going on. To this day, no one knows the whole truth of the Gorsline-Rastall journey to De Russey's Lane. Four years after the murders, however, a new team of detectives learned much more than Mason and Mott had known. They learned that Gorsline, with Rastall in the Apperson beside him, had driven to a parking spot next to the lovers' lane where Edward W. Hall and Eleanor Mills were presumably sharing their wonder-heart love and romantic dreams. Or possibly the minister and his mistress were planning their future course of action.

Gorsline and Rastall reached their own destination, one secluded lane away from the minister and the choir singer, at ten-fifteen that night. They parked, lights out, approximately three hundred feet over from the crab apple tree.[8]

Within a minute or two they heard a murmuring of unrecognizable voices, not loud or quarreling, but merely conversing, or so they testified in 1926, followed by the crack of gunfire. Just how much else they saw, heard, or knew remained a mystery. Alexander Simpson questioned them at length on the witness stand, but they never went beyond their similar but limited testimony.

What does seem clear is that the ten o'clock trip to De Russey's Lane, its precise timing and specific destination, were probably not mere coincidence. The odds against such a coincidence are just too great. More likely there was a nonlibidinous reason for Gorsline to be where he was, when he was, and even accompanied by a member of the choir. Finding out that reason would go a long way toward solving the perplexing mystery of the slayings. Simpson's investigative team worked

Ralph V. Gorsline. A vestryman and choir signer at St. John's, Gorsline was seen on the night of the murders in his green Apperson with a young woman not his wife. They had parked in a lovers' lane near the crime scene. (photo 1926)

hard to try to get the pair in the Apperson to tell the whole truth.

Throughout the earlier inquiry, Gorsline and Rastall had clung successfully to their nearly identical stories. No matter what David, Totten, and Mott knew, or thought they knew, they got no help in adding to their information base from either occupant of the dark green touring car. The detectives had no choice but to try to piece together for themselves the motives and impulses that prompted the tomcat of the St. John's vestry (Miss Rastall was considered merely a walk-on that night) to make his neatly pinpointed ten o'clock trek to the Phillips farm. The investigators developed a variety of theories.

The theory that mattered most in 1922 was that of detective Mason and prosecutor Mott. It seems a rather tenuous theory in view of what credible witnesses had told them about the occupants of the Apperson.

Mason and Mott decided that Ralph V. Gorsline had driven Mrs. Hall and Henry Carpender to the Phillips farm. He had done so for the purpose of having them confront the clergyman and his mistress with a sheaf of letters proving their illicit love affair.

That was the plan. It went awry. Disaster followed almost immediately upon the arrival of the three accusers. Murder, no less. And now Gorsline was in a pretty fix. By having first-hand knowledge of the unexpected slayings, then driving the guilty pair home, and then not coming forward with the truth, the meddlesome vestryman, in the official theory of events, became an accessory after the fact. He was the third person against whom Wilbur A. Mott sought an indictment.

A headline in the New York Times of November 9, 1922, read, "SECOND MAN IAGO OF CASE," and the article, while not identifying Gorsline by name, cited him as the "most fla-grant case of refusal to give the authorities information."[9] Anyone who had been following the case knew who *that* fellow was—a man not unlike Shakespeare's crafty villain in *Othello*.

From the prosecutors' standpoint, Gorsline was at best an uncooperative witness, at worst a villainous conspirator. He was one of the many residents of New Brunswick who wanted as little as possible to do with the investigators' search for answers. He qualified as an irritant to them, but it seems doubtful that he was an accessory in quite the way they sup-posed.

Catherine Rastall's presence in Gorsline's touring car that evening argues strongly against his having acted as the killers' chauffeur. The Apperson was parked in the general vicinity of the crab apple tree at the time of the murders. There could be no doubt about that. At least one unnamed but believable wit-ness (not Jane Gibson), who somehow managed to keep his name out of the newspapers throughout the entire 1922 investi-gation, had seen Miss Rastall in the vestryman's automobile near the scene of the crime.[10]

No one except the Pig Woman, then or ever, claimed under oath to have seen Mrs. Hall or Henry Carpender anywhere near De Russey's Lane. Nor had anyone reported seeing the rector's wife and the stockbroker that night in the green Apperson. If Gorsline had acted as the killers' chauffeur, Mott could produce nobody to confirm it.

When indictments failed in 1922, Ralph V. Gorsline, like Mrs. Hall and Henry Carpender, went back to his daily routine. For Gorsline this meant running the Reckitts bluing factory. Helen Gorsline, as forgiving as Frances Hall had once been, accepted her husband's plea of innocence regarding Catherine

Rastall's Thursday night automobile ride. The headline crime-and-sex story of the day slipped into limbo.

But thorny questions remained. If Gorsline and Rastall *had* been near the scene of the crime . . . Why? The obvious answer, if one chose to ignore the coincidences of time and place, was that they went there, in the idiom of the day, to spoon. After all, what else do couples do in lovers' lanes?

When Alexander Simpson's investigators bore down hard on prospective witnesses in 1926, harder than Mott's men ever had, Catherine Rastall, after a soul-wrenching talk with Rev. J. Mervin Pettit, Hall's successor as minister at St. John's, finally cracked. She admitted that she and Gorsline had not gone directly to her home on Senior Street that night. The story that she and the vestryman, trapped in a lie, now told was that Gorsline had picked her up, as both had said four years ago, at about ten o'clock on Thursday night, a few minutes after Catherine left the State Theatre's nine o'clock showing of *Slim Shoulders,* with Irene Castle. They had driven not to her parents' house but to De Russey's Lane, where they parked and were about to settle into a comfortable intimacy when a sudden disturbance in a nearby lane interrupted them.

Their stories were well coordinated in the 1926 version, just as they had been in their 1922 account. They gave similar testimony on the witness stand, with only one discrepancy. Here is Gorsline explaining the key moments to prosecutor Simpson:

Q—And what was the first intimation you had that there was anything wrong?

A—We heard—I heard a mumbling of voices which sounded like men's voices.

Q—Did they come nearer to you or go further away from you?

A—I could not say as to that. To me it seemed to be just off in the distance.

Q—Then what was the next you heard?

A—One shot.

Q—Yes. Then what did you hear?

A—And a woman screamed.

Q—Then what did you hear?

A—I heard three shots in quick succession.

Q—Then what did you hear?

A—And a moaning.[11]

While this was not exactly a technicolor description of a double murder three hundred feet away, it did more or less match the rudiments of Mrs. Gibson's story, which in turn pretty much mirrored the extensive newspaper accounts of what other, more reliable witnesses had heard.

Did Gorsline and Rastall investigate the origin of the shots? No, they said. Did they leave the lovers' lane immediately? Yes, said Rastall. They backed out and took off in a hurry. No, said Gorsline. They stayed there for perhaps three to six minutes and then left without undue haste. Why did they stay? He offered no explanation.

The vestryman's revised story pained Mrs. Helen Gorsline deeply, but she said she would stand by her husband "to the limit."[12] Perhaps she was touched by his comment to the press that by telling the truth about Catherine Rastall he was ruining his life. On reflection, however, Mrs. Gorsline resolved to redefine the limit of her loyalty. Deciding the limit had already been reached, she left her husband soon after the trial. Many years later, in 1935, she received a final decree of divorce.[13]

Meanwhile, back in New Brunswick in 1922, Mason and Mott became convinced that the gaunt vestryman had been instrumental in bringing about the lovers'-lane encounter between Mrs. Hall and her straying spouse. In this scenario, Gorsline had decided the time had come to pull the plug on the Edward-Eleanor romance. He may have been doing so for the good name of the church, at the instigation of Mrs. Hall's relatives, out of personal spite, or for some other reason.

The investigators believed he enlisted the aid of Eleanor Mills' friend (or rival, or both), Mrs. Addison Clark, who lived almost as close to Reverend Hall's church as Eleanor did. Minnie Clark, active in St. John's Sunday school, had one of the keys to the church and may have discovered the lovers' private post office at the church.

The location of this post office was the subject of much speculation in the press. One person who professed to know where the rector and the choir singer hid their love notes was Eleanor's daughter, Charlotte. She disclosed the hiding place in her trial testimony. The lovers, she said, put their letters in a large book on the second shelf from the bottom of a bookcase in the rector's study.[14]

This book was meant to be a secret spot, safe from prying eyes. But Eleanor occasionally expressed concern to the rector that someone else would learn where they were hiding the letters. One of her letters, undated like the others, began: "My dear, dear boy. When I said I would leave a note, I forgot that it may not be wise, but I may take a chance, for I cannot have you disappointed, even tho' it isn't much." Later in the same note she wrote, "I guess I'd better not leave this but give it to you tomorrow." Another letter began: "Wasn't I happy to find a sweet note, for I did not expect you would risk leaving one for me yesterday."[15]

It's a good guess that someone eventually did locate the

hiding place. The detectives' odds-on favorites as the snoops who found the private post office and passed on whatever epistles were in the big book to Mrs. Hall were Ralph V. Gorsline and Minnie Clark. Gorsline and Mrs. Clark stoutly denied any such activities.[16]

Gorsline had another problem too. The very day after Mott's investigators questioned him about his whereabouts and activities on the night of the murders, the vestryman's green Apperson caught fire and burned. "I seem to be the victim of unfortunate circumstances," he said. "It is true that I had a green car, and that green car was burned beyond repair on the day after I was questioned." But he went on to say that he was not driving the car when it ignited. He had lent it to Alfred Doucet, proprietor of the State Highway Garage, where Gorsline kept his automobile.

Doucet picked up the story. "It was so sudden that I cannot explain how it happened. I had been over to Princeton with Mrs. Doucet and had reached Livingston Street on the return trip. Suddenly flames and smoke shot out from under the seat. The car was in motion at the time. I just had time to get my wife safely out when the whole business was on fire. I did not even have time to reach for the extinguisher with which the car was equipped."[17]

Investigators were understandably suspicious of this fire. They could think of a reason or two why Gorsline might want to get rid of the Apperson if it had had anything to do with the commission of the Hall-Mills murders. And even if the car had been more or less fortuitously at the murder scene, its destruction would make it impossible for a witness to point and say, "Yes, that's the car." Whatever the truth about the charred Apperson, the circumstances of its immolation on Livingston

Avenue cast further doubt on Gorsline's plea of noninvolvement.

Alexander Simpson's investigation added more fuel to the fire. A witness turned up in the late summer of 1926 who said that Gorsline had come in off the street, quite literally, to admit having been at the scene of the crime. This slow-to-surface witness was one William Garvin, a pudgy, balding former manager of the New York office of the William Burns Detective Agency, located in the Woolworth Building, Manhattan. Garvin told a tale worthy of the Pig Woman at her giddiest. It seemed that on October 1, 1922, Ralph V. Gorsline had wandered into the detective agency's office and, wholly unprompted, announced that his conscience bothered him and he wanted to unburden himself to the stranger behind the desk.

According to this ex-Burns man, Gorsline told him that, having heard some shots near the crab apple tree, he climbed down from his Apperson, rushed in the direction of the sound, and saw . . . Henry Stevens. The sportsman from Lavallette was carrying a revolver. As Gorsline approached the crime scene, Stevens snarled, "What the hell are you doing here. This is none of your affair. Get the hell out of here." The angry Stevens then fired two shots at the ground. (It must have been a mute revolver, because none of the several witnesses heard these two shots.) Gorsline immediately fled the scene at Henry Stevens' show of wrath. The gaunt vestryman, said Garvin, also told him a tale about having been "taken to a lodge room and made to swear that he would never tell it."[18]

Defense attorney Robert H. McCarter opened his cross-examination with the question, "Mr. Garvin, are you the man that is commonly known as 'Greasy Vest'?" Simpson exploded with an objection—"He may be known as Ali Baba, but that would not make him Ali Baba." Justice Charles W. Parker overruled the objection. McCarter went on to lead Greasy Vest Garvin (for indeed it was he) through an account of the improbable route that had brought him to the witness stand in Somerville to point the finger of guilt at Henry Stevens. A thousand-dollar reward figured in the narrative.[19]

Ralph V. Gorsline denied the truth of Garvin's testimony. While Gorsline may well have been something of an Iago in the vestry, given all the self-serving revisions and evasions in his testimony—and with that classy touring car of his suspiciously in the junkyard—nevertheless he was a more believable witness than Greasy Vest Garvin. Of course, the real target of Garvin's testimony was not Gorsline but Henry Stevens, the man from Lavallette with the copper-riveted alibi. Mrs. Hall's trap-shooting brother was proving damnably hard for the special prosecutor to place at the Phillips farm at the time of the murders. Garvin put him there, but not convincingly.

It looked as if Simpson might be willing to put on the stand a preposterous witness or two to try to prove his and Mrs. Gibson's theory of the crime.

15 A Tabloid Crusade

"They are not doing anything; they never did do anything to solve the mystery," James Mills said disgustedly, two years after the murder of his wife and Reverend Hall. "They know who did it as well as I do, but they haven't done anything about it."[1]

Despite occasional assurances from state and local authorities that the case would not be forgotten, it was. Timothy N. Pfeiffer promised to direct an independent investigation, but he never did.[2] New Jersey's attorney general, Thomas F. McCran, vowed he would appoint a new special prosecutor to succeed Wilbur A. Mott, but he never did.[3] Ferd David continued to work on some angles of the investigation, but they came to nothing.[4] At least one state trooper, Henry L. Dickman, also stayed on the case, likewise to no avail.[5] Interest in the mystery waned.

Two months after the grand jury failed to return indictments, Mrs. Hall boarded the Italian liner *America* for a long period of rest and recreation in Italy.[6] Her close friend and confidante, Miss Sally Peters, accompanied her on the trip. After a fourteen-month sojourn abroad, Mrs. Hall returned to New Brunswick, where she stayed for a while at the home of her cousin, Mrs. William G. Bearman. She then returned to her Nichol Avenue mansion, "greatly improved in health."[7]

Few newspaper articles mentioned the Hall-Mills case over the next four years. The press had more immediate stories to cover. In August 1923 the president of the United States, Warren G. Harding, died unexpectedly, and Calvin Coolidge became the nation's chief executive. A year later the Ku Klux

Klan held a massive rally in Washington, D.C., in which 40,000 white-robed klansmen and klanswomen marched down Pennsylvania Avenue. A year after that, in July 1925, the Scopes monkey trial was held in Dayton, Tennessee. Clarence Darrow's barbed defense went for naught, as the jury convicted John T. Scopes of teaching the theory of evolution, and the court fined him a hundred dollars.[8]

The Roaring Twenties were in full swing, the mood of the nation euphoric. Old murders were cold copy. Still, there were others besides Jim Mills who remembered the Hall-Mills mystery and thought it had been buried all too quickly. The brutal crime remained unsolved, the killer or killers still at large. Since the press had lavished so much attention on the initial investigation, it was a good bet that any well-scripted revival would bring America's journalists running once again. Some kind of new evidence would be needed, though, and there was not much indication that anyone involved in the first inquiry was trying to find it. How, then, to reopen the case?

The answer came from a small, aggressive newspaperman with round, dark-rimmed eyeglasses and a reputation for uncovering scandal. He was Philip. A. Payne, thirty-two, who had recently been named managing editor of the New York *Daily Mirror*. Payne had entered journalism after his graduation from St. Michael College, Toronto, where he had majored in chemistry. Abandoning the laboratory for the newsroom, he took a job as sportswriter for the *Perth Amboy Chronicle*, later moving on to the *Hoboken Observer*. By the time the First World War broke out, Payne had risen to the position of city editor at the *Hoboken Dispatch*.

After the war he worked for major tabloid newspapers in Chicago and New York. In June 1925 he was dismissed as managing editor of the New York *Daily News* for paying more attention, in person and in print, to an attractive divorcee than to his assigned tasks. He soon became managing editor of the New York *Daily Mirror,* William Randolph Hearst's challenge to the *Daily News.*[9] In an era of yellow journalism these two papers were fiercely competitive, and Payne was on the lookout for a big story to boost the circulation of the *Mirror.* He found it, or possibly created it, in an unusual way. It began with an annulment petition filed on July 3, 1926, by a disgruntled husband from Roselle Park, New Jersey, in the Court of Chancery at Trenton.

The petition was filed by Arthur S. Riehl, a music store clerk and piano tuner in New Brunswick, who had married one of the Halls' two resident servants, the tall, attractive parlormaid, Louise Geist. Their marriage, in July 1924, had soured almost immediately, and Riehl now wanted to call it quits. When his petition for annulment, which was neither sworn to nor signed, fell into the hands of Philip A. Payne—skeptics suggested that Payne's hands may have helped to write it—the *Daily Mirror* launched a barrage of front-page articles demanding that the Hall-Mills case be reopened.

Arthur S. Riehl had peppered his annulment petition with provocative statements that, according to a prolix *New York Times* reporter, "aroused suspicion that it was framed with a view to exploiting sensational stories of the Hall-Mills case composed of the local gossip current at the time of the murder and not hitherto published because no substantiation for it could be found." Further adding to the skepticism was the fact that the petition was written in narrative rather than legal form.[10]

In it Riehl maintained that his wife Louise, along with Mrs.

Hall, Willie Stevens, and Peter Tumulty, a family retainer, had gone a-motoring on the night of the murders. Specifically, they had gone out to the Phillips farm, to a spot close to where the bodies were found. According to Riehl, his wife had told him she knew about Reverend Hall's plans to elope with Eleanor Mills. The implication was that Mrs. Hall would permit no such scandal to stain her life.

At about ten o'clock on the night of September 14, 1922, Louise Geist, Frances Hall, Willie Stevens, and Peter Tumulty set off in Reverend Hall's automobile (presumably the Case touring car), with Tumulty at the wheel. Their aim was to confront the would-be elopers out on their Easton Avenue road.[11] What else may have been planned is not mentioned in the petition. Louise Geist either didn't know or else thought it unwise to tell.

For her part in the adventure—whatever her part was, other than going along for the ride and keeping quiet about it afterwards—Louise Geist allegedly received $5,000.

It seems safe to say that only the most gullible *boobus Americanus,* as H. L. Mencken liked to call his fellow countrymen, believed Louise Geist's tale (via Arthur S. Riehl) about having been invited along on the expedition to confront the rector and Mrs. Mills. The real suspicion surrounding the parlormaid had less to do with events under the crab apple tree than with how much she had heard of the 7:00 p.m. telephone conversation at 23 Nichol Avenue between the two victims on the night they died. She was an important witness in the matter of the phone call. It was an incident that would dominate the questioning of the former parlormaid at the trial, but about which Arthur S. Riehl had nothing to say.

The idea that Peter Tumulty was pressed into service to

drive the trio to the Phillips farm struck investigators as equally far-fetched. Tumulty, according to a Middlesex County judge who knew him, "is one of the old type of Irish who go to church every Sunday. He would have gone right to the authorities had he learned of such a crime."[12] And while Tumulty, a hearty man with white hair and an engaging smile, became a chauffeur after the crime (at the time of the trial he was stockbroker Henry de la Bruyère Carpender's driver), he served mainly as a gardener and handyman for the Halls in 1922. He washed their two automobiles now and then, as his trial testimony revealed, but his duties seldom extended to driving them. The Reverend and Mrs. Hall did their own driving. Tumulty said he went home at 5:00 p.m. on the day of the murders, just as he did on other work days.[13]

One of the more intriguing of Riehl's allegations, all of which Timothy N. Pfeiffer called "so ridiculous it is useless to say anything about them," was this: "Respondent told your petitioner Willie Stevens was a good shot and that there was always a pistol in the Hall library drawer."[14] How Louise Geist could have judged Willie's marksmanship was never explained, but as a parlormaid she might well have known about the presence of a pistol in the library.

Riehl's petition supplied no specifics about what Louise Geist had seen or heard at the murder site. When investigators in Middlesex and Somerset Counties attempted to question him, they found he had disappeared. He remained missing, or incognito, and played no further role in the investigation. Although his annulment petition launched the series of events that made front-page headlines for the rest of 1926, Riehl never expanded upon his allegations, nor did he appear as a witness at the trial.[15]

Louise Geist. Parlormaid at the Hall residence on Nichol Avenue in 1922, she may have heard the phone conversation between the minister and the choir singer that led to their fatal assignation. At the time of the trial, she was married to Arthur S. Riehl, whose petition for annulment had reopened the case. (photo 1926)

Barbara Tough. Upstairs maid at the Hall residence, she knew of the affectionate relationship between Eleanor Mills and Reverend Hall. Reporters seemed more interested in her Scots dialect than in her visit to the Parker Home on the afternoon of the day of the murders. (photo 1926)

Louise Geist Riehl called her husband "crazy" and said his charges were all "a pack of lies." At her home in Davidson's Mills, near New Brunswick, she told reporters that his annulment petition was an act of revenge. Several months before, she said, he came to her home "and threatened to drag me into an investigation of the Hall-Mills murders if I did not go back to him."[16]

As for his annulment petition, Riehl eventually withdrew it and filed an action for divorce on the grounds of desertion. The decree was denied, and Louise Geist Riehl countered with a divorce action of her own, claiming that her husband left her a few weeks after their marriage and never provided support. She asked to resume the use of her maiden name.[17]

Once the Hall-Mills case had been reopened, there was no easy way to close it. The old ills flew forth, as from Pandora's box, and were sped on their way by a throng of journalists who saw in the four-year-old crime all the elements of a blockbuster story. Philip A. Payne had assessed the public interest and his press cohorts accurately. There was a tendency to judge him harshly for this. At the trial, defense attorney McCarter referred to him as "Mephistopheles," a characterization, wrote Damon Runyon, "that would undoubtedly have astonished the mild-mannered editor."[18]

The soft-spoken but tough-minded Payne handled himself creditably on the witness stand. Pressed on cross-examination about the much-traveled calling card, Exhibit S-17, that supposedly showed Willie Stevens' fingerprints, Payne denied having paid Edward A. Schwartz, the state's fingerprint expert, any money for being allowed to borrow the card on behalf of the *Daily Mirror*. McCarter did not believe him. The questioning went like this:

Q—You say you gave him [Schwartz] nothing whatever for the card?

A—Nothing financial, no.

Q—Well, if it was not financial, what did you give him? Why don't you answer me? . . . Does it require a great deal of thought to remember what it was?

A—No.

Q—Then why don't you answer?

A—I told Schwartz, if he—

Q—I have not asked what you told him. I asked you what you gave him?

A—I told Schwartz that if he could help clear up this crime, he was doing a service to the State of New Jersey. That was the only consideration he got.[19]

Still, Payne could not deflect the suspicion that his main interest in reopening the Hall-Mills case was to increase the circulation of the *Daily Mirror*. But most of the flak he took ignored the fact that this *was*, after all, an unsolved mystery. At least one person, and perhaps more than one, had gotten away with a very ugly crime. To suggest, as some writers did, that reviving the investigation was a needless opening of old wounds among the gentlefolk of central New Jersey seems fatuous. It seems doubly so if one or more of them committed the murders.

Bruce Bliven, a columnist for *The New Republic*, admitted on December 1, 1926, that he was "bored sick by the Hall-Mills case," but nonetheless he provided some insight into why it had become such a huge spectacle:

"I am bound to add [Bliven wrote] that it does have at least four other values which attract the public interest, beyond the great attribute that it is still unsolved and can be picked at like a wire-nail puzzle. First of these is the enigmatic central figure,

Mrs. Hall. Is she a stone image, concealing guilt behind the most perfect poker face since the man in the iron mask? Can one middle-aged widow of a small-town pastor outbluff the State of New Jersey (easy) the sharp wits of tabloidia (harder) and even (climax) the neighbors?

"And again, did wealth buy immunity four years ago? Is Jersey justice like Jersey lightning, greased?

"Further, the case is quadrupled in viscosity because the bad actor was a clergyman. How the general population yearns to see a gentleman of the cloth stub his toe! And how discouragingly seldom does he oblige!"[20]

When Bruce Bliven wrote those words, the jury's verdict was not yet in. His comment about the case being "still unsolved" indicates how poorly the trial was going for the prosecution. Payne had provided the opening for a new investigation, but the trail was cold by 1926. When the trial finally began, some of the more promising witnesses, including firearms expert Charles E. Waite, were dead. Others proved no more forthcoming than they had been four years earlier, and the evidence that had been missing or mishandled from the outset had not been found or undergone any improvement in quality.[21]

Nevertheless, the drumbeat publicity of the *Daily Mirror's* circulation-building campaign in July 1926, coupled with the recognition on the part of state officials that the whole thing had indeed been botched in 1922, led Governor A. Harry Moore to appoint a new special prosecutor to look into the case. The man he chose would become as synonymous with Hall-Mills as the spotlight-seeking Pig Woman. He was Alexander Simpson, a short-statured lawyer from Jersey City, which also happened to be Governor Moore's home town, as well as the home town of Frank ("I Am the Boss") Hague. Like several other participants in Hall-Mills redux, Alexander Simpson was a state senator. Known for his flashy clothing, including bright yellow and green shirts, and sometimes referred to as the Napoleon of New Jersey, he entered the fray with a reputation for aggressiveness that would soon be verified in word and deed.[22]

NEWARK EVENING NEWS, THURSDAY, JULY 29, 1926

Hall-Mills Case Reopened, Widow Charged with Murder

Air of Mystery Maintained as Officers Are Silent on Evidence

Suit Furnished Clew

Mrs. Hall Confers with Attorneys in Somerset Jail—Arrest Comes Late at Night

Staff Correspondent

SOMERVILLE, July 29.— New evidence on which Mrs. Frances Stevens Hall was arrested for murder shortly before midnight last night at her New Brunswick home is withheld by Prosecutor Francis Bergen.

Mrs. Hall is charged in separate complaints with the four-year-old murders of her husband, Rev. Dr. Edward Wheeler Hall, and his choir singer, Mrs. Eleanor Mills.

The investigation that preceded her arrest followed an allegation in a recent annulment suit brought by Arthur S. Riehl of Roselle Park that his wife had told him that she had knowledge of the murder. At that time she was Louise Geist, a maid in the Hall home.

The interest that would inevitably attach to the reopening of this most famous case with the spectacular arrest is enhanced by the air

Newspapers throughout the United States gave extensive coverage to the Hall-Mills case in both 1922 and 1926. Interest was especially intense in the New York metropolitan area. Although the *Newark Evening News* followed the case in some detail, neither it nor any other New Jersey newspaper matched the saturation coverage of the *New York Times.*

16 Jail for the Widow

Just before midnight on Wednesday, July 28, 1926, two auto-mobiles pulled into the circular driveway of the big red brick home at 23 Nichol Avenue. Six men got out and climbed the steps to the porch. One of them pushed the button of the electric doorbell.[1]

The maid who answered the bell was asked to summon Mrs. Hall. Although the maid seemed taken aback by the cluster of sober-faced men at that hour of the night, she hastened upstairs to convey the message.

The person who first appeared on the staircase was not the rector's widow, but the widow's eccentric older brother, the bushy-haired man Damon Runyon thought looked like a successful delicatessen owner.

"Hello, Willie," said Captain John J. Lamb of the New Jersey State Police. "I came here to see Mrs. Hall right away. I have important business of an official character to transact with her."[2]

Willie Stevens called up the broad staircase to his sister, and within a few minutes she came down, fully dressed, clad in black. The contingent of men facing her included, besides Captain Lamb, two state troopers, Matthew McManus and Joseph Hutton; a Somerset County detective, Joseph Hanlon; and two members of the Jersey City Police Department, Captain Harry Walsh and Sergeant Richard Burke.[3]

"Good evening, gentlemen," she said. "Your visit is a rather late one. I suppose you want to question me again."

Captain Lamb gave Mrs. Hall the unwelcome news. "I have a warrant calling for your arrest. I have been instructed to take you to Somerville at once."

"May I be permitted to read the warrant?" Mrs. Hall asked.

Actually, there were two warrants, one charging Mrs. Hall with the murder of her husband, the other charging her with the murder of Eleanor Mills. They had been sworn out by Francis Bergen, prosecutor of Somerset County, and granted by Justice of the Peace William R. Sutphen of Somerville.[4]

Captain Lamb handed one of them to her and she looked it over carefully. After examining it, she handed it back to Lamb and asked, "May I telephone my attorney?"

The captain agreed, and Mrs. Hall called Russell E. Watson of New Brunswick. The lawyer arrived within ten minutes, studied the warrants, and advised Mrs. Hall that for the time being there was nothing she could do but go with the officers.

And so it was that Mrs. Frances Noel Stevens Hall spent the rest of that night in custody, behind bars at the Somerset County jail, from about 3:00 a.m. on Thursday morning, July 29. She remained there until her release on bail two days later.

In his book on the Hall-Mills case, William M. Kunstler raises an issue that was cited by the journalists of the day: "For some reason no attempt to apprehend the suspect was made until more than thirteen hours after Sutphen had issued the orders." Admittedly, this appears odd. But, in fact, the first few words of Kunstler's next sentence provide a hint as to the reason for the timing of the arrest: "A few minutes before midnight. . . ."[5]

The reason for the delay was that although William R. Sutphen signed the arrest warrants on July 28, he dated them July 29: "Given under my hand and seal, this twenty-ninth day of July," they read.[6] Thus, the officers arrived at 23 Nichol Avenue just in time for the warrants to be valid. They made the arrest not belatedly but at the earliest possible moment.[7]

The speculation as to why it happened like this swirled mainly around the role of the *Daily Mirror* in getting the case reopened. Some suspected that managing editor Philip A. Payne had been told in advance that the arrests were coming on July 29, thus getting a jump on the competition. If that was what occurred, it suggested that the handling of the case by the press and the police might be no more prudent in 1926 than it had been four years earlier.[8]

Mrs. Hall remained in custody for forty-three hours, occupying one of six detention rooms reserved for women. The second-floor room, not really a cell, had gray walls and a steel-grilled door, with two wooden beds, two wooden chairs, and a small table. Its two windows overlooked the business center of Somerville. Throughout the day on Thursday, small boys gathered on the lawn below the jail and pointed to the windows of the room where they imagined the wealthy widow to be imprisoned.[9]

One of Frances Hall's growing army of attorneys, Robert H. McCarter, visited her in the detention room. He found her to be calm and self-possessed. She was no doubt uneasy and a bit surprised, but she was nonetheless "withstanding the ordeal bravely." McCarter, who would soon be heading the Million Dollar Defense team in the case, told reporters, "She hasn't wept a tear."[10]

On the first night of her stay and well on into the next morning, she shared the sparsely furnished room with a close friend, Elovine Carpender, the wife of Edwin R. Carpender, one of Mrs. Hall's many cousins in New Brunswick. Four years earlier, Edwin had been the emissary who came to 23 Nichol Avenue to inform Frances of her husband's murder. Now (prior to the arrival from New York of Sally Peters) the granite-jawed Elovine was the person who kept Frances company through the ordeal of her arrest and confinement.

Carpender, the maiden name of Frances's mother, was a highly respected name in town. Two Carpender families lived within a short distance of the Halls. Today there is a truncated Carpender Road not far from where the Halls lived at the time of the tragedy.

Edwin R. Carpender and his wife Elovine lived on the next street over from the Halls, at 10 Townsend Street. The dapper Edwin, like the rest of Carpenders, enjoyed a substantial inheritance and, like Willie Stevens, was a mustachioed man of leisure. Although Edwin had apparently been under no suspicion in Mott's investigation, special prosecutor Simpson soon took a hard look at him as a possible after-the-fact carrier of sensitive papers of some kind from the Hall household.[11]

Down the street at 45 Nichol Avenue (next door really, but the grounds were too extensive to make the term seem appropriate) lived cousin Henry de la Bruyère Carpender and his wife Mary. Mrs. Carpender came from the socially prominent Neilson family. Henry, forty years old, was a New York stockbroker, thought by special prosecutor Wilbur A. Mott to have been the Henry of Mrs. Gibson's nagging "Oh, Henry" quote. Four years later Simpson reached the same conclusion at first, but further investigation made him change his mind and pursue a different Henry.[12]

Some distance away from these two Carpender families, at 15 Union Street, New Brunswick, lived another cousin, Arthur S. Carpender, and his wife, Helena, she also of Neilson lineage.

Arthur was a career naval officer, a graduate of the United States Naval Academy. At the time of the trial, he often served as a dashing escort for Mrs. Hall when she made her way to the courthouse in Somerville. Newspapers always referred to him by rank—Commander Carpender—though technically he was a lieutenant commander. Arthur S. Carpender would be highly decorated for his service two decades later in the Second World War. He retired from the Navy in 1946 as an admiral.[13]

Mrs. Hall received staunch and continuing support from these three Carpenders and their wives. More surprisingly, she also received it from Reverend Hall's two married sisters. One of them, Mrs. Fannie Voorhees, lived on Clifford Avenue in Jersey City. The other, Mrs. Theodora Bonner, lived on Park Avenue, Manhattan. Both women liked their sister-in-law and sympathized with her. In the preceding four years Mrs. Bonner had occasionally entertained Mrs. Hall at her upper Park Avenue home. Evidently, she did not consider the rector's widow to be a murderess.

Upon learning of Mrs. Hall's arrest, Frank Voorhees spoke for both his wife Fannie and himself in dismissing the idea of any new evidence having been uncovered. "As far as we are aware of the facts," he said, "it seems as if the case has been reopened solely on the statements made in the recent annulment proceedings brought by Riehl against his wife." It did look that way from the newspaper accounts. And Voorhees added, "All our sympathy is with Mrs. Hall."[14]

Theodora Bonner was equally supportive. She felt "sorry for the trouble that has been brought on Mrs. Hall" and declared herself "thoroughly convinced that she knows nothing about the crime." Mrs. Bonner then made the somewhat curious promise that the beleaguered widow would stay "right here in New Brunswick until the charge against her has been disposed of." That noon, the second day after she was released on bail, Frances Hall entertained Mrs. Bonner and Mrs. Voorhees at a luncheon in her Nichol Avenue home.[15]

There can be little doubt that Willie Stevens was distraught by his sister's sudden arrest and confinement. He went into seclusion, reportedly staying with friends. When Russell B. Watson, Frances Hall's New Brunswick attorney, was questioned about Willie's whereabouts, he replied acidly that Mrs. Hall's brother was in a place where the authorities would be unable to "get him out of bed at two o'clock in the morning." The next day, however, Willie returned to the Hall mansion, where he remained closeted, inaccessible to the press but available for questioning by investigators, if that was thought necessary.[16]

Reverend J. Mervin Pettit, the murdered rector's successor at St. John's, issued a statement of his faith in Mrs. Hall, saying that he was personally convinced of her innocence. He cited her recent Sunday school teaching as evidence of her moral character.[17] He pointed out that the prominent citizens of New Brunswick, particularly the women, were staunchly behind the widow, just as they had been four years earlier when she had seemed to be facing indictment.

Back then, as the grand jury in Somerset County was holding its second session, a letter appeared in the New Brunswick *Daily Home News.* It was signed by seventy-six women, none of them members of the Church of St. John the Evangelist. It read:

New Brunswick,
Nov. 21, 1922

A few of the friends of Mrs. Frances Stevens Hall desire to express their unswerving faith in her absolute and unswerving devotion to truth and integrity and to all the highest ideals of Christian character. They refuse to believe that in any crisis she would in any respect abandon the high principles which have always guided her life. To them she is now and always has been a woman of the highest type, above suspicion and above reproach, incapable of thinking, much less doing, evil.[18]

One of the sponsors of the letter, Ethel W. Webb, wife of the president of the Webb Wire Company, denied that the purpose of this carefully worded endorsement was to influence the grand jury in any way. Cecilia Lipman, whose husband, Dr. Jacob G. Lipman, headed the staff of the State Agricultural Experiment Station, was another driving force behind the letter-writing campaign. The date of publication, the women said, was wholly coincidental. The idea for the letter dated back to the week after the bodies were discovered, and might possibly have originated with Mrs. Hall's confidante, Sally Peters.[19] The signers were women of status in the community, one of whom would soon become a national celebrity. She was Emily Post, the arbiter of American manners and social customs. Mrs. Post, the forty-second signee, lived in New York City and summered at Bar Harbor. Her book *Etiquette* was first published in 1922.[20]

A person of high standing who seemed not to be in Mrs. Hall's corner in 1926 was the governor of New Jersey, A. Harry Moore. When asked immediately after her arrest about the possibility of bail, Governor Moore, a Democrat from Hudson County, said from his summer home in Sea Girt that the state would oppose it, owing to the seriousness of the crime. He added that he regarded the case as one "of such importance that it should be wound up one way or the other, and not allowed to remain an unsolved mystery." Governor Moore, who was beginning the first of his three nonconsecutive terms in the statehouse, noted that he was assigning Captain Harry Walsh of Jersey City to investigate the facts.[21]

The day after the governor made his remarks, Chief Justice William S. Gummere of the New Jersey Supreme Court, at his summer home in Point Pleasant, ordered Mrs. Hall released on $15,000 bail, $7,500 for each of the two counts of murder. The judge saw no "great evidence or presumption of guilt" in the information given him by Francis L. Bergen, the Somerset County prosecutor. Justice Gummere seemed a mite miffed when Bergen refused to reveal any of the purported new evidence against Mrs. Hall.

A horde of photographers, reporters, and curiosity seekers met the widow as she emerged on Friday afternoon from the Somerset County jail. Her stoicism nearly deserted her for a moment, but, after conferring with her counsel—Russell E. Watson, Timothy N. Pfeiffer, and Augustus Studer—she suppressed her annoyance and allowed the photographers to take pictures. She turned this way and that, smiling as requested, and then proceeded with her entourage down a slope behind the jail and into Edwin Carpender's automobile. Upon reaching her home, she refused further public appearances.

Later that afternoon Russell E. Watson appeared at the front door of the Hall mansion, clearly irritated by the events of the preceding two days. "She has been outrageously treated," he told reporters. "What's the use of her talking about it? What's the use of my talking about it? She made an affidavit today denying all knowledge of the crime. What more can she say? What more can anyone say?"[22]

17   Like a Small Town Sport

On the same day that Judge Gummere granted Mrs. Hall's request for bail, Governor Moore named a special prosecutor to investigate the Hall-Mills case. The previous special prosecutor, Wilbur A. Mott, had been a distinguished but rather cautious attorney. What was needed, Governor Moore believed, was a dynamo, a lawyer who would probe fearlessly, shake up the New Brunswick establishment, and somehow, after all these years, come up with enough evidence to convict the guilty.

The man the governor chose for this formidable task was a lean, tiny fellow with big political ambitions, State Senator Alexander Simpson, a Democrat from Jersey City. Journalist Damon Runyon described Simpson as "a small jockey-sized, fox-terrier-like little man with a wheedling voice. You can call it personality. He dresses like a small town sport, fancy colored shirt, black leather spats and a dark suit with a pin stripe. His hair is gray and curly and oiled."[1] A consummate showman despite his low-key though sometimes abrasive courtroom manner, the new special prosecutor was a political ally of Governor A. Harry Moore, a Jersey City native, and he had close ties to Hudson County boss Frank Hague.

It was assumed that Simpson had his eye on the governorship himself and that the assured high exposure he would get as special prosecutor on the Hall-Mills case would help him climb what nineteenth-century British prime minister Benjamin Disraeli called the greasy pole.

But the ordinary citizens of Middlesex and Somerset Counties, who had little interest in the ins and outs of state politics, could well wonder, and did wonder, if the administration of local justice was being handed over not just to outsiders but to a special clique of outsiders. Hudson County outsiders. Frank Hague outsiders. They wondered how much it would cost, and where the money would come from, to pay for this senseless, belated fishing expedition, as many viewed it.

The Somerville *Unionist-Gazette* began to assail the new special prosecutor before the first week of his tenure had ended. "The Hall-Mills case," fumed an editorial in the paper, "has been taken out of the hands of Somerset County officials and is being directed either from Trenton or Jersey City." That development was bad enough, but lest anyone forget, "It cost the county $10,000 when Wilbur Mott was sent here to clear up matters four years ago and not a thing was accomplished that prosecutor Azariah Beekman [of Somerset County] had not brought to light."[2]

The *Unionist-Gazette* had a point, and one day later the Somerset *Democrat* joined in the attack. Even before Simpson had settled into the job, it noted editorially, he had started calling for a flurry of indictments. One woman and three men, the new special prosecutor announced, would be charged with murder. Now, how could the brash little lawyer do that? Had Somerset's own prosecutor, Francis Bergen, already solved the mystery before Simpson arrived? Maybe so. Surely, Simpson hadn't had time enough to solve it—and Mrs. Hall had been arrested before he arrived on the scene. As the *Democrat's* editorialist observed with tempered sarcasm, "Senator Simpson is a most able criminal lawyer, and in the event that the case came to trial he could be of great assistance to the prosecutor [Bergen]. But that time has not yet arrived, and in the meantime the taxpayers of the county are saddled with an extra expense and for work which has apparently been accomplished before Senator Simpson entered the case."[3]

That was not quite true. Alexander Simpson's problem, as voiced by Mrs. Hall's skeptical in-law Frank Voorhees and others, was that neither Francis Bergen nor anyone else had new evidence of any kind, only the questionable allegations in the annulment petition filed by Louise Geist Riehl's disgruntled husband. Simpson might think—as many people in New Brunswick presumably thought—that they knew well enough, at least in broad outline, what had happened out there under the crab apple tree. The difficulty, as Middlesex detective Ferd David had lamented a few days after the murders, was that the authorities had no proof against a specific individual or individuals that would stand up in court.

When Simpson took over as special prosecutor, he had no new evidence to present to a grand jury. The allegations in the Riehl annulment petition were hearsay. Francis Bergen had not solved the case. Nobody had solved it. Simpson's best hope, as he must have known from the outset, was to unravel the mystery, gather some credible evidence that no one had been able to obtain in 1922, and then prosecute the person or persons responsible for those two neatly arranged corpses.

And it truly *was* a mystery. A classic mystery. Contrary to Ferd David's cheerful dictum, the case was too complex to be a cinch. A comment in a front-page article in the *New York Times* of July 30, 1926, put it well, describing the Hall-Mills case as a "fascinating and perfectly balanced mystery, where each scrap of evidence and each conjecture has been cancelled by an opposing scrap of evidence and an opposing deduction."[4]

What kind of expertise did Alexander Simpson bring to his daunting task? Not much—at least not much as a criminal prosecutor. He was a journalist turned lawyer-politician. Born on June 12, 1872, in Jersey City, he graduated from Jersey City High School and went to work. He began as a newspaper reporter for the *Jersey City Argus.* Next he moved to the *New York Reporter* and later to the *World* and the *Globe.* While covering his beat as a part-time journalist in New York City, he also worked for a judge and studied law at Columbia Law School. Although he never completed his studies there, owing to a lack of money, he was admitted to the New Jersey bar in 1894. At the time he hung out his shingle he was doubling as a reporter for the *Jersey City News.* The paper, learning of his law practice, dismissed him for trying to pursue both careers, He turned his attention to politics, briefly at first, then persistently.[5]

In 1898, prior to the rise of Frank Hague, Simpson served one term in the New Jersey State Assembly. He returned to the Assembly eighteen years later and became minority leader, a position he held in both the 1916 and 1918 sessions. In April 1918 he filed for the Democratic nomination for U.S. Senator, but lost to George M. LaMonte, who subsequently lost to the Republican nominee, Walter E. Edge. Simpson, lowering his sights a bit, ran for and won a New Jersey Senate seat. His term began in 1922, and Simpson, a freshman senator, served as Democratic floor leader. Three years later he won reelection easily.[6]

Not surprisingly, Simpson was an activist senator, a politician who made noise and news. An important cog in Hague's increasingly powerful political machine, a spokesman for the workingman, and an urban populist, he was a blunt and articulate opponent of Prohibition and Sunday blue laws. He empathized with the poor. In 1922 he had come down foursquare for a five-cent fare on municipally franchised trolleys.[7]

When in the summer of 1926 he got the call to act as special prosecutor in the widely publicized Hall-Mills case, it seemed like an exquisite opportunity to advance his political career. The publicity would be unrelenting, if the press frenzy of 1922 could be taken as any guide.

Not that a successful prosecution would be easy. Simpson knew it wouldn't be. But being an outsider, and a brash one at that, he had certain advantages. For one, he could assemble an experienced team of detectives from Hudson County, investigators not tied to the local politics and power structure of Middlesex and Somerset Counties. On this score he did well. He brought in Patrick Hayes, Hoboken's chief of police, to coordinate the investigation. From the Jersey City Police Department he recruited, with Mayor Hague's approval, Captain Harry F. Walsh, detective John J. Underwood, and several others. He gave them free rein, and they served him well, if unavailingly.[8]

The problem was, it was too late to investigate. Simpson quickly learned that some of the none-too-damning evidence from the 1922 investigation was missing, including Willie Stevens' handgun, which had long since been returned to its owner.[9] Nevertheless, the new prosecutor exuded confidence. "We are still looking for some documents," he told Hague. "The visiting card of the clergyman found in his shoes, his eyeglasses, shirt collar, and cuff buttons."[10] From the items Simpson listed, it seems clear he was hoping to find one or more long-preserved fingerprints.

But he was hedging his bets. He realized early on that he might have to go to the grand jury and on to trial with little more than the inconsistent eyewitness testimony of the Pig

Woman. Therefore, like Wilbur A. Mott before him, he praised the loopy Mrs. Gibson as if she were some kind of bucolic heroine. "I am absolutely convinced that Jane Gibson tells a truthful story," he informed reporters three days after assuming his new duties. "I shall report to the governor that she is not the type of person who, through sheer imagination, could invent any of the evidence she gives for the night of the murder. She tells me the story of recognizing the woman and two of the men."[11]

Two of the men? If Jane Gibson had been consistent about anything at all four years back it was that she had seen one woman and one man arriving at the scene to confront the minister and his mistress. Now the new special prosecutor was talking about indicting "a woman and two men, perhaps three."[12] Alexander Simpson should probably have waited a few days before giving a ringing endorsement to the Pig Woman—waited, that is, for her to change her story to fit *his* theory of the crime, not hers. Instead, he seems to have leaped to the conclusion that her tale, the first time he heard it, was the unvarnished truth.

Simpson plunged ahead as if the pieces of the puzzle were falling neatly into place. They weren't, but the special prosecutor refused to be discouraged or deterred. As the press, the public, and the governor awaited prompt, decisive action, Simpson did his best to provide them with at least a semblance of it. He had a few successes. Between his assignment to the case in late July and the beginning of the trial in early November, he and his investigators managed to uncover several leads, facts, and witnesses that Mott and Mason either had not known about or had not fully exploited in 1922.

Since Mrs. Gibson loomed larger in the new investigation

Alexander Simpson. When the Hall-Mills case was reopened in 1926, Simpson, a state senator from Hudson County, was named special prosecutor. He tried hard but unsuccessfully to convict Mrs. Hall and her two brothers. (photo 1926)

than Simpson might have wished, he needed some way to corroborate the Pig Woman's presence in De Russey's Lane on the night of the murders. Her unsupported word would not be enough. The Bible itself, Deuteronomy 19:15, maintains, "One witness is not enough to convict." Mrs. Gibson's calendar-diary entry would be insufficient too; it was far too sketchy for Simpson to offer as evidence.

Back in 1922 Nellie Lo Russell, a feisty black woman who lived in a one-room shanty near the Gibson farm, had testified that Jane Gibson came to her house that fateful night. The two of them were together, she said, at the time the murders presumably occurred. Their topic of discussion was Mrs. Russell's lost dog, which the Pig Woman had found (rescued from a thieving foreigner, she said) and which Mrs. Russell reclaimed later that evening. If Nellie Lo Russell gave the same testimony at the 1926 trial, it would be damaging to Simpson's case.[13]

Enter Robert Erling, a wheelwright and truck driver, a slender young fellow with tousled hair who claimed he had been wooing one Jenny Lemford in De Russey's Lane on the night of the murders. While the two of them were cuddling in his sporty runabout with the headlights out, who should come riding by on her mule but Jane Gibson. Erling knew the Pig Woman fairly well from having had his laundry done by a girl who had once worked on the Gibson farm. Mrs. Gibson brought her mule to a halt and peered at the parked car. Fearful that he would be recognized in an embarrassing situation, Erling scrunched down. So did Jenny Lemford. After a moment or so, the four-legged Jenny—the Pig Woman's mule, that is— plodded on.[14]

Whether this incident ever occurred is open to question. Jenny Lemford, who by 1926 was Jenny Wahler, a wife and

mother, denied parking with Robert Erling that night in De
Russey's Lane. In an affidavit signed in early August 1926 she
admitted riding with Erling down De Russey's Lane, but insisted they hadn't parked there.[15] At the trial in November she
testified she had been with Erling all that day, but said they had
made no amatory stop in De Russey's Lane.[16] Neither of them
had seen Mrs. Gibson on her mule, she said.

There is a curious irony in the Erling story, one that casts
doubt on Jenny's protestations of maidenly reticence. Unmentioned in 1922, it came to light in 1926 because of a conversation the young wheelwright had with Nellie Lo Russell in
1924, while the case was in limbo. According to Mrs. Russell
(no friend of the Pig Woman or the prosecution), Erling, whom
she knew as "Snappy," told her about his date with Jenny Lemford and about seeing Mrs. Gibson in De Russey's Lane on the
night of the murders. It was the same story he later told on the
witness stand.

Robert Erling's account, if true, would confirm that Mrs.
Gibson and her mule had been in De Russey's Lane on the
night of the murders. It would, at the same time, indicate that
Mrs. Russell had been mistaken in 1922 when she swore that
she and the Pig Woman had been discussing a lost dog that
evening.[17] Nellie Lo Russell may well have concluded in 1924
that she had made an error as to when she had talked with Mrs.
Gibson about the lost dog—as in fact she had.[18] The conversation had been a week earlier than she remembered. Someone
on the McCarter team must have reached the same conclusion,
because the Million Dollar Defense did not call Nellie Lo
Russell as a witness in 1926.[19]

Another minor accomplishment of the Simpson investigation was getting James Mills to acknowledge once and for all

that he had been aware of the ongoing affair between his wife and Edward W. Hall. Despite Jim's initial defense of Eleanor's honor (not to mention the rector's and his own), he admitted to Simpson's men that the relationship was no secret and was probably not platonic. Actually, Jim Mills' ambivalence about his wife's fidelity had been evident even in 1922. A month or so after the murders, while being questioned about Mrs. Hall's absolute belief in husband's faithfulness, a belief that held up even in the face of the publication of Eleanor's love letters to her "babykins," Jim Mills mused, "Mrs. Hall had better get a new pair of glasses."[20]

Yet Jim continued to hedge, claiming his wife was true-blue. She was just a silly romantic, he said, writing perfervid but meaningless nonsense to no one in particular.[21] Only under the Simpson team's insistent prodding did he concede he had known about the love affair between his wife and the clergyman all along. Each had angrily threatened the other with divorce.[22]

In pursuit of further evidence, Alexander Simpson was determined to track down any eyewitnesses who had seen and could identify automobiles in De Russey's Lane or on Easton Avenue near the Phillips farm at the estimated time of the murders. The presence in the lane of Ralph V. Gorsline's green Apperson touring car was a given, as it had been from the beginning. The Apperson's proximity to the murder scene was surely one of the reasons Wilbur A. Mott had sought an indictment against Gorsline in 1922. Mott doubted that the car had been there by happenstance.

Simpson also took an interest in some of the other automobiles that may have been in the vicinity. And he made some headway. Charles J. Alpaugh, a railroad employee from Somerville, was working as a bus driver on the night of the crime. At about midnight, as his bus rumbled along Easton Avenue with a busload of firemen returning from a picnic in Red Bank, he saw two cars parked on Easton Avenue near De Russey's Lane. One was a Cadillac coupe, parked on the Parker Home side of the road and pointing toward Bound Brook. The other was a Dodge sedan, parked on the Phillips farm side of the road and pointing toward New Brunswick. Alpaugh saw "two or three persons . . . standing on the bank" beside the Dodge. As his bus approached, they "slid down [the bank toward] the car."[23]

Alpaugh was not the only one to see a Dodge sedan parked on Easton Avenue at about twelve o'clock that night. William F. Randall, a rural letter carrier, and his wife were returning to Bound Brook after attending a show at the State Theatre in New Brunswick. On Easton Avenue between the Parker Home and De Russey's Lane they saw a Dodge sedan parked with its lights off and its curtains drawn. The car, pointing toward New Brunswick, had one door open toward the Phillips farm. The Randalls saw no one near the car.[24]

Charles J. Alpaugh and William F. Randall were straight-forward, believable witnesses who gave Simpson's theory of the crime somewhat more credibility than Mott's earlier conjecture. Of course, a Dodge sedan parked on Easton Avenue near De Russey's Lane, while intriguing, did not automatically translate into Mrs. Hall's Dodge sedan with the aggrieved wife at the wheel and a brother or two along for the ride, particularly since the car had been seen at midnight rather than an hour and a half earlier. Still, Simpson may well have thought he was weaving a tight web of circumstance that would snare at least two of the rich and powerful Stevenses—Frances and Willie—in a confrontational adventure that had ended in tragedy.

When Simpson took over, the state lacked any strong physical evidence pointing to a specific suspect or suspects. They had some .32-caliber bullets and cartridge cases, but the pistol that fired them was never found.[25] They had no pocket knife, or kitchen knife, or razor, or garden shears that could be tied definitely to the slash wound on Mrs. Mills' neck. They had no bloodstained garments except Mrs. Mills' polka-dot dress. The handkerchiefs were useless. They had no footprints, no tire tracks, no hairs, no fibers—nothing that would erase reasonable doubt from the minds of the jurors. They did have, however, one lone fingerprint, supposedly that of Willie Stevens, lifted from the rector's calling card that was propped against his foot when the bodies were discovered. How this fingerprint evidence would play in court, and how the defense would counter it, remained to be seen.[26]

Simpson's one unquestioned coup in the Hall-Mills investigation involved Ralph V. Gorsline and Catherine Rastall. In the original investigation Mott and Mason had known that Gorsline was lying when he denied being anywhere near De Russey's Lane on the night of the murders. Gorsline had been seen there, his car had been there, and Catherine Rastall had been there. Nonetheless, both Gorsline and Rastall denied those facts repeatedly in 1922. The stonewalling ended in 1926, when Catherine Rastall admitted having been near the scene of the crime and having heard the four shots fired. Gorsline was thus forced to own up to his presence there as well. Unfortunately for the special prosecutor, the two would tell only half, or less than half, of what had happened during their evening together. The rest of it remains unknown. It seems likely that Gorsline could have broken the case open for Simpson—but probably not without being charged as an accessory before or after the fact. His motivation for being so near the scene of the murders was never definitely established.[27]

The Simpson detectives came up with one other witness who had noticed something unusual in the early morning following the murders. He was Harry A. Kolb of New Brunswick, a salesman, who at the time of the crime had been a milkman for the Paulus Dairy Company. Between four and five o'clock on the morning of September 15, 1922, Kolb arrived with his horse and wagon at 23 Nichol Avenue to make his usual milk delivery. For the only time in his seven months on the job, he found a rear door of the Hall mansion standing open as he approached from the Redmond Street side. He closed it to allow his horse and wagon to pass, made the milk delivery, and thought no more about it.[28]

None of these Simpson findings, separately or together, added up to conclusive proof, but they all seemed to point toward the likely involvement of Mrs. Hall and perhaps Willie Stevens in the events of September 14 and 15, 1922. Time would tell whether the special prosecutor could weave them into a tapestry that showed the killer or killers in colors striking enough for a jury to vote guilty.

18   Hippodroming

Alexander Simpson felt certain of one thing: Mrs. Frances
Noel Stevens Hall was somehow involved in the events under
the crab apple tree four years earlier. She had escaped justice
then, but she would not escape it now, although Simpson knew
that the obstacles facing him were substantial. When he accepted the appointment as special prosecutor in the case, Mrs.
Hall was already in jail, the New York *Daily Mirror* was calling for prompt action, and the townspeople and the responsible
press were beginning to wonder if this was more a witchhunt
than a serious search for the truth.[1]

William Phillips was also in jail. He was the burly night
watchman who had observed the "woman in gray" hurrying,
alone, toward a side door of the Hall mansion after 2:00 a.m. on
the night of the murders, and darting inside. Phillips was being
held in lieu of $5,000 bail, a predicament his wife and family
were unable to fathom and a sum they were unable to raise.
While Mrs. Hall, a presumed murderess, was soon released on
$15,000 bail, Phillips, one of the witnesses against her, stayed
locked up.[2]

Even after his bail was reduced to $2,500, and after Simpson
had taken over, the unhappy Phillips (whose memory had gone
blank with the passing years, doubtless to the annoyance of the
special prosecutor) remained behind bars. One night his wife,
incensed after her plea to visit him had been refused, was returning from the jail to her home at 72 Dennis Street when she
was accosted by reporters. She complained bitterly to them:
"He didn't fire any shots. He didn't commit the murders. Why

do they hold him this way? I don't understand it."[3]

Maybe the Simpson team thought that jail time would refresh Phillips' memory. It didn't. Released on bail a few days later, he returned home by trolley, where he immediately got into a fight with a news photographer. As Phillips retreated into his house, his wife fumed once more at the clutch of press representatives. "Why don't you go to the right people? We don't know anything about the murder. What do you want to bother us for?"[4]

William Phillips, one of Simpson's potentially strong witnesses, had turned truculent and uncommunicative. He could hardly be blamed. The revived case was off to a rocky start.

Two days after Phillips' release, Simpson ordered two more arrests: Ralph V. Gorsline as an accessory after the fact and Nellie Lo Russell as a material witness. The state troopers assigned to the case were supposed to obtain the warrants and take the pair into custody. For reasons of their own, they balked at Simpson's request, and the special prosecutor, briefly chastened, withdrew his demand for the arrests but said he would like to have the warrants on hand anyway, just in case.[5]

A few days later he called for three more warrants. Scheduled to be arrested in this roundup were Barbara Tough, the Halls' upstairs maid; Peter Tumulty, the Halls' gardener and occasional chauffeur; and Mary Gildea, a person whose name was new to almost everybody. All were to be held as material witnesses. Mrs. Gildea, it seemed, had been a cook in the Hall household in 1922. Her name hadn't made the news back then, but the cook, who lived at 24 Prosper Street, New Brunswick, had supposedly said during the two days of uncertainty about the rector's whereabouts, "They have been murdered. They have been murdered."[6]

None of the warrants for material witnesses were executed, then or later. Nor was Mary Gildea even called to testify at the trial. Mrs. Hall, who had gone into seclusion at her home following her release on bail, continued to be the only person charged in the case.

Senator Simpson, as the newspapers generally called him, began to draw criticism, and not just in Somerset County. *The Hudson Journal* of Union City, a Democratic paper on Simpson's home turf, in an editorial headlined "On the Brink of a Fall," questioned whether "a mere wave of a magic wand" could solve the puzzling four-year-old mystery and suggested that the impulsive senator was "in danger of being toppled from his pedestal."[7]

The Jersey Journal, a Democratic paper in Jersey City, was even more outspoken. It editorialized: "There has been so much rushing back and forth, mysterious 'tips' that later vanished into the air, 'missing' witnesses who suddenly turned up and proved they hadn't been missing at all, orders for warrants, then counter orders, numerous statements followed by almost as many denials, that those who would evidently like to upset Senator Simpson's applecart have been provided with the opportunity they were looking for to accuse him of 'hippodroming' [putting on a stunt-filled performance], rather than conducting a sane and orderly inquiry into an outrageous crime."[8]

Whether the hippodroming ended with the arrests three days later of Willie Stevens and Henry de la Bruyère Carpender is a matter of conjecture. No one supposed that Mrs. Hall alone had committed the murders on the Phillips farm. Still, there seemed little to support the thesis that the eccentric gadfly Willie Stevens and the respected stockbroker Henry Carpender had accompanied Mrs. Hall on the grievous errand that made her a widow. A cynic might conclude that Alexander Simpson was moving forward simply to avoid staying in place. The extensive press coverage had put him on the hot seat, and inaction could very well injure his political reputation.

On August 12, 1926, William Stevens and Henry Carpender were arrested on warrants issued to Captain John J. Lamb of the New Jersey State Police. According to Simpson, the arrests were based on "new evidence," a term often used to mean that Mrs. Jane Gibson, the Pig Woman, had added some new embroidery to her story. Simpson promised he would clarify the nature of this new evidence the next day.

Willie Stevens was at home at 5:15 p.m. when Captain Lamb, accompanied by three Jersey City detectives, served the warrant. "I knew it would come to this," Willie said, lowering his head.[9] Mrs. Hall, composed as always, asked to read the warrant. While she was doing so, a fierce storm broke. Lightning flashes lit the darkening sky, thunder cracked and rumbled, and the lights in the Hall home were turned on to allow Mrs. Hall to finish her reading.

Henry Carpender was informed by phone that a warrant had been issued for his arrest. Obligingly, the broker, who had just returned from his firm in downtown Manhattan, agreed to come at once to 23 Nichol Avenue to accept service. When he entered the Hall home, wearing a gray suit and carrying an umbrella, he was smiling. The tall, balding Carpender, so erect "as to suggest military training," acted nonchalant about his arrest. And why not? He had an alibi that none of the investigators had seemingly bothered to check.[10]

Jim Mills, when told of the arrests, thought he saw right away what Simpson was up to. "The arrests," said the laconic school janitor, "must be on the strength of that Pig Woman's

Somerset County Courthouse. The Hall-Mills trial took place at this courthouse in Somerville, New Jersey, in November and early December 1926. The trial was front-page news throughout the United States. (photo 1926)

story. Well, that Pig Woman didn't say anything at all about the murder until several weeks after it happened and she'd had plenty of time to read the newspapers." Even the trustful Jim, however, couldn't believe the whole case was going to rest on Mrs. Gibson's fancied observations. He concluded, "If they're arresting Willie Stevens and Henry Carpender they must have got some new witnesses."[11]

Mrs. Jane Gibson was the headline story the next day, three columns on the front page of the *New York Times.* Her pretrial appearance before County Judge Frank L. Cleary at the Somerset County Courthouse was nothing short of a triumph. "I had never before seen her," said Judge Cleary, "but fancied her an uncouth person, illiterate. Instead she seemed to be a woman of intelligence who displayed no illiteracy in the excellent choice of words with which she told her story straightforwardly." The Pig Woman's testimony, if believed, left no doubt as to who had fired the fatal shots:

Q—When you say you saw a flashlight, do you mean an electric light?

A—No, I saw a light; someone had a flash.

Q—Like a pocket lamp?

A—Like a pocket flashlight.

A—Yes.

Q—You saw it flashing around.

A—Yes, sir.

Q—What was the next thing you saw?

A—Then I saw something glitter and I saw a man's face.

Q—Whose face did you see? Can you pick him out in this courtroom?

A—This here man.

Q—Go down and put your hand on him.

A—This man here.

Q—Pointing to Henry Carpender?

A—Yes, sir.

Q—As he flashed the light around, something glittered in his hand?

A—Yes, sir.

Q—After you saw him with something glittering in his hand, did you hear any report?

A—Yes, right quick.

Q—What was it you heard?

A—A shot.

Mrs. Gibson went on to testify that she heard three more shots as she hastily mounted her mule and headed for home.[12]

What happened to that testimony over the next few weeks makes magician David Copperfield's vanishing Ferrari look like a trick performed by a school kid on amateur night. What occurred between August and September was nothing less than the substitution of someone else—an alternative Henry—for the man Mrs. Gibson positively identified as being at the scene of the crime. The Pig Woman's first choice for the Henry in her widely reported "Oh, Henry" quotation was Henry Carpender, the man who had held "something glittering in his hand" and, inferentially at least, fired one shot, followed moments later by three more shots. Her pointing him out under oath was forthright and unequivocal.

No matter how articulate and persuasive the Pig Woman was, she could hardly hope to wiggle out of such a direct accusation. But she did—and it didn't take her long.

Why she tried to bail out on the naming of Henry Carpender is an intriguing question. Her identification of him as the gunman at the scene, Willie Stevens as the "bushy-haired man," and

Mrs. Hall as the "woman in gray" placed three people at the crime scene, one more than Mrs. Gibson had previously reported. No matter. She could deal with that. But it did seem surprising that she—or Alexander Simpson—would now want to add yet another character to the scene. With the glitteringly armed first cousin, the oddball brother, and the sinned-against wife all clustered under the crab apple tree, why did the special prosecutor feel obliged to turn his attention to a brother of Mrs. Hall who lived fifty miles away?

The reason, explained Simpson, was a tale told by Paul F. B. Hamborszky, a former minister at the Hungarian Reformed Church in New Brunswick. Reverend Hamborszky's story had surfaced in the original investigation, hard on the heels of a $5,000-reward offer in a Magyar-language newspaper for information leading to the arrest and conviction of the Hall-Mills killer or killers. First published in *Amerikai Magyar Nepazava,* a daily published simultaneously in four major U.S. cities, the Hamborszky revelations were quickly picked up in English and thereafter appeared at length in a signed statement—not an affidavit—dated November 16, 1922.[13]

Reverend Hamborszky, a youngish, good-looking man, pictured himself as a close acquaintance of Reverend Hall, a friend in whom the St. John's minister would sometimes confide. Hamborszky's lengthy account of their conversations made it clear that Reverend Hall was deeply in love with Eleanor Mills and that he planned to divorce his wife and marry his mistress. The key passage, in Simpson's opinion, was this: "I do not know what I will do," said Hall. "All I know is I have to get out. I am in constant fear. [Henry Stevens] has threatened me and told me that he will finish me if I do not give up Mrs. Mills."[14]

None of this should be taken too seriously. Although Reverend Hamborszky did sign an affidavit in 1926,[15] he pointedly avoided testifying in court, just as he had in 1922. On the eve of his scheduled appearance at a pretrial proceeding in August 1926, the former Hungarian clergyman dropped out of sight.[16] Undaunted, Simpson kept him on the witness list for the trial. Hamborszky briefly reappeared. Then on the day before the trial opened, the special prosecutor was forced to admit that the ex-preacher, now a real estate salesman residing in Astoria, Queens, but selling building lots in Ocala, Florida, had once again flown the coop.[17]

The real reason Simpson turned his attention to Henry Stevens was probably unrelated to Paul F. B. Hamborszky. It was far more likely connected to the problems that Henry Carpender was giving him as Mrs. Gibson's designated triggerman. For one thing, Carpender had an apparently valid alibi about dining with the Rices in Highland Park on the night of the murders. For another, Mrs. Hall would not have yelled "Henry" at the pistol-packing stockbroker; she would have yelled "Harry." Simpson ought to have known both of these things before he bought into the Pig Woman's latest version of events. His oversight could prove disastrous. If Simpson continued to insist that Carpender was the man under the crab apple tree, he could surely expect a finding of reasonable doubt from any intelligent jury.

He needed a more vulnerable Henry. What better candidate than Frances Stevens Hall's other brother, the fellow in Lavallette who had made his living as an expert marksman? So off to Lavallette sped the stars of the Simpson investigative team, Captain Harry Walsh and Sergeant Richard Burke, followed a day later by Patrick J. Hayes, Simpson's chief aide, plus the special prosecutor himself. Apparently determined to place Henry Stevens at the scene of the crime, they questioned him at length about his familiar bluefishing-with-the-boys alibi. They intimated that his various witnesses were not nearly as impressive as Mason and Mott had found them four years earlier. Simpson noted inconsistences in their stories, not necessarily fatal to the alibi, true, but inconsistencies nonetheless. Henry's wife, Ethel, suggested caustically that for a lesson on inconsistencies the detectives should read the New Testament scriptures of Matthew, Mark, Luke, and John.[18]

When the investigators asked about a rumor that the speedometer on Henry Stevens' Ford indicated the car had been driven about 150 miles on the night of the murders, Stevens smiled. "That has been one of the most amusing things about this whole case to me," he asserted. "The old Ford was literally falling to pieces, its tires were almost off the rims, nothing was in proper shape except the brakes, and it had never had a speedometer on it."[19]

Although his neighbors in Lavallette, including the mayor of the town, continued to support Henry Stevens' account of his activities on the night of the murders, Simpson wasn't buying. He found holes and discrepancies in whatever he was told. When asked about a possible arrest, the bantam rooster from Jersey City replied, "We are going to concentrate on breaking the alibi first."

The case as Simpson envisioned it was taking shape. Three days into the assault on Henry Stevens' alibi, John J. Underwood, the Jersey City detective, went down to Toms River to check out the new suspect for himself. Before he left, he told reporters that it "has been established that there were three men and a woman at the scene of the murder that night."[20]

Less than two weeks later, on September 15, 1926, the Somerset County grand jury voted four indictments for murder in the Hall-Mills case. Mrs. Hall, expecting the news, had her bag packed for a return to jail. Henry Carpender and Willie Stevens were already locked up. Henry Stevens, learning of his indictment from a newspaper reporter in Lavallette, seemed unruffled. "What do you think about that?" he said, puffing on his pipe. "Now I'll have to show them they are wrong, won't I?"[21]

No one knew precisely what role each of the accused was supposed to have played in the drama near De Russey's Lane. It was widely believed that while Mrs. Hall had been present at the scene of the crime, she had been more horrified than elated when the shots were fired. Henry Carpender was presumed to have wielded the glittering .32 caliber pistol. But the public lacked any clue as to how the Stevens brothers, Willie and Henry, fit into the Simpson scenario. To learn that, they would have to wait for the trial.

Alexander Simpson wanted to try the four defendants separately. The defense lawyers wanted to try them all together. After much maneuvering and debate, the contending attorneys got a mixed answer from Supreme Court Justice Charles W. Parker and Common Pleas Judge Frank L. Cleary. Mrs. Hall and her two brothers would be tried together. An order of severance would be issued for Henry Carpender. He would be tried separately at a later date.[22]

Early in the Simpson inquiry, an editorial in the Somerville *Unionist Gazette* had expressed distaste for the reopening of the Hall-Mills case. Its words remained relevant on the eve of the trial. "So the show is on," the writer declared, "with a Hudson senator as ringmaster."[23] The implication of hippodroming was strong. And it had the ring of literal truth, for the star of the upcoming show, Mrs. Jane Gibson, claimed that she had once been a circus performer.[24]

The three defendants. With defense attorney Augustus C. Studer, Jr., (at left), defendants Willie Stevens, Frances (Stevens) Hall, and Henry Stevens watch the courtroom proceedings. (photo 1926)

19   The Prosecution Begins

Seventy-nine prosecution witnesses took the stand between November 3 and November 19, 1926, as Alexander Simpson attempted to prove beyond a reasonable doubt that Frances Stevens Hall, Henry Stevens, and Willie Stevens had sallied out to De Russey's Lane on the night of September 14, 1922, and (with or without Willie present), confronted Edward W. Hall and Eleanor Mills under the now-famous crab apple tree, argued briefly with the ensnared couple, struggled with one or both of them, and fired four shots. The trial concerned only the murder of Eleanor Mills, although it was assumed that whoever killed her had also killed the rector. Henry Carpender remained in jail, awaiting a later trial.[1]

The month-long trial, with enterprising press coverage to match the prior publicity mania surrounding the "great crime of the century,"[2] took place in the main courtroom on the second floor of Somerset County's white marble courthouse, a gleaming Italian Renaissance-style building on East Main Street in Somerville. On the first day of the trial, more than two hundred journalists—sixteen from the New York *Daily News* alone, thirteen from the New York *Daily Mirror*—telegraphed 130,175 words during the eight hours the court was in session.[3]

Two judges sat on the bench. The presiding judge was Charles W. Parker, a distinguished-looking justice of the Supreme Court, a man in his mid-sixties, a resident of Morristown who was "known both for his severity and his devotion to justice."[4] Beside him sat Frank L. Cleary, a Common Pleas judge, who midway through the trial took his six-year-old daughter and five-year-old son to see the giant portable telegraph loop board in the basement of the courthouse, with its 120 positions, recently deployed at the Tunney-Dempsey heavyweight boxing match in Philadelphia. It had been set up in a special office in the basement of the courthouse, and when the trial opened it stood ready to handle the flurry of telegraphic dispatches from the swarming host of reporters. Judge Cleary next took his children to the third floor, where he showed them the teletype-writers installed there. Said the judge, "They will probably never again see such a sight."[5]

Nor would Cleary himself ever again see such a sight as this trial. Especially notable was the prosecution's star witness, Mrs. Jane Gibson, the notorious Pig Woman, whose apparently terminal illness kept her under medical care and off the witness stand until November 18, two weeks and a day after the trial began. Several postponements, accompanied by Simpson's fearful talk of her dying before she could tell her story, built suspense. Defense attorneys sensed hippodroming, but Mrs. Gibson was genuinely ill, although the cancer wouldn't claim her for another four years.

Morris Markey, writing for the nascent *New Yorker* magazine, was struck by the setting for the trial, the small white courthouse in Somerville. "It is really a pity that you cannot be here," wrote Markey, "that you cannot hope to worm your way past the women packed at the door, and move cautiously down the sloping aisle to settle yourself in one of the high-backed open chairs and stare down into the well where the action is carried out. For one who is here, it is an absorbing thing, and yet it seems not quite real. It is not quite palpable—the thought that this square room, not very large, with its tiers of dull-faced people banked from the edge of the well itself up the sharp slope to the white wall beyond, is the center of attention for a whole race of humans."[6]

The first two witnesses for the prosecution made it clear that Alexander Simpson, with or without Jane Gibson, was in plenty of trouble, nearly as much trouble as the three defendants—although it was only the special prosecutor's reputation and political future that were at stake, not his freedom. The witnesses, two of Simpson's promised surprises, were Mr. and Mrs. John S. Dickson of North Plainfield, a town seven and a half miles north of New Brunswick.

Mr. Dickson, an accountant with a Wall Street firm, testified that while he and his wife were at their home on Rock View Avenue at about 8:30 on the night of the murders, an agitated and perhaps intoxicated Willie Stevens knocked on their front door and asked directions to "the Parker House," saying he thought it was somewhere "down the lane." Charlotte Dickson confirmed her husband's testimony, adding that the man they identified as Willie seemed not merely distraught but "terror stricken."

On cross-examination the Dicksons added various details about their visitor's appearance, actions, and words. The unsteady Willie Stevens, John Dickson declared, had on a derby, sported a gold watch on a chain, and wore no eyeglasses. Charlotte Dickson, a forceful woman in a severe brown dress, said that Willie stuttered and admitted to being "an ep-, ep-, ep-epileptic."[7] These details, far from bolstering Simpson's case, cast serious doubt on the Dicksons' story, for Willie Stevens never wore a derby, carried a silver watch and chain, always wore eyeglasses, didn't stutter, and, according to his family doctor, had never suffered from epilepsy.[8]

No doubt the Dicksons encountered somebody on their

doorstep that night, but it wasn't Willie Stevens. The prosecution's first two witnesses were resounding flops.

Simpson's next witness, on the other hand, had something of importance to say. She was Charlotte Mills, the daughter of the slain choir singer. In retrospect, Charlotte seems a rather pathetic figure in the Hall-Mills saga, despite her saucy self-confidence. Sixteen years old when her mother died, Charlotte was "pretty, with fair skin, blue eyes, straw-colored hair, and a turned-up nose."[9] "An alert girl of the modern type," observed a *New York Times* reporter in 1922, quoting the teenager to the effect that "Mrs. Hall does not like flappers, and I'm a flapper."[10] Charlotte emphasized that the dislike was mutual, and she may well have thought Mrs. Hall to be a murderess. "A woman did it," she told reporters a few days after the bodies were discovered, "and it was a woman who was jealous of my mother and wanted revenge."[11]

Not long after the 1926 indictment of the four defendants, Jim Mills cautiously expressed the hope that Simpson knew what he was doing. Charlotte, by then twenty and employed in the office of the International Motor Company in New Brunswick, had no reservations. "Hurrah!" she shouted when told that Mrs. Hall would be tried on a first-degree murder charge. "I think Simpson's great. Whatever he does is just right with me."[12]

Charlotte claimed to have been a confidante of her mother in the year before the murders. Mother and daughter got along well, slept in the same attic room, and shared at least some confidences about Eleanor's involvement with the rector. To investigators Charlotte maintained that "Mrs. Hall was aware of it [the love affair]." Her mother, she said, made frequent allusions to Mrs. Hall's vexation at Eleanor's role in her husband's life.

At the same time, Eleanor told her daughter about her growing dissatisfaction with her own life, saying, "I made a mistake marrying a man with no push or go."[13]

On the witness stand at the trial Charlotte Mills looked colorfully chic in a rose jersey sports suit and green velour tam. Her cheerful outfit did nothing to lessen the pain of the ordeal, and she fought for control throughout her testimony, weeping when asked to identify a portrait of her mother. Simpson questioned Charlotte about what she had done immediately after learning of the death of her mother. She replied that she had gone to 23 Nichol Avenue to see Mrs. Hall.

Q—What happened at the house when you went to see her?

A—I rang the bell, and the maid came to the door, and she directed me that Mrs. Hall was around the back, and as I started for the back I saw somebody running to the house, but I could not tell who it was. I came around and I thought I would leave, but just at that time I heard a heavy footstep on the front porch of their home, and it was Mr. Pfeiffer. He asked me what I wanted.

Q—Go ahead, tell us what occurred.

A—I told him I would like to see Mrs. Hall. He asked me why. I told him that I just wanted to see her and talk with her about all what had happened. He said, being her lawyer, he did not think it was well at that time. He told me they were very much interested in me and extended their sympathy, that they had often spoken about my welfare. They were interested in it ... and wanted to know if I would not like to go away from this for a while, say to an institution or religious home of some kind.

Q—Did you want to go to a religious home?

A—No.

Q—Did you see Mrs. Hall afterward riding around in an

automobile?

    A—Yes, frequently.

    Q—Did she pay any attention to you?

    A—No.[14]

Although Charlotte's testimony made Mrs. Hall appear insensitive, the victim's daughter lacked any real knowledge of what had happened under the crab apple tree. She could insist that the standoffish Mrs. Hall knew about Edward and Eleanor's trysts, but neither she nor anyone else could prove that they had led to murder. The people on the Mills side of the affair were generally willing to share the rumors, conversations, and anecdotes that grew out of the liaison. Those on the Hall-Stevens-Carpender side were unwilling to speculate on who knew what. Or, more accurately, they found it pointless to speculate, or said they did. Given Mrs. Hall's rectitude and gentility, they denied that there could be anything improper to tell.

Perhaps the most revealing comment Mrs. Hall ever made about the fatal love affair came in 1922 when, responding to a reporter's question about the published letters and the effusive love diary that seemed to picture her husband carrying on an intimate affair with Eleanor Mills, the Iron Widow, as journalists often called her, replied icily, "I know him too well for him to be in love."[15]

Another person besides Charlotte who realized that the minister and the choir singer were more than pen pals was Millie Opie, a rotund dressmaker who lived at 51 Carman Street, next door to the Mills. She testified that the phone calls and visits between the lovers had become a matter of neighborhood gossip. The rector came to Mrs. Mills' upstairs apartment "most every day, she said, and remained there "half an hour or an hour." The visits occurred in mid-morning or mid-afternoon, when the Mills children were at school and janitor Jim was at work—albeit directly across Abeel Street in the Lord Stirling School.

Alexander Simpson questioned Miss Opie:

Q—I understand you to say, preceding September 14, that Mr. Hall was calling there too frequently?

A—Yes.

Q—And you are quite sure that was limited to the last two months preceding the fourteenth of September?

A—Yes.

Q—Now, whom did you hear indulging in that talk?

A—Well, there was a Mrs. Lathan.

Q—Yes.

A—And a Mrs. Hardy.

Q—Yes, anybody else?

A—Not to me, but these parties spoke about the other neighbors there.

On cross-examination, Clarence Case got Miss Opie to admit that those trysts "every day" in July and August did not include—could not include—the time the rector spent at Point Pleasant and Islesford, which together totaled almost an entire month. When Case asked about the nature of the neighborhood gossip, the plump dressmaker replied, "Mrs. Lathan said that if Mr. Hall could call on one of his parishioners eight or nine times a week and not call once a year on her she was going to another church."

When the laughter subsided, Simpson asked her what, if anything, she had heard going on at the Mills residence during the rector's visits. "You never heard them singing?" he inquired. *"Gloria in Excelsis Deo,* or anything of that kind, did you?"

Miss Opie responded, "No, and the windows were open too."[16]

Another woman who gave testimony about the doomed love affair was Elsie P. Barnhardt, one of Eleanor's several sisters. A resident of Paterson, and thus removed from the uneasy atmosphere of New Brunswick and the charged climate of Somerville, Mrs. Barnhardt was a congenial woman in her early thirties, at ease on the witness stand. Judge Parker appeared entranced by Elsie, even stepping down from the bench at one point to take a closer look at her.[17]

The incident Mrs. Barnhardt related to bear out her belief in the affair between her sister and the St. John's minister is charmingly innocent by today's standards. One day, about eighteen months before the murders, she went to the church to see her sister, presumably having not found her at home. Reverend Hall emerged from his study at the rear of the church and told her that Eleanor was "around dusting somewhere." Elsie and the rector began to look for her. After searching vainly for a while, they saw Eleanor coming out of the very study where the rector had just been. She was "all flushed," Mrs. Barnhardt said, and offered only a curt "Hello."[18]

Not long after this episode Eleanor began to confide in Elsie about her involvement with the rector. Mrs. Mills told Mrs. Barnhardt, with evident pride, how Reverend Hall "had got up out of his sickbed to visit her in the hospital when she had her operation." Elsie wondered if such an action might arouse the suspicion of Mrs. Hall and others.

Simpson asked Mrs. Barnhardt:

Q—Did you talk with her, have any conversation with her about the wisdom or unwisdom of being so bold about this?

A—Yes.

Q—How long before she was murdered?

A—I think it must have been about a year.

Q—What did you say?

A—I told her she was a little unwise.

Q—Well, what did she say to you?

A—She said she did not care who knew it. She was not going to hide it from anyone.[19]

Still, Simpson could produce no evidence that the married sweethearts were sneaking off to hotel rooms to carry on their dalliance. Seven or eight months before the murders, Eleanor Mills arrived at the Barnhardts' home in Paterson and asked to stay overnight. She explained that she was meeting Reverend Hall in New York City the next day. They were planning to attend a play together. It was called *Shuffling Along,* Mrs. Barnhardt recalled. Eleanor stayed in Paterson that night and left for Manhattan early the following morning.[20]

It took no great prosecutorial skill for Simpson to prove that Edward W. Hall and Eleanor Mills were lovers and that their affair was widely known. In a sense, that was the crux of the prosecution. Revenge for infidelity. The arrangement of the corpses alone told the story. The fervent letters and diary entries, familiar to nearly every newspaper reader in the country, were introduced into evidence. Even the two Hall maids who lived in the mansion, although sympathetic to Mrs. Hall, admitted that the affair was common knowledge.

Barbara Tough (pronounced "Too"), a maid in the Hall household for seven years, told a story that predated Mrs. Barnhardt's "flushed face" tale by several years. "We were at the church," Miss Tough testified in her lilting Scottish brogue, referring to Reverend Hall as "the dominie." "We were going to one of the girls' houses, and it was arranged that we would meet at the church at half-past seven. When I went down I did not

Charles W. Parker, a justice of the Supreme Court of New Jersey, was the presiding judge at the Hall-Mills murder trial. Justice Parker, who served on New Jersey's highest court from 1907 to 1947, wrote the 1935 decision upholding Bruno Richard Hauptmann 's conviction in the Lindbergh kidnap-murder case. (photo 1926)

Frank L. Cleary, a judge in the Court of Common Pleas of Somerset County, assisted Justice Parker at the Hall-Mills trial. Judge Cleary had two children, ages five and six, whom he brought to the courthouse to see the telegraphic and teletypewriter equipment being used by journalists. (photo 1926)

see anyone, so I went in and I called twice while I was in the Sunday school room, and no one answered me. And I knew Dr. Hall had left the house before I did. So I walked on and was going to walk to his study and ask him had he seen any of the girls, and . . . as I reached the guild room door there Eleanor Mills jumped off Dr. Hall's knee."

Q—Where was Dr. Hall sitting, in his study?

A—No, in the guild room.

Q—What happened after she jumped off his knee?

A—Eleanor began to laugh hysterically, and then she says, "Oh, it is only Barbara." Dr. Hall did not speak, but he looked very angry like at me.

Q—Then what did you do?

A—Then we went out—you see, we were going to Highland Park—so Eleanor that night and I walked down together, and we went down to meet the other girls.

Q—That was about four years ago, you say, before she was murdered?

A—Oh, yes.

Q—Well, what do you know, if anything, about the associations of Dr. Hall and Eleanor?

A—Well, by that time gossip was beginning—

Senator Case—I object to that. What do you know?[21]

Case had a point. While Simpson could and did prove that many acquaintances of the rector and the janitor's wife knew of their relationship, and that they gossiped about it, he could not legitimately make the inferential leap to Mrs. Hall's knowledge of her husband's unfaithfulness. As Case noted, "It has happened in the lives and observation of all of us that the one most concerned, the one to be affected most, most injured by a situation about which gossip is rife, is the one last to learn of it."[22]

And if Frances Hall stuck to her claim of ignorance, as she did unwaveringly, it would profit Alexander Simpson very little to show that everyone *else* in town seemed to know of the long-term affair. Of course, if the prosecutor could prove that Mrs. Hall had seen the letters before the murders were committed, that would put her claim in a different light. She could still maintain her disbelief in any real, as opposed to literary, intimacy between Edward and Eleanor, (as she stubbornly did maintain after the letters were released to the public) but her claim would be less persuasive.

Barbara Tough furnished no alibi for Mrs. Hall or Willie Stevens between the hours of 10:00 p.m. and 2:00 a.m. on the night of the murders. Thursday was her day off, she explained, and she arrived back at 23 Nichol Avenue at precisely ten o'clock at night. She found lights burning in the lower hall, the library, the kitchen, and the second-floor hall. Seeing and hearing no one, she put out the kitchen light and went directly to her third-floor bedroom.

At 2:00 a.m., she said, she heard Mrs. Hall walking in the second-floor hallway, going from her bedroom to the bathroom and back again. She was sure of the time. She heard no knocking on Willie's door, no attempt to rouse him during this early morning break. Miss Tough went back to sleep, unaware that anything was amiss.[23]

The second live-in maid in the Hall household, Louise Geist (Louise Geist Riehl at the time of the trial) testified that she went up to her room "sometime between nine and ten" on the night of the murders. She did not hear Barbara Tough arrive home. Indeed, she heard nothing, she said, until the "noise of the shutters" awakened her early the next morning.

Much of Louise Geist Riehl's testimony dealt with the

phone call from Eleanor Mills to Reverend Hall at his home at about seven o'clock on the night of the murders. Alexander Simpson expressed annoyance at her testimony on this important incident, testimony which he said differed substantially from what she had told the grand jury in 1922. Simpson's irritation may or may not have been justified. There is no way to know, since most of the grand jury testimony was never made public.[24]

Mrs. Riehl, whom Simpson insisted on calling Miss Geist, made a marked impression on the journalists in the courtroom. "Defiant, stagey, talky—what you might call 'fresh'"—wrote Damon Runyon, "but by no means hard to look at, as the saying is," Mrs. Riehl "cocked her head like a bird, and rolled her big circular eyes . . . up at the stained glass skylight" as she testified.[25] To the *New York Times* reporter she "seemed a trifle cocksure on the stand and was ever ready to match her wits against the nimble ones of the state's representative." The *Times* reporter also noted her outfit, "the registering features being a blue coat and a small toquelike hat of vivid red."[26]

Arthur S. Riehl, in his petition for annulment, asserted that Louise had taken a $5,000 bribe to keep quiet about her knowledge of the Hall-Mills slayings. If so, she hardly earned the money, based on her trial testimony regarding Willie Stevens. When recounting her conversation with Willie on the morning after the murders, she came close to pointing the finger of guilt at the eccentric man of the house who chased fire engines.

Simpson, after asking the bland question, "Did you come down then?," drew the following response from Mrs. Riehl:

A—As soon as I heard the shutter come down, I got up and came down into the dining room, and there I saw Mr. Willie Stevens, and I says to him, "What are you doing up so early?"

He said, "I would rather not tell you. I would rather have Mrs. Hall tell you." I said, "What are you doing up so early—what is the matter?" He said, "There was something terrible happened last night, and Mrs. Hall and I have been up most of the night."

Q—Did you ask him what the terrible thing was?

A—No, sir.

Q—Did he say anything about your not telling what he told you?

A—Yes. He said, "Don't tell Frances I told you."

Q—What was his manner when he told you that? Can you describe his manner?

A—Well, he seemed a little nervous. I did not look at him very good.

Q—Didn't you describe it to the grand jury in 1922 in the following language: "He looked as if he had katzenjammer"?[27]

Mrs. Riehl could not remember using those exact words. But when she left the witness stand there could be little doubt that by shading her story about the 7:00 p.m. telephone call she had supported Mrs. Hall's claim of knowing nothing about the rector's love affair, whereas by describing Willie Stevens' words and demeanor the next morning she had undermined his alibi of having slept peacefully through the tragic events on the Phillips farm.

20   Simpson at Apogee

Despite the prosecution's shaky start with the easily disproved testimony of the Dicksons, several witnesses supported one or more aspects of Simpson's theory of the crime. The testimony of Charlotte Mills, Millie Opie, Elsie Barnhardt, and Barbara Tough made it obvious that the rector's affair with the choir singer was well known. Louise Geist Riehl's account of Willie Stevens' words and demeanor on the morning after the murders suggested that Mrs. Hall's oddball brother knew something about what had happened the evening before.

Mrs. Anna L. Hoag, a small, pale woman who had lived on Green's farm in 1922, a few hundred feet from the scene of the crime, testified to having heard four shots at about ten o'clock on the night of the murders. This confirmed the more specific statements of Ralph V. Gorsline and Catherine Rastall, when they finally owned up, four years after the fact, to having been parked in a lovers' lane next to the one with the crab apple tree.[1]

A more important witness than Mrs. Hoag was Elija K. Soper, a well-dressed salesman of about fifty, with gray hair and horn-rimmed glasses, who lived at 76 Lawrence Avenue, New Brunswick. He had been attending a Masonic meeting in Somerville on the night of September 14, 1922. Returning home around midnight in a Ford sedan driven by a friend, Soper saw an open touring car, dark green or black, parked at the side of the road on Easton Avenue near De Russey's Lane. There were three people in it—two men in the front seat and a woman wearing a light coat in the back seat. Soper knew Willie Stevens by sight but was unable to identify any of the passengers in the touring car.[2]

Ira B. Nixon, a slim man with a square face who had worked with Soper in 1922 at the National Oil and Supply Company in Newark, testified that on the morning of Saturday, September 23, 1922, he and Soper, while picking up their checks at the cashier's window of the oil company, had discussed the Hall-Mills murder case. At that time, Nixon said, Soper told him that the three people in the touring car were "Mrs. Hall and her two brothers." He said he couldn't imagine why Soper on the witness stand had testified to not knowing the identities of any of the three passengers.[3]

Simpson had a few other encouraging moments during the trial. On the same day he read into the record the rector's ardent letters to his mistress, he questioned a fresh-faced, fair-haired young man, William J. Grealis of New Brunswick, on the subject of Willie Stevens' wardrobe. Grealis, fourteen years old at the time of the murders, had been employed part-time by Lyons & Parker, a clothing store on Church Street in New Brunswick. He delivered a new three-piece suit to the Hall residence on Nichol Avenue at about 8:00 p.m. on the day the bodies were discovered. A nervous Willie Stevens met Grealis in the curving front driveway and told him to go around to the back of the house, since Willie wanted to give him a suit to take back to the store "to be cleaned and scoured."[4]

Grealis delivered the new suit and received from Willie a soiled suit tied with a rope. Leaving by a side door at Willie's insistence, the youngster returned to the clothing shop where he and his older brother Austin untied the rope and examined the suit. They found dark-colored spots on the vest and around the waist of the trousers. The suit did not get cleaned as Willie had instructed, but instead was turned over to one of the detectives working on the case. Grealis next saw it about two weeks later in the Middlesex County prosecutor's office. By the time of the trial in 1926 Willie's soiled suit had become one of the many pieces of evidence that had somehow disappeared.

Although Simpson expected jurors to infer that the spots on Willie's suit were bloodstains, defense counsel would have no part of that. "Don't you know," Clarence Case asked Grealis on cross-examination, "that he [Willie] had a way of getting his food on the front of his vest or clothing, and that it had to be frequently cleaned?" The young man, now eighteen, admitted to having known that spots and stains were fairly common on Willie's suits. He balked, however, at Case's suggestion that Willie was understandably nervous that night because the rector had been found slain earlier in the day. Did the youthful deliveryman really find this nervousness strange under the circumstances? Case inquired with a touch of sarcasm. "Well," replied Grealis, "the way he acted, I did think it was strange."

On redirect, Simpson attacked Case's implication that the spots were food stains.

Q—You did not know what his table manners were?

A—No.

Q—You had never dined with him?

A—No.

Q—Or lunched with him?

A—No.

Q—Or acted as his waiter?

A—No, sir.[5]

The verbal dueling between Simpson and Case sometimes became "nos-tee," as Case pronounced *nasty*.[6] When Case tried to learn why Simpson thought William Grealis had asked to go out the front door of the Hall mansion instead of leaving the way he had come in, the special prosecutor, sensing nit-picking over the entreaties of a fourteen-year-old delivery boy, snapped, "Why does the junior counsel sob so?" Simpson's question was a double insult—the loaded word *sob*, of course, but also the reference to Case as "junior counsel." It made the fifty-year-old Republican senator from Somerset County sound like a young underling on the defense team, and a crybaby at that. What prosecutor Simpson, a Democrat from Hudson County, hoped to gain by needling one of Somerville's favorite sons in front of a Somerset County jury is hard to imagine.[7]

Grealis performed well on the witness stand, but in the absence of any clarification from the prosecutor, the jury was left to decide for itself whether the spots on Willie's suit were bloodstains or gravy stains.

Alexander Simpson assigned the task of reading Eleanor Mills' love letters in court to Francis L. Bergen, the Somerset County prosecutor, who clearly did not enjoy doing it. His sing-song voice dropped a bit as he hurried over passages such as "Sweetheart, my true heart, I could crush you. Oh, I am wild tonight. . . ." And, "Darling, my life is nothing except I have all your love. . . . I am holding my sweet babykins' face in my hands and looking deep into his heart. . . ."[8]

As Bergen read Eleanor's letters, Mrs. Hall remained as unperturbed as ever. Willie Stevens did not. He sat ramrod straight, his hands on his knees, listening intently to every word. Several times during the reading, Damon Runyon observed, the firehouse buff "lifted his protruding mustache in a snarl that showed his white teeth. . . . Willie seemed greatly annoyed."[9]

The letters, while embarrassing, revealed nothing new. By far the most worrisome item of evidence to the defense team was Willie Stevens' alleged fingerprint on Reverend Hall's calling card. The card, found propped against the shoe of the rector's corpse, became the focus of much testimony and loomed large in the presentations of both Simpson and McCarter. Despite the card's checkered history and casual journeys, Simpson put on a persuasive, single-minded show concerning it. McCarter, on the other hand, spellbinder though he was, seemed to confuse matters for the jury by offering two mutually exclusive explanations of the evidence. One was that the fingerprint on the calling card, exhibit S-17, was a forgery transferred directly from a Willie Stevens print in the prosecutor's office, and thus indisputably Willie's. The other was that the fingerprint on the card belonged to someone else. McCarter offered expert witnesses to support both positions and in his summation he gave equal time to each. Although the jury could toss out S-17 on other grounds—the broken chain of custody being the most obvious—it is hard to see what McCarter expected the jury to make of his vigorously argued but irreconcilable conclusions.[10]

Simpson wasted no time in putting the fly-specked calling card with its allegedly damning fingerprint into evidence. On the second day of the trial, November 4, the special prosecutor called three expert witnesses to try to place Willie Stevens, via the imprint of Willie's left index finger on S-17, at the scene of the crime. The first expert on the stand was Lieutenant Frederick Drewen of the Jersey City Police Department, a nattily dressed young man brimming with self-confidence. Drewen claimed ten years of experience in dealing with whorls, loops, and arches. When asked if the print on Reverend Hall's calling card matched any of Willie's fingerprints taken by the police in early August 1926 (and never before), the lieutenant testified that "one of them compared with the fingerprints of the index finger of William Stevens."

Simpson, edgy as always, said "What do you mean 'compared'? Is it or is it not a print of William Stevens?"

"It is," replied Drewen. He went on to testify that the print came from Willie's left index finger and that it appeared on the back of the calling card at the extreme left.[11]

The next expert to take the stand, Edward A. Schwartz, a thin, balding man, identified himself as Superintendent of the Bureau of Records of the Newark Police Department. He agreed with Lieutenant Drewen that the print on the back of the rector's calling card matched the left index finger of Willie Stevens. But something of far greater interest to the defense team than Schwartz's title or his expertise was the fact that he had been the person in possession of the calling card from the time Mott and Mason's investigation collapsed in 1922 with the grand jury's no-bill until just a few months before the 1926 trial, when Simpson's investigators claimed it. McCarter and Case hoped that the tangled tale of the card's wanderings, a story that involved Schwartz, would cancel any belief the jurors might have in the authenticity of the fingerprint, no matter how sure Simpson's experts said they were about the match-up.[12]

Still, the day went well for the prosecution. As Damon Runyon reported, "The fingerprint testimony seemed disturbing to the party gathered around the table on the defense's side of the room. There was much whispered consultation, and both Case and McCarter fought hard to keep out the fingerprints for the time being."[13]

One of Simpson's best prepared and strongest witnesses anchored the trio of fingerprint experts. He was Joseph A. Faurot, recently retired as Deputy Police Commissioner of New

York City and, many years before, the first law enforcement officer to use fingerprint evidence in an American court. Faurot brought to court a stack of twenty photographs, two transparencies, and a big brown light box for viewing the transparencies. A slow-moving man with a bald head and a mustache, he explained the theory and procedures of fingerprinting in considerable detail, pointing out that Willie Stevens' type of print was the arch (as opposed to the whorl, the loop, or the composite) and that only about five percent of the population fit that classification. Like Drewen and Schwartz, he found a direct and specific match between Willie's left index finger and the print on the back of the fly-specked calling card.[14]

These three witnesses were a major plus for Simpson's case, but there were minuses as well. For one, there was George D. Totten, Somerset's top detective in 1922 and a man who, along with Middlesex County prosecutor Joseph E. Stricker and Middlesex's fingerprint expert, William Fitzpatrick, had looked closely, indeed microscopically, at the rector's calling card in November of that year. Stricker and Fitzpatrick were now dead, leaving Totten to report their observations. Even before the Drewen-Schwartz-Faurot trio began their recital, the ex-Somerset investigator had sworn vehemently on the stand that in early November 1922 the card contained no fingerprint of the kind Simpson put into evidence.[15]

Moreover, if there had been an unidentified fingerprint on the card, why wouldn't Fitzpatrick have taken Willie Stevens' prints—and those of many other possible suspects—during the first investigation?[16] Simpson was aware that Willie had not been fingerprinted in 1922. In cross-examining one of the expert witnesses for the defense, he hammered home the point that no successful forgery of Willie's print could have been made until after August 12, 1926, when Willie was fingerprinted for the first time. "Just like a forged signature," Simpson insisted—"If you have not got a man's signature, you cannot forge it. If you have not got a print, you cannot forge it."[17]

The defense expert readily agreed.

The testimony of Drewen, Schwartz, and Faurot seemed to leave the Million Dollar Defense with one obvious option—to prove that the fingerprint on the calling card was forged. If George Totten and the deceased Stricker and Fitzpatrick were right, if no print existed in 1922 in the place on the card where Simpson's three experts found one in 1926, then forgery appeared not only possible but probable. The defense team did have two of their several fingerprint experts, Gerhardt Kuhne and James Herbert Taylor, pursue the theory of forgery. Curiously, though, at the same time they were opting for forgery they were coming to the contradictory conclusion that the disputed print belonged to someone other than Willie Stevens.

One of the defense experts, James Herbert Taylor of the U.S. Navy Department, testified to both defense propositions. On November 23, McCarter asked:

Q—Have you [James Herbert Taylor] examined State's exhibit 17?[18]

A—Yes, sir.

Q—And have you examined the enlargements?

A—Yes, sir.

Q—Are they the fingerprints of the same person?

A—They are not, sir.

Q—Have you any doubt about that?

A—None in the least.[19]

So much for the forgery idea. Why forge someone *else's* fingerprint if the aim was to frame Willie Stevens? But wait. Six days later Taylor was back on the witness stand explaining at some length how the fingerprint *was* forged. "It might have been put on in several ways," the Navy expert said. "It might have been transferred to the card from a plate handled by the subject, the plate subsequently to be developed and then bathed in a solution which would enable a person to transfer it on the fingertip of a rubber glove to any object upon which the print was desired."[20]

He went on to describe other methods of forgery, apparently oblivious to the fact that the fingerprint either was forged or it wasn't. And Taylor had company in his confusion. Gerhardt Kuhne of the Central Bureau of Identification of New York City went through the same logical flip-flop, managing to do it on a single, brief trip to the witness stand. After stating positively that Willie Stevens' fingerprint and the print on the calling card belonged to different persons, he proceeded to show, with equal certainty, how the disputed print, the one that was supposed to be Willie Stevens', had been added later. The whole card, Kuhne explained, had first been developed with lampblack or boneblack. Then, at a later time, the forged fingerprint was put on (anybody's fingerprint apparently would do), and the card was developed again, this time with charcoal or graphite.[21]

The testimony of Taylor and Kuhne seems to be a variation on the old saw, "I wasn't there; but even if I was there, I didn't commit the crime." Applied to this case: "The fingerprints belong to two different persons; but even if they belong to the same person, the print on the calling card is forged."

Alexander Simpson's case was hardly demolished by the defense team's fingerprint experts. By the end of the trial a reasonable person could conclude that maybe, just maybe, even after the rector's fly-specked calling card had been up hill and down dale, across the Hudson and up the river, pooh-poohed by Totten and ridiculed by McCarter, it might possibly, just possibly, have borne the arches of Willie's left index finger from the very beginning.

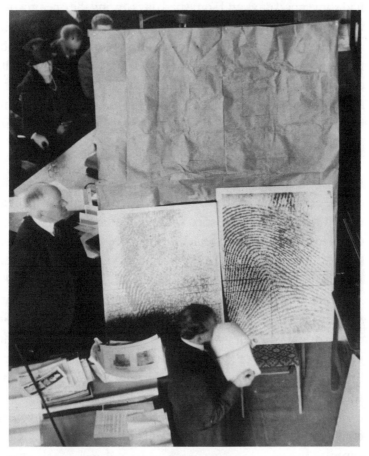

Enlarged fingerprint from Hall's calling card. The prosecution maintained that this print belonged to Willie Stevens and had been on the card since the night the murders were committed. The defense disagreed. (photo 1926)

21   A Liar, Liar, Liar!

The state of Jane Gibson's health remained a topic of conversation throughout the first two weeks of the trial. Simpson had some good days and some bad days during the opening two weeks, but few doubted that without the Pig Woman's eyewitness testimony the prosecution stood no realistic hope of obtaining convictions. Mrs. Gibson was truly ill, gravely ill, the cancer was real, and however stage-managed the defense team might believe her last-minute, made-for-media appearance to be, she was in bad shape. It would take an extraordinary effort for her to appear at the Somerset County Courthouse.

Finally, when she was ready to testify, Mrs. Gibson was taken by ambulance from Jersey City to Somerville. Curious onlookers along the way shouted advice and encouragement at the woman in the ambulance with gold letters reading "Jersey City Hospital." There seemed to be more wisecracking than sympathizing. "Oooh, the Pig Woman!" yelled one spectator. Another shouted, "Now's yer chance, Jane. Do yer squealin'!"[1]

When Mrs. Gibson arrived at the courthouse, she was carried into the courtroom on a stretcher, then transferred to an iron hospital bed from which she testified. In her 1922 grand jury debut, she had persuaded no one. How well she would perform this time, in the main event, surely had to concern the special prosecutor. The Pig Woman gave it her all.

New York Times reporter Bruce Rae wrote the lead story for this signal moment in American courtroom history. It began:

"Propped in a bed in the hushed courtroom, her face as

waxen white as the coverlets, Mrs. Jane Gibson told her story yesterday in the Hall-Mills murder trial at Somerville, N.J. The recital took her only twenty minutes, and a white-clad nurse stood at one side of the bed and a physician at the other as the painfully slow sentences of accusation were uttered.

"It was a story of shots in the darkness and of faces dimly seen in the flare of a flashlight, a narrative of mumbled voices, curses, and a struggle, and the dull sound of the falling of the Rev. Edward W. Hall and Mrs. Eleanor R. Mills before four bullets. A story that was simple, yet one that clutched the auditors in a spell of silence broken only by the words issuing from the parched lips."[2]

Ishbel Ross, Bruce Rae's wife of four years, was covering the trial for the rival *New York Herald Tribune.* Her opinion of the Pig Woman's testimony, and her style of writing, differed considerably from that of her husband. Judging by Ross's reportage, she was skeptical of the Pig Woman's tale and identified with the plight of Mrs. Hall. "[Mrs. Gibson's] wild eyes," she wrote, "blazed from their sunken sockets at Mrs. Hall. Her skinny arm was leveled at the still form in black. A faint smile of pitying scorn touched the lips of the rector's widow. Her calm was untouched in the midst of a hysteria that she visibly despised."[3]

As Bruce Rae noted, Mrs. Gibson's direct testimony lasted only twenty minutes. It was a trimmed-down account of what she now claimed to have seen and heard on the fateful night. Inevitably, her recollections differed in several respects from the previous tellings. The search for corn thieves became the overriding theme this time, even to the extent of replacing her lost moccasin as the reason for her second trip to De Russey's Lane. Mrs. Gibson spoke of a clearly identifiable Mrs. Hall kneeling over "two shadows." In past accounts the widow had been weeping in apparent distress. In this, her final and decisive remembrance, the Pig Woman testified that "She [Mrs. Hall] let out a screech."

Her testimony concerning the murders was less vividly detailed than before. After tying up her mule Jenny (a new twist), she approached to within fifteen feet of the people near the crab apple tree. Senator Simpson asked:

Q—Were you able to make out any words when they got closer to you?

A—Yes.

Q—What words?

A—Well, the men were talking and a woman said very quick, "Explain these letters."

Q—And what did you hear the men say, if anything?

A—They were saying "G— D— it," and everything else. All that kind of stuff.

Q—What do you mean, a man or a woman?

A—A man hollered.

Q—And immediately after that what did you hear?

A—Then somebody threw a flash toward where they were hollering.

Q—A flashlight?

A—Yes, and I see something glitter and I see a man, and I see another man like they were wrestling together.

The strain of testifying had begun to show on Mrs. Gibson, and at this point a nurse leaned over the bed and put cold cream on her lips. The attending doctor counted the pulse of the witness. While this was going on, Simpson spent his time dropping coins from one hand to the other. He then resumed his questioning.

Q—Did you see any faces there?

A—Yes, I see two faces.

Q—Have you identified those two faces since?

A—Yes.

Q—Who were they?

A—One was Henry Stevens.

Q—You need not identify the other one. Did you see Willie Stevens there?

A—No.

Q—But there was one man you saw, and Willie Stevens?[4]

A—Yes.

Q—After you saw Henry Stevens' face did you hear anything?

A—Yes. The light went out and I heard a shot.

Q—Then what did you hear?

A—Then I heard like something fall heavy. Then I run for the mule.

Q—Did you hear a woman say anything?

A—Yes. There were two women.

Q—Did you hear a woman's voice after you heard the shot?

A—One said, "Oh, Henry"; easy, very easy; and the other began to scream, scream, scream so loud.

Q—. . . Did you hear anything in the way of shots after the first shot?

A—I ran for the mule after the first shot, but that woman was screaming, screaming, trying to run away or something; screaming, screaming, screaming, and I just got my foot in the stirrup when Bang! Bang! Bang!—three quick shots.

Q—Then what did you do when you got your foot in the stirrup?

A—I stumbled over a stump and I ran home then.[5]

Who *were* these people? Presumably, the two women were Mrs. Hall and Eleanor Mills—Mrs. Hall breathing, "Oh, Henry," and Mrs. Mills screaming, screaming, screaming. Then there was Henry Stevens, neatly skewered by name. Common sense suggests that the other man—whom Mrs. Gibson was told she "need not identify"—was the rector. The rector, after all, was the man on the receiving end of the first shot.

But if these were the four people under the crab apple tree, where was Henry Carpender? He was the man the Pig Woman had identified without hesitation at the preliminary hearing as the person who waved that glittering "something" at the scene of the crime. From her iron bed at the trial, however, the Pig Woman neither stated nor denied that both Henrys were on hand for the slayings. She skimmed past the issue. A bit of now-you-see-him-now-you-don't legerdemain had subtly, and amazingly, substituted Henry Stevens for Henry Carpender.

And where was Willie Stevens? Mrs. Gibson had an answer for that. Although she hadn't seen Willie near the crab apple tree, she had seen him a few minutes earlier, standing with Mrs. Hall in the glare of headlights. Both before and after identifying Willie by name, Mrs. Gibson referred to him many times as the "colored man."[6] He was also, presumably, the "bushy-haired man" of the Pig Woman's 1922 memories.

Jane Gibson's aged mother, Mrs. Salome Cerenner, had a front-row seat for her daughter's testimony. Mrs. Cerenner was not a supportive mom. "I am ashamed of being her mother," she told reporters, "and I am going to tell all about her." Which she did. "She's a liar, she's mean, and she's not a good woman," Mrs. Cerenner said. "Her first name is not Jane. Her last name is not Gibson. She never was a circus rider."[7] Mrs. Cerenner continued in that vein, taking issue with a wide variety of her daughter's reported statements. At the trial, the old woman, spare, gray-haired, and dressed in black, stared balefully at her afflicted daughter and muttered from her front-row seat, "She's a liar. A liar, liar, liar!"[8]

Mrs. Gibson (or Mary Jane Easton, to be strictly accurate about it) was certainly that. Clarence Case, who cross-examined the bedridden witness, might have gotten a good many laughs from his probing of the Pig Woman's "real" name if the thin, cancer-wracked patient hadn't appeared to be so near death's door. Case introduced the following additional names that Mrs. Gibson had purportedly used: Mary Jane Eisleitner (her birth name), Mary Jane Leitner (a shortening of Eisleitner), Janet Hilton (which she denied), Anna King (which she denied), Mary Kesselring (her first married name, which she denied, although the defense had uncovered a marriage certificate in Paterson dated August 13, 1890, and a divorce decree in which Frederick Kesselring charged her with adultery). Senator Case alleged that she had also lived with two men, Harry Ray and Stumpy Gillan, without taking their last names.[9]

As for Mrs. Gibson's testimony, Senator Case on cross-examination—which lasted much longer than Simpson's direct—caught Mrs. Gibson in contradiction after contradiction between what she had just said under oath at the trial and what she had sworn to on prior occasions. Still, the scrappy Pig Woman, notwithstanding her nickname and lack of education, was a shrewd and intelligent adversary. She had a remarkable talent for meshing, or appearing to mesh, irreconcilable facts. When she saw no satisfactory way to fudge, she would simply deny the truth of what Case was saying. Or else, instead of answering yes or no, she would bounce a question back at him: "Why would I do that?" "Why would I say that?" In particular, why hadn't she included Henry Stevens in her testimony at the preliminary hearing in August? Simple enough, she said. She hadn't been asked about him. Like any accomplished liar, the Pig Woman was beyond embarrassment.

Her exit from the courtroom was as dramatic as her entrance had been. Here is how Bruce Rae's lead story in the *New York Times* described it:

"Mrs. Gibson settled her disordered, gray-streaked head back on the pillow. Her eyes closed and her fingers pulled nervously at the blankets. Two attendants moved forward at either end of the stretcher to lift it. Mrs. Gibson's eyes opened in their caverns and for a second stared at the ceiling.

"The jury was filing out and all save two had gone through the oaken door. The black-robed judges, Supreme Court Justice Parker and Common Pleas Judge Cleary had left the bench. But the three defendants, with Mr. [Henry] Carpender bending over the back of them, remained in their places.

"Summoning a reserve of vitality, Mrs. Gibson half-raised herself from the canvas carrier. A wasted hand was thrust suddenly at the accused, each absorbed in watching her. Mrs. Gibson's voice rose shrilly, with an eerie break in it. Then it died away in a choking sound.

"'I have told them the truth!' she cried. 'So help me, God! And you know I've told the truth!'

"She fell back on the stretcher. Bessie Lockwood, the nurse, quickly drew a sheet over the patient's head."[10]

She had not told the truth. Or, at best, she had told an imaginatively embroidered version of the truth. Her cryptic diary entry, "Must have been what I heard and saw on the 14th," had turned into a gripping, first-person narrative, ever changing, with named characters, shadowy settings, sparse but

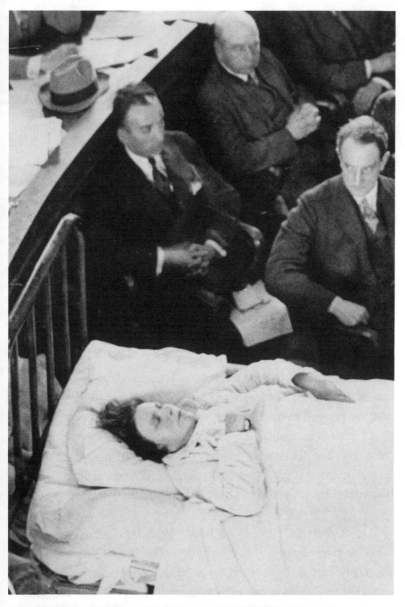

The Pig Woman testifies. The high point of the Hall-Mills trial was Jane
Gibson's delayed courtroom appearance, testifying from a hospital bed. She told
her ever-changing story of corn thieves and shots in the dark. (photo 1926)

telling dialogue, and a plot revolving around an intrepid farmer's search for corn thieves.

Arthur Sutphen Meredith, a former Superior Court judge in Somerset County, spent years studying the Hall-Mills case. Meredith, who lived in a house once owned by Clarence Case, put no faith whatever in the Pig Woman's testimony. "I think she was just a publicity-seeker," he said.[11] If so, she was a brilliant success at her calling, based on the amount of publicity she generated. But few publicity-seekers go so far as to make multiple false accusations of murder. She did. Her testimony caused Damon Runyon to ask, on the day he reported her trial testimony, "If she hadn't told the truth, and nothing but the truth, what motive could have possibly prompted her to risk her life to relate a story that may send four people to prison, if not to the electric chair?"[12]

It's a good question, and one that cannot be answered with any assurance. In Mrs. Gibson's lifetime, which ended in 1930, a psychiatrist or clinical psychologist (an alienist in those days) might have made a useful diagnosis. It seems clear beyond any doubt that the Pig Woman was a compulsive liar. Her mother had her pegged correctly. Mary Jane was a born prevaricator, and a very accomplished one. On the basis of her personality traits and her documented behavior it seems arguable that she was a psychopath, "a person having a character disorder distinguished by amoral or antisocial behavior without feelings of remorse."[13]

Dr. Robert D. Hare in his book, *Without Conscience,* presents a twelve-point "Psychopathy Checklist"—preceded, it should be noted, by a warning in boldface type not to use the checklist to diagnose oneself or others.[14] Fair enough, but Dr. Hare's book does read like an extended character sketch of Jane

Gibson. The psychopath, he writes, is "glib and superficial. . . can tell unlikely but convincing stories. . . . A signpost to the trait is often a smooth lack of concern at being found out." Entertaining and articulate, psychopaths are "egocentric and grandiose," with a narcissistic and grossly inflated sense of their self-worth and importance. They "take offense easily and become angry and aggressive over trivialities." [15]

As if responding to Damon Runyon's puzzled question about Jane Gibson's motivation and her seeming insensitivity toward what might happen to the defendants, Dr. Hare writes that psychopaths show "a stunning lack of concern for the devastating effects their acts have on others." Psychopaths lack empathy and are deceitful and manipulative. They "seem proud of their ability to lie. . . . Lying, deceiving, and manipulation are natural talents for psychopaths. With their powers of imagination in gear and focused on themselves, psychopaths appear amazingly unfazed by the possibility—or even by the certainty—of being found out. When caught in a lie or challenged with the truth, they are seldom perplexed or embarrassed—they simply change their stories or attempt to rework the facts so that they appear to be consistent with the lie. The results are a series of contradictory statements and a thoroughly confused listener. Much of the lying seems to have no motivation other than what psychologist Paul Ekman refers to as a 'duping delight.'"[16]

And so it goes. Psychopaths are impulsive and have a need for excitement—"they long to live in the fast lane or 'on the edge,' where the action is. In many cases the action involves breaking the rules." They lack a sense of responsibility, yet are frequently "successful in convincing the criminal justice system of their good intentions and their trustworthiness." They are skilled storytellers, although their scripts lack logical consistency.[17]

In short, psychopaths are a lot like Jane Gibson. Dr. Hare is surely right about the folly of trying to analyze anyone by long distance, over a lapse of time, or from newspaper accounts. Still, it is hard to avoid the conclusion that a clinical evaluation of the Pig Woman, using Dr. Hare's "Psychopathy Checklist," would find a great many matching symptoms.

Wilbur A. Mott and Alexander Simpson, astute and intelligent prosecutors, both thought they could believe the improbable tales Mrs. Gibson was spinning for them. Dr. Hare's book excuses the two special prosecutors to some degree. He cites several instances where experienced psychologists, knowing full well they were dealing with psychopaths, were taken in by them anyway. One young staff psychologist even went so far as to run off with a dangerous, smooth-talking rogue with whom she had fallen in love.[18]

The Million Dollar Defense team mounted a concerted attack on the Pig Woman's veracity. And they went a bit further, showing considerable insight (as an elite team should) into Mrs. Gibson's character. Feeling obliged to come up with a plausible alternative to Simpson's three-Stevenses-and-a-Carpender theory of the crime, however fuzzy the details of the prosecution's scenario might be, they settled on two possible killers. One of them was Jane Gibson.[19]

22 The Million Dollar Defense

The Hall-Mills case, like many other murder cases in which the accused has a sizable bank account, was a cornucopia for the defense lawyers. In 1922 Mrs. Frances Stevens Hall's local attorney, W. Edwin Florance of New Brunswick, had quickly backed away from the case, deferring to the young, highly regarded New York attorney, Timothy N. Pfeiffer. When no indictments were returned that year, Pfeiffer resumed his flourishing career across the Hudson River. By the time the case was reopened in the 1926, Mrs. Hall's local counsel was Russell E. Watson of New Brunswick, and again Pfeiffer got an urgent call to come to the aid of the rector's widow.[1]

In 1926 her situation looked serious. Indictments against the widow, her brothers, and Henry Carpender had been easily obtained, convictions could bring the death penalty or long prison terms, and the well-to-do defendants had no wish to gamble on a trial jury's buying into the special prosecutor's theory of the crime, whatever that theory might turn out to be. Mrs. Hall engaged seven lawyers to represent the embattled Stevenses. The press quickly dubbed this coterie of legal talent the Million Dollar Defense.

Pfeiffer remained as Mrs. Hall's personal attorney, but another man, one of the most distinguished lawyers in New Jersey, took over as chief counsel of the defense team. He was Robert H. McCarter, born in Newton, New Jersey, a graduate of Princeton University and Columbia Law School, founder of the highly regarded McCarter & English law firm, and Attorney General of New Jersey from 1903 to 1906. Sixty-seven years old at the time of the Hall-Mills trial, McCarter, who lived in Rumson and practiced in Newark, was primarily a corporation lawyer, one of the most successful in the Northeast.[2]

Assisting McCarter on the Million Dollar Defense team was Clarence E. Case, a native of Jersey City and a resident of Somerville. Case, like Simpson, was a state senator at the time of the trial. Unlike the special prosecutor from Hudson County, Case was a Republican. A Rutgers Phi Beta Kappa graduate with a law degree from New York Law School, he was fifty years old in 1926.[3] Damon Runyon observed that Case "looks like a schoolmaster and talks like one. . . . He is a spare-built man, resembling the late Woodrow Wilson. He holds himself tightly—squeezed up so to speak." Yet when Case warmed to his courtroom task, he began "swinging his arms until his coattails flapped, his face got red and the frat key on his watch chain waggled furiously."[4]

In addition to McCarter and Case, who tried the case in court, the Million Dollar Defense team consisted of Pfeiffer and Watson along with the less-publicized Robert H. Neilson, Augustus C. Studer, Jr., and Nathaniel Palzer.[5]

The defense strategy could hardly have been simpler. McCarter the bulldog and Case the whippet insisted that the three defendants (and Henry Carpender, too) had unbreakable alibis. They said that each defendant would testify to having been elsewhere when the minister and his mistress were gunned down at the Phillips farm. And each of them did. Henry Stevens took the stand on November 20, Willie Stevens on November 23, and Mrs. Frances Stevens Hall on November 27.

This sequence of appearances made good sense. Henry, the lifelong sportsman from Lavallette, came armed with an apparently rock-solid alibi, one that was backed by a drove of supporters from his Jersey shore community. Willie, on the other hand, had to be considered a question mark. Except for defense counsel—and perhaps even they had some slight apprehension—no one knew just what to expect on the stand from the eccentric and volatile firemen's gofer. Few doubted that Simpson's best chance for a conviction or convictions lay in trapping the supposedly vulnerable Willie into confessing his guilty knowledge of the murders (assuming he had any such knowledge) when the prosecutor's chance came to cross-examine. Given a disastrous admission or two from a rattled Willie, the defense could conceivably take a serious hit, or even collapse.[6] Yet no matter how poorly Willie might do, McCarter, Case, Pfeiffer, and the other defense attorneys knew they could count on the poised and capable Mrs. Hall to testify effectively on direct examination and then to hold her own when cross-examined by Simpson.

At a few minutes past ten o'clock on Saturday morning, the thirteenth day of the trial and the day after Clarence Case opened for the defense, John Buss, Somerset County bailiff and court crier, announced, "Henry Stevens to the stand." The witness, his graying black hair carefully combed, his bristling black mustache well trimmed, stepped briskly to the oaken chair at the front of the courtroom. He wore a dark, neatly pressed suit, a white shirt with a starched turned-down collar, and a black tie with a blue stripe, "a nifty bit of haberdashery," as Damon Runyon saw it. Settling back, the eldest of the Stevens siblings gazed at the jury through amber-rimmed spectacles, his manner relaxed and pleasant.

"Mr. Stevens, how old are you?" asked Senator Case.

"Fifty-seven," Henry Stevens replied in a firm voice. He smiled. "It happens to be my birthday today, sir."[7]

Under Case's questioning, Henry Stevens denied being at the scene of the crime, having any foreknowledge of it, or participating in it "in any way, directly or indirectly." As he began to testify, his younger brother Willie beamed at him for a few moments, but then, tapping a yellow lead pencil on the table in front of him, turned his attention to a window through which he could watch some birds fluttering in the trees. Mrs. Hall moved her usual chair to the table of defense counsel, taking a seat next to Robert H. McCarter, where she could observe the drama at close hand. To reporters in the courtroom she looked more strained than she had during the earlier phases of the trial.[8]

Henry retold his fishing-at-Lavallette story in detail—how on the evening of the murders he had been surf casting, how at about dusk he had met a fellow fisherman, Arthur Applegate, with a fine bluefish, and how he had offered to weigh it with his small pocket scales. Applegate accepted the offer. The big blue weighed in at six pounds. When asked, "How does that range among bluefish, fair or large?" Henry replied, "A pretty good-size fish."[9]

Stevens testified that later that night he and William H. Eger, a real estate dealer in Washington, D.C. who owned a summer home at Lavallette, fished together on the beach for a while. At about nine o'clock, Henry left for his home to clean the four fish he had caught. Eger joined him later at the Stevens' house for "a drink of ginger ale, or root beer, some soft drink that we had in our icebox, and we talked two or three minutes, and then Mr. Eger went home." Henry estimated Eger's time of leaving at about 10:00 p.m. and his own bedtime at about an hour later.[10]

According to Henry's testimony, he arose before sunrise the

next day, which was Friday the 15th, put on his boots, went out to the beach, and spent the next half hour or so catching mullet for bait. He recalled having an early lunch that day, prepared and served by Mrs. Anna Evanson, the Stevens' cook at their Lavallette home. Henry's wife, Ethel, meanwhile, was busy in New York City, getting their apartment at 120 East 31st Street ready for the annual move from the shore to the city for the winter.

At about 1:30 p.m. on Friday, Henry took his friends, Mr. and Mrs. Charles S. Wilson and their two daughters, to the train station in Point Pleasant, eight miles away. The Wilsons were on their way back to Jersey City after summering at the shore. Stevens, their next-door neighbor in Lavallette, drove them in his brown Ford station wagon, a Model T with natural-wood trim and wooden wheel spokes. The Model T was a car without a gearshift—the only kind he could drive.[11] Henry carried the Wilsons' bags to the depot, then took their little black spaniel to the baggage car.

When Henry returned to Lavallette after running a couple of errands, he resumed his fishing, caught a four-pound blue-fish, and later had dinner at his home on Brown Avenue, pre-pared, he remembered, by Mrs. Evanson. In the evening he vis-ited the Egers, returned to his own summer house, and went to bed at eleven or a little before.[12] Thus ended Friday, with Henry Stevens as yet unaware of the disappearance of Edward W. Hall.

Henry's fishing-at-the-shore alibi segued into Saturday. He got up early, as always, made his own breakfast, as was his custom, went to town, did some work on his hot water heater, delivered that four-pound bluefish from the day before to Mrs. Eger, who promised to cook it for dinner. She invited Henry over to their house for the evening. The Saturday-night dinner never took place, although Henry, a bit confused in his testimony, began to recount something about it anyway. Senator Case cut him off and redirected his attention toward an urgent telegram that had arrived on Saturday afternoon.

The indefatigable sportsman was once again surf casting on the beach in front of his house when the Western Union stationmaster showed up with the telegram. Clarence Case introduced it at the trial as exhibit D-16:

> NEW BRUNSWICK NEW JERSEY 1:16 P.M. HENRY R. STEVENS LAVALLETTE NEW JERSEY EDWARD W. HALL HAS BEEN KILLED COME AT ONCE MY HOUSE E. R. CARPENDER

Henry gathered up his fishing tackle, dashed for his Brown Avenue home, checked the railroad schedule, packed a bag, and managed to catch the 4:25 p.m. train to New Brunswick. He changed cars at Sea Girt and changed again at Monmouth Junction, where he caught sight of a banner headline in the New Brunswick *Daily Home News.* Buying a copy of the paper, he learned to his astonishment and dismay the basic facts of the double homicide. This newspaper account, he testified, was his first inkling of what had happened to his brother-in-law, Edward W. Hall, and a woman whose name he had never heard, Mrs. James Mills.[13]

Prosecutor Simpson's cross-examination of Henry Stevens began with a series of questions that must have seemed peculiarly off-target to the jury:

Q—You say Mr. William Stevens is your brother?

A—Yes.

Q—Is he your full brother?

A—Yes.

Q—Where was he born?

A—Aiken, South Carolina.

Q—You know there is no birth record of him in the church in South Carolina where there is a birth record of yourself and your sister, do you not?

A—No, I do not.

Q—Have you any knowledge on the subject?

A—No.

Q—Are you older than he is, or is he older than you?

A—I am older than he.

Q—How much?

A—About two years.

Q—You say he is your full brother and is by the same mother as you?

A—Yes.

Q—He is not by a mulatto?

A—No.

Q—He has the same father and mother as you, according to you?

A—Yes.

Q—Can you explain the difference in your faces?

A—I cannot.[14]

What was Simpson driving at? He supposedly believed that Henry Stevens was the man under the crab apple tree with the "glittering" thing in his hand. Henry Stevens was the prosecution's presumed killer.[15] Why, then, did Simpson open his cross-examination with an attack on the parentage of Willie Stevens? Mrs. Gibson's eyewitness account had not even placed Willie among the struggling foursome at the scene of the crime.[16]

The answer may lie in a segment of pretrial dialogue and in Willie's reaction to it. At the hearing back on August 26, the

Clarence E. Case. One of the two principal trial attorneys of the Million Dollar Defense, Case was a state senator from Somerset County. His devastating cross-examination of the Pig Woman cast doubt on her purported eyewitness story of the murders. (photo 1926)

Timothy N. Pfeiffer and Robert H. McCarter. Pfeiffer served as Mrs. Hall's personal attorney in 1922 and again in 1926. McCarter headed the Million Dollar Defense team at the trial in Somerville. (photo 1926)

eccentric younger brother's "demeanor changed like a flash" when Simpson remarked that Willie "looks like a colored man, with his kinky hair and his dark complexion." Up to that point Willie had been composed and attentive, often tapping "his pudgy fingers with a yellow lead pencil." His only show of anger at the trial had come when Eleanor Mills' letters were read aloud.[17] But Simpson's earlier comment about Willie's supposedly Negroid features had shattered his calm. It had enraged him instantly. His "color flamed, his eyes bulged, and he half rose in his excitement. The gush of anger passed quickly and once more he was placid."[18] James Thurber wrote that Willie "bared his teeth, as if about to leap on the prosecutor."[19]

It was an extraordinary display of emotion, quite unlike the picture of a sweet-tempered Willie limned by the defense. Simpson may have hoped to get a similar explosive response in his opening parry with brother Henry. If so, he was disappointed. Willie Stevens, wrote Damon Runyon, looked "a little startled," but his reaction was far from a reprise of that earlier paroxysm.[20] Simpson scored few points in his cross-examination of Henry Stevens, although he did catch the defendant in several minor memory lapses. On the whole, however, Henry's fishing-at-the-shore alibi held up. The retired exhibition marksman testified that he was an expert shot only with a shotgun, not with a pistol or a revolver. One of the oddest exchanges occurred when Simpson asked Henry Stevens if one would "have to be any kind of a marksman" to do the shooting that killed Reverend Hall and Eleanor Mills "at 10:20 or 10:25 on a dark night with no moon out, six feet away, and nothing to direct his aim except the voice. You say a man could do that without being a good marksman?"

Senator Case objected, and after a discussion with Justice

Parker, during which Simpson scoffed at the "persiflage of the Senator," Henry Stevens was allowed to answer. He said: "I think that any ordinary marksman might at times place the bullets in the space designated if he was able to see the object that he was firing at."

But Simpson persisted with his strange hypothetical question (for the shots were known to have been fired at a much closer range than six feet, and almost certainly at least one flashlight had been aimed at the victims): "If he did not see it and had only the voice to locate it and made those wounds, would he be a good marksman or not?"

How could Henry possibly answer the question? He replied, "I think it has nothing to do with the marksmanship."[21]

If Simpson gained anything in his cross-examination, it lay in his exposing Henry Stevens' indifference toward his younger sister and brother in the hours following the murders and then after their separate arrests. But this revelation of an older brother's apathy cut both ways, for if Henry had shown little concern for his family's personal and legal problems after the murders, it might well suggest that he had shown little interest in their domestic problems before the murders—which, in fact, appears to have been the case. Henry had his own life to live, and, as he noted on the witness stand, "I have a great many relatives in New Brunswick who were closer than I was."[22] He probably meant geographically, but he might as easily have meant emotionally.

The people Henry liked best were those he fished with at Lavallette, and they in turn liked him. One by one they came to the witness stand and supported their friend's alibi. Arthur Applegate remembered that big blue of his as if he had hooked it only yesterday. His wife Mazie chimed in with confirmation.

William H. Eger and his wife recalled clearly the exculpatory incidents that Henry had just related in court. Anna Evanson reviewed her 1922 cooking schedule and found that it matched Henry's mealtimes. Mr. and Mrs. Charles Wilson and their two daughters, Alice and Elaine, both students at Mount Holyoke College, gave strong support to Henry Stevens' claim that he was indeed in Lavallette, not New Brunswick, when the dire deed was done.

Several others, neighbors and anglers—one of them Enoch Titus Van Camp, the mayor of Lavallette in 1922—also placed the defendant either on the beach or in town during the critical hours. Even if Henry Stevens had not kept a diary in which he mentioned weighing Arthur Applegate's six-pound bluefish (Henry had kept a fishing-and-game diary for thirty years, so this was no hastily compiled night-of-the-crime journal), the Million Dollar Defense team would have managed to cast Henry Hewgill Stevens convincingly in a surf-casting rather than a gunslinging role at the time the rector and his mistress went to their reward.[23]

If the jury believed Henry Stevens' alibi, and there was every reason to suppose they would, the prosecution was left without a shooter. It was too late now for the Pig Woman to switch the shiny object back into the hands of Henry (Harry) Carpender. As for Mrs. Hall, while she was the aggrieved person in the liaison, along with the cuckolded Jim Mills, no one had ever supposed her to be the Annie Oakley of De Russey's Lane. And then there was William Stevens, gentle and childlike, a butt of jokes at the firehouse, a harmless buffoon. He seemed utterly miscast as a ruthless killer, rather like Lou Costello trying to play Don Corleone.

23   Willie Comes Through

Two days after Henry Stevens took the witness stand to testify in his own defense, it was his younger brother's turn to explain where he had been on the night of September 14, 1922. The press, the public, and the jury waited eagerly to see whether William Stevens, sometimes called "Crazy Willie," could put himself at home, in bed, on Nichol Avenue, New Brunswick, as convincingly as Henry had put himself on the beach at Lavallette. When Willie was called to the stand, his face lit up with a smile. Not so Mrs. Hall's. His beloved sister, who had protected him for much of his life, looked tense and worried.

Willie's usual lumbering gait propelled him to the witness stand. He sat down heavily, his knuckles whitening as he gripped the corner of the chair, and his smile faded as the questioning began. He wore a dark suit and vest, a white shirt with a bat-wing collar, and a neatly knotted brown silk tie. A heavy silver watch chain fell in a semicircle over his rounded midriff. His prominent eyes looked even larger through the magnifying lenses of his thick spectacles. On the stand Willie fiddled continually with a yellow pencil, as he had throughout the trial.

Senator Clarence Case, who had questioned Henry Stevens so effectively two days before, approached the witness. He asked, "Mr. Stevens, how old are you?" Willie replied, "I am forty-four." Case smiled. "Isn't it fifty-four?" Willie, with a sudden, beaming smile, replied, "Yes." He leaned forward in what the *New York Times* reporter called "a burst of boy-like gaiety, as though amused he could make such a mistake."[1]

That was Willie, all right, just as he had been portrayed from the beginning by his defense attorneys: a town character, an awkward oddity, a good-natured dimwit. Naturally, he would make some foolish mistake on the witness stand such as getting his age wrong by ten years. And so he would, especially if coached to do so. Willie Stevens made just that one amusing miscue—and no others—in his testimony that day and the next. Whether fifty-four or forty-four, he seemed equal in acuity to the lawyers who examined him. When he was asked on cross-examination about certain police actions, he countered with the question, "Do you mean the city police or the members of the detective staff of the County of Middlesex?" When asked if he would object to having a physician talk with him about the symptoms of epilepsy, he replied, "I would rather consult my lawyers."[2]

Throughout his appearance on the stand, Willie remained composed and spoke slowly, as if weighing each word before he said it. His supposed gaffes, committed earlier—beginning in September 1922 with his amusing challenge to the press, "I'm not a half-wit, as you have been saying, and I'm not a sissy"—were most likely not random incidents.[3] The Stevens' lawyers had kept Willie under a tight rein, usually inaccessible to journalists, during the 1922 proceedings and again in 1926. When he did get to speak in public, he drew laughs, his remarks calculated, it seemed, to show him in an amusing light. The humor of what he said came less from Willie's simplemindedness than from the defense team's apparent aim to present their client as a likable oaf.

Take his arraignment, four months earlier. When the clerk called his name, Willie stood up with an odd little jerk of his shoulders. After Simpson read the indictments charging him with the murders of Eleanor R. Mills and Edward Wheeler Hall, the defendant was asked, "How do you plead, guilty or not guilty?"

Willie stiffened, his face grave, and he said, "I am innocent."

"But how do you plead, guilty or not guilty?"

"Not guilty!" he shouted.

Later, on his way back to the jail, he met James P. Major, warden of the Somerset County jail. "Warden, did I holler loud enough for them?" he asked, laughing heartily. Major joined in the merriment.[4]

Unless one believes that the Million Dollar Defense lawyers failed to inform Willie that his choices at the arraignment would be "guilty" or "not guilty," the obvious conclusion is that his "I am innocent" response was intentional, not a blunder. A good bet is that Willie Stevens said exactly what his lawyers advised him to say.

The same preparation can be inferred from his trial testimony. When Alexander Simpson failed to ask Willie directly if he had been prepped by his lawyers for the trial (Willie having denied on cross-examination that he had ever been coached for a police interrogation), the defendant took matters into his own hands. "May I say a word?" he asked the judge, after Simpson attempted, over Case's objection, to get Willie to trace for the third time his elaborate murder-evening itinerary. Simpson explained to Judge Parker that he was trying to discover if the defendant was merely repeating his testimony word-for-word. The special prosecutor hoped to show that Willie had been carefully taught, that he had memorized the route.

"All I have to say," Willie said, "is I was never taught, as you insinuate, by any person whatsoever." His prior testimony was "my best recollection from the time I started out with my sister to this present minute."

But Willie was surely "taught" to some degree before the trial. If he was not taught, then the Million Dollar Defense team was derelict in its professional duty. According to the late, well-known trial attorney Henry B. Rothblatt, "The defendant *must* . . . be subjected in advance to a thorough cross-examination by you [defense counsel]. You have an idea of what the prosecutor is going to ask. . . show him [the defendant] how easily he can be led into traps."[5] No competent defense lawyer would let his or her client face cross-examination wholly unprepared.

Of course Willie had gone over his all-important alibi. Of course he had been coached. He had repeated the sequence of streets on that nighttime walk countless times with his lawyers. He may not actually have memorized the route—he knew it from more than half a century of living in New Brunswick and walking its streets—but his "best recollection" on the witness stand could hardly have been spontaneous and unrehearsed.

The word *recollection* is sprinkled throughout Willie Stevens' answers to Alexander Simpson's questions. It is usually preceded by the word *no* rather than by the word *best*. While Willie had undoubtedly forgotten many minor facts over the four-year period between the murders and the trial, his "no recollection" answers attached themselves most often, and most tellingly, to what would have been potentially damaging admissions. Did Willie remember telling Louise Geist on Friday morning that "something terrible" had happened the night before? "I have no recollection of that, sir." On that same Friday did he tell the firemen that "something was going to happen"? ". . . no recollection. . . ." Were the Halls having troubles of any kind at home? "Not that I remember." Did

Timothy Pfeiffer ever ask him if he had been at the scene of the murders? ". . . no recollection. . . ." Had Willie told defense counsel the story of his nighttime walk with Frances more than once prior to the trial? ". . . no recollection. . . ."[6]

One of the surprises in Willie's testimony came in response to Simpson's further probing on the question of the defendant's movements on the night of the murder. Simpson asked:

Q—How do you explain that you never told your movements on this night until the time you were arrested [on August 12, 1926].

A—That is very easy: Simply because I was not asked. . . .

Q—Nobody asked you?

A—No, sir.

Q—Didn't the Middlesex [assistant] prosecutor have you here [at the Somerset County Courthouse in 1922] in a long examination which takes twenty-three pages of typewriting? Didn't he ask you to describe your movements?

A—No, sir. He did not.

Q—Then, as I understand you, Mr. Stevens, nobody has ever asked you to describe your movements up till the time you did it in the jail and here, when I asked you to do it?

A—That is what I mean.[7]

No one had ever asked? What about the long interrogation that had so angered Willie Stevens in October 1922? John E. Toolan, then assistant prosecutor for Middlesex County, kept questioning Willie persistently during that session, cursing him again and again, from about eight o'clock at night until after three in the morning. What, if not his movements on the fatal night, did Toolan (along with Ferd David and Sergeant J. J. Lamb of the State Police) want to learn? Why had Toolan, David, and Lamb spent those eight hours leaning on poor,

Willie Stevens testifies. Polite and articulate, the bachelor brother of Mrs. Hall proved to be an excellent witness in his own defense, occasionally correcting prosecutor Simpson on minor points during cross-examination. (photo 1926)

cowed Willie? According to Willie Stevens' trial testimony, it was "because I could not tell them what simple little conversation my sister and I had going down to the church."[8]

At the trial Willie could remember the route to the church in minute detail, but back in 1922, only days after the murders, he had adamantly refused—for eight grueling hours—to discuss a "simple little conversation" he and his sister had "going down to the church." Why? One reasonable inference is that he had not been told how to respond to that line of questioning, and in the absence of such instruction, he had been advised by counsel to say nothing.

Sergeant Lamb, as Willie recalled in a forgiving mood at the trial, had cursed him only once, and David not at all. All three men had questioned him harshly, the defendant said, but it was Toolan—presently the Middlesex County prosecutor—who had really laid on the invective. Despite this all-out effort, Toolan, David, and Lamb had not cracked Willie's alibi in 1922, and Simpson was not cracking it now.

In fact, Willie Stevens even undertook to correct his cross-examiner on a couple of points. In an exchange about the rector's mother, Simpson asked, "How far is the Bayard from your house?" Willie responded not with an answer but with the correct pronunciation of "the By-ard." Simpson, unruffled, asked his question again, using Willie's pronunciation.

Later in the cross-examination, when Simpson asked a question involving "Dr. Hall's church," Willie replied tangentially, "He was not a doctor, sir. He was the Reverend Mr. Hall." Since the investigators, the witnesses, and the press, including the *New York Times,* had routinely referred to Hall as "Dr.," both in 1922 and 1926, Willie's news came as a surprise to many, including the special prosecutor.

"He was not Dr. Hall?" Simpson asked.

"No sir."

"He was not a doctor of any kind?"

"No, sir," said Willie.

"I am glad you corrected me on that." (Simpson nevertheless continued to refer to the rector as "Dr. Hall.")[9]

In his cross-examination the special prosecutor treated Willie Stevens with courtesy tinged with condescension. "He did not attempt to harass or excite Willie," Damon Runyon wrote. "Simpson undoubtedly realized, from the beginning, that great sympathetic appeal to the jury [of a good-natured witness of limited intelligence], and he took care not to appear in the light of bully-ragging the grown-up man who remains in many ways a mental child."[10]

At one point Simpson, adopting what Runyon described as a "strangely confidential manner," tried to get Willie to admit that failing to knock on the door of the Mills' darkened house sometime after 2:00 a.m. on the night the rector disappeared didn't ring quite true.

Simpson said: "You have a good deal of experience in life, Mr. Stevens, and have read a good deal, they say, and know a lot about human affairs. Don't you think it sounds rather fishy when you say you got up in the middle of the night to go and look for Dr. Hall and went to the house where you thought he was and never even knocked on the door, with your experience of human affairs and people that you met, and all that sort of thing, don't that seem rather fishy to you?"

Case objected. Judge Parker found the question "a little broad" but allowed it. Willie responded evenly, "The only way I can answer it, Your Honor, is that I don't see that it is at all fishy."[11]

In theory, Simpson's approach to questioning Willie was correct, and Runyon, for his part, found the bland cross-examination "amazingly skillful." After all, as Henry Rothblatt advised, "Do not brow-beat the stupid witness. The jury will resent such tactics. Instead, be gentle and help him along. He may become your friend and offer you some favorable testimony."[12]

Yes, but the witness must be a bona fide simpleton. Willie Stevens was not a simpleton, and he gave Simpson no favorable testimony whatever. The "stupid witness," as Simpson must have prejudged him, carried the day. Willie corrected the special prosecutor's language, chided his logic, took issue with him on the facts, and refused to corroborate any statement by any witness that tended to cast doubt on his story of an early bedtime and a predawn stroll with his sister. He made his shaky, unsubstantiated alibi look remarkably strong.

The *New York Times* headlined its next-day story, "WILLIE STEVENS ON STAND DENIES MURDER; REMAINS CALM UNDER CROSS-EXAMINATION . . . WITNESS A GREAT SURPRISE." The New York *Daily Mirror,* which had played a major role in reopening the case, trumpeted, "WILLIE IS A GOOD WITNESS." The Morristown *Daily Record* praised him in bold type: "LEFT STAND SPLENDID WITNESS FOR HIMSELF, PROSECUTOR BEING UNABLE TO BREAK DOWN SINGLE ESSENTIAL POINT."

It was a personal triumph for Willie and a professional triumph for his attorneys, who had adroitly portrayed him to the press and public as a timid incompetent, a bushy-haired baby who needed protection from life's cruelties. They had shown him as a befuddled fellow who ran from photographers like a scared rabbit and who might easily crumble before the dynamic cross-examiner from Hudson County.

Prior to the trial the Simpson scenario had put Willie Stevens under the crab apple tree, but the Pig Woman's most recent version of events failed to support that story line. Moreover, in the beginning Simpson had Willie carrying the murder weapon. In September the Hudson County investigators believed that the widow's bachelor brother was the one who brought the handgun (maybe his own Iver-Johnson revolver, maybe the rector's rumored pistol) to the Phillips farm, unbeknownst to either Mrs. Hall or Henry Stevens.

Willie, they posited, exploded with anger when he saw the intimate scene before him. His sister, whom he adored, was being flagrantly, heartlessly betrayed. He drew his weapon, and then . . . and then . . . Henry Stevens, being the better shot, grabbed the "glittering" firearm from his brother's hand and dispatched the lovers: Reverend Hall first, then his screaming mistress.[13] It wasn't quite the Pig Woman's tale, even back then, but it was close, and it gave each of the three defendants a role to play beneath the crab apple tree.

By the time of the trial, however, the Pig Woman's reminiscences had put Henry Stevens at the scene and Willie Stevens somewhere out of sight.

Simpson's failure to make a credible case against Willie Stevens stemmed in part from Mrs. Gibson's tale-telling and in part from the special prosecutor's own lack of interest in Willie's character and personality. Today one would expect to see a battery of psychologists and psychiatrists for both the prosecution and defense, but in 1926 Simpson did not call a single expert witness to analyze the "not absolutely normal" defendant. Defense counsel, interestingly enough, offered the only insight into the mind of Willie Stevens by calling to the stand Willie's personal physician for the prior twelve years, Dr. Lawrence Runyon.

Dr. Runyon, "bald and a bit belligerent, and not entirely up to the Runyon type in pulchritude," quipped his reporter-name-sake,[14] took the stand for the defense. In response to Case's questions Dr. Runyon stated that Willie did not suffer from epilepsy and did not stutter.

On cross-examination Simpson had his chance to find out what it was that made Willie such a town character. But Dr. Runyon, clearly no fan of the prosecutor, sketched a vague and inconsistent picture of his patient. Willie, although not absolutely normal, was "able to take care of himself perfectly well," Dr. Runyon said. Simpson wondered if the defendant's intelligence was below average. Not at all, replied the doctor. "He is brighter than the average person," although "he has not advanced as far in school learning as some others."

When Simpson pressed Dr. Runyon on this brighter-than-average claim, the New Brunswick physician said, "He reads books that are above the average and knows the answer and makes a good many people look like fools." (This testimony came on the day before Willie began making a fool of Alexander Simpson.) What kind of books? Simpson wanted to know. "They are books on engineering, books on that type of reading," said Dr. Runyon.[15] In fact, Willie's main intellectual interests were metallurgy, entomology, and botany.[16] "Is he reading any books on surgery?" asked Simpson. "Not to my knowledge," the doctor replied.

The most quoted line in this Simpson-Runyon exchange occurred when the prosecutor asked, "Well, is he brighter than the average person, a sort of genius in a way, I suppose?" Willie's family doctor, although disqualifying himself as a "brain specialist," agreed with Simpson's characterization: "Yes, that is just what I mean."[17]

At this late date it is impossible to categorize Willie's mental abnormality with any certainty. His public appearances in late 1922 and 1926 were choreographed by the defense to the extent possible, but they were hardly designed to make him appear normal. Quite the contrary. Willie had a mental aberration of some kind, and everybody knew it. One psychologist has suggested that he showed many of the traits associated with Asperger's Disorder.[18]

According to the American Psychiatric Association, "The essential features of Asperger's Disorder are severe and sustained impairment in social interaction. . . and the development of restricted, repetitive patterns of behavior, interests and activities." It is marked by impairment in occupational functioning. There are no significant delays in language and cognitive development, nor in adaptive behavior except in the area of social interaction. Those with the disorder are often clumsy and may exhibit stereotyped and repetitive mannerisms. The disorder lasts a lifetime.[19]

But didn't Willie Stevens spend nearly every day interacting, repetitively, to be sure, with the firemen at Engine Company No. 3? The answer is yes and no. He certainly spent his time there, playing cards and dominoes, polishing the brass, running errands. By all accounts the firemen teased him, almost as they might have teased a team mascot, but they also recognized his social and economic position in the community. The Hall-Stevens-Carpender nexus wielded considerable power in New Brunswick, which the firemen could not ignore. They humored Willie Stevens, put up with him, and accepted his eccentricities, but they were not really his friends. They did not spend their

off-duty hours with him. Indeed, there is nothing on the record
to suggest that Willie had any close friend except his sister. He
never married, never courted a woman.[20] He spent twenty-two
of his summers at Bay Head, New Jersey, and many of his winters at St. Petersburg, Florida, traveling alone to both places.

His older brother and younger sister attracted a galaxy of
character witnesses in 1922 and 1926, but Willie attracted none.
The firemen at Engine Company No. 3 did not line up to proclaim Willie's innocence. The only word from the firehouse—
and most of the firemen were as determinedly close-mouthed as
the parishioners at St. John's—tended to punch holes in Willie's
alibi. In 1922 Captain Michael Regan had quoted several comments by Willie that implied he knew of the murders before the
bodies were found. Had Regan not died prior to 1926, he might
well have been a helpful witness for the prosecution.[21]

The only fireman who did testify at the trial was John J.
Kline of Engine Company No. 3. A witness for the defense,
Kline had known Willie for twenty years. His testimony on
Willie's behalf was mainly to the effect that he had never seen
Willie wearing a derby and had never heard him stutter, thus
refuting the Dicksons' first-day trial testimony once more.

In his cross-examination of Kline, the special prosecutor
quoted a firehouse remark of Willie's that presumably had
made the rounds but that no fireman would corroborate on the
record. "Well," Simpson asked, "did you ever hear him say one
day as he saw Mrs. Mills pass the firehouse, 'I'll get that bitch
yet. She's made more trouble for my sister than anyone
living'?"

"No," said Kline.

Willie smiled. He had every reason to. Nothing went right
for the prosecution in its case against Willie Stevens.[22]

24 The State's Case Collapses

With Henry Stevens evidently (and evidentially) fishing on the beach at Lavallette and Willie Stevens unshakably at home in bed, except for that early morning walk with his sister, Alexander Simpson could hardly have been sanguine about his chances. Mrs. Frances Hall, the last defendant in the trial to testify, had already proved herself able to field tough questions with calm assurance and would no doubt do well on the witness stand. Simpson might treat her less deferentially on cross-examination than he had her brother Willie, but the prosecution's case had already come close to collapse.

The only piece of physical evidence introduced by Simpson that worried the defense team was Reverend Hall's calling card with Willie Stevens' fingerprint allegedly on it, and it had traveled too many places, passed through too many hands for the jury to accept it uncritically. No one today can say with absolute certainty whether the fingerprint on the calling card was a lucky find that convinced Simpson of Willie's involvement in the murders, or whether it was, as the defense contended, a forgery produced by overenthusiastic investigators. Either way the erratic odyssey of the card spoke damningly against it.

Few of the prosecution witnesses had come through the trial unscathed. Some had emerged looking foolish. The testimony of Mr. and Mrs. Dickson, Simpson's surprise witnesses on the first day, had been quickly and thoroughly discredited. Whoever the North Plainfield couple had seen on the evening of the Hall-Mills tragedy, it was not Willie Stevens, lost and agitated on his way to the Parker Home. The prosecutor's trial-opening gambit had run into a persuasive litany of rebuttals from other witnesses.

Henry L. Dickman, one of the New Jersey troopers who had investigated the murders in 1922, had also turned out to be a catastrophic witness. The New Jersey State Police, an ambiguous presence in the Hall-Mills case, apparently assigned Dickman, a young, good-looking graduate of their first training class, to stay on in New Brunswick after the 1922 grand jury found no bill. Dickman claimed that in April 1923 Henry Carpender, in the presence of Azariah Beekman, had offered him $2,500 in cash to drop his one-man investigation of the case. Accepting the bribe, Dickman went off on a forty-one day drinking binge—thus effectively resigning from the State Police. Carpender, predictably, insisted he had never seen Dickman in his life and had never paid him a bribe.[1]

Dickman's testimony at the trial conflicted with his earlier sworn statement. On the witness stand he said he had received the $2,500 not from Henry Carpender, as he had previously sworn, but from Azariah Beekman, by then dead, with no mention of Carpender having been present. The trooper's trustworthiness was further called into question by the fact that he had deserted not only from the State Police in 1923 but earlier, in 1909, from the U.S. Navy. Then in 1925, two years after his New Jersey desertion but before the *Daily Mirror*'s Hall-Mills crusade, he scored the hat trick by deserting from the U.S. Army. At the time of the trial he was serving time in Alcatraz for his latest AWOL bender. Why Simpson considered it a good idea to bring Dickman east and put him on the witness stand is a mystery. The Million Dollar Defense had a merry time dissecting the ex-trooper's résumé, leaving his testimony—which added nothing to Simpson's case anyway—as questionable as the Pig Woman's reminiscences.[2]

Frank Caprio, who identified himself as a private detective from Long Branch, proved to be another ruinous witness for the prosecution. Caprio, a bald man with shifty eyes, wore a boldly striped suit and a pinky ring with a large diamond. He claimed to have worked for the Somerset County prosecutor's office for about three weeks in 1922. In the course of his duties, which mostly involved watching the Hall residence, he had spotted a razor and a German-looking automatic pistol on the deceased Azariah Beekman's desk. After the grand jury failed to hand up indictments, Beekman, for some reason, allegedly let Frank Caprio take the razor "with a fingerprint sheet of paper wrapped up around" it. The razor thereafter lay undisturbed in the private detective's desk drawer in his Long Branch or Red Bank office for four years—until the case was reopened and Caprio saw that it might be helpful to the prosecution.

Dubious as this testimony was on its face, it became an increasingly hilarious joke upon McCarter's cross-examination. It turned out that Frank Caprio ("My name is Fortunato, not Frank") had a criminal record, although he had great trouble remembering it.

Q—Were you convicted in the Monmouth County Court of Quarter Sessions on or about the 7th of July, 1919, of false pretenses on five indictments and sentenced for a period not exceeding three years to State's Prison in New Jersey at hard labor?

Simpson—I think we ought to have the record straight. There is no crime of "false pretenses."

The Court—What are you chewing, Mr. Caprio?

A—Gum.

The Court—Would you mind taking it out?

A—Yes.

McCarter and Caprio continued sparring over the alleged three-year prison term. Caprio admitted he had been convicted of taking money under false pretenses, agreed that the judge had sentenced him, but insisted, "I didn't do no three years in State's Prison."

McCarter tried again:

Q—Were you convicted of that offense in Monmouth County?

A—Well, Monmouth County—

Q—Were you?

A—You won't give me a chance to explain myself. Monmouth County is a place where they sentence prisoners for nothing.

After it was established that everyone knew Caprio as Frank and not as Fortunato, a question arose as to where his office was located. Caprio stated on the witness stand that his office was in Long Branch. McCarter then told of a visit by Caprio to the McCarter & English law firm in Newark's Prudential Building. Caprio had mentioned the name of a friend whose case he thought would interest the well-known lawyer. Caprio denied the visit. McCarter pressed on:

Q—And didn't you tell me that your office was in Red Bank?

A—My office is in Red Bank.

Q—Why did you tell [me] just a moment ago it was in Long Branch?

A—I lived in Long Branch. My office is in Red Bank, has been there five years.

And so it went. By the time Caprio stepped down, the transcript of his testimony read like a comedy skit.[3]

Then there was Mrs. Demarest, a member of St. John's choir

and a cousin of Minnie Clark. A buxom, fiftyish woman with a self-confident air, Marie Demarest claimed that she and Henry Stevens had known each other since childhood. She admitted to being "about forty-eight" but had not the slightest idea how old Henry might be. Mrs. Demarest, who lived in Highland Park, had testified for the prosecution to having seen Henry Stevens in downtown New Brunswick on Friday morning, the day before the bodies were discovered. Her testimony was loud and positive. She obviously disliked Senator Case, barking angry answers at him as the audience in the courtroom tittered. It came down in the end to the question of whether the jurors chose to believe Mrs. Demarest's one-woman sighting in New Brunswick or the collective memories of the residents of Lavallette.[4]

After the defense had brought Henry's legion of friends into the fray, and after fireman Willie had charmed the courtroom audience, Simpson could still perhaps entertain a wild hope that the jury—having heard only the latest version of Mrs. Gibson's recollections, not all the other versions—would accept the story she had told, and, by extension, accept the prosecution's scenario of the crime, based primarily on that story.

But Simpson, many of whose witnesses had fared so poorly, would have to do better in his cross-examination of Mrs. Frances Stevens Hall than he had done against either of her brothers. He could count on the Iron Widow to make a strong showing on direct examination. Simpson's cross-examination was the fulcrum. If he failed to cast serious doubt on Mrs. Hall's alibi during his cross-examination, the already strong possibility of acquittals would verge on certainty. Mrs. Hall, short, wispy, and motherly-looking, her hair sprinkled with gray, wearing widow's black and a string of pearls, took the witness stand at two o'clock on the afternoon of Saturday, September 28, 1926, a self-assured smile on her lips. Her composed demeanor lasted throughout her direct testimony, impressing most observers in the crowded courtroom, although a few regarded it as "bordering on iciness."[5]

Robert H. McCarter, the senior member of the Million Dollar Defense team, conducted the direct examination. It was one of the high points of the trial. The "bulldoggish looking, old-fashioned spellbinder," as Damon Runyon called him,[6] led his client carefully through her recollections of the events preceding and following the tragedy on the Phillips farm.

She insisted she knew nothing about an affair between her husband and Eleanor Mills. She reiterated her love for her husband, spoke of her faith in his undiminished love and devotion, and flatly denied having anything to do with the murders. To McCarter's question, "Were you in or about De Russey's Lane or Phillips farm or in the neighborhood of what is known as the crab apple tree on the evening of September 14, 1922," she answered, "I was not."[7]

Some of her testimony contradicted what she had told authorities earlier, as Simpson took pains to point out. But if the jury believed her updated version, she was home free. Still, there were points in her testimony that Simpson might well have explored but didn't. Mrs. Hall claimed she hadn't heard a word of the telephone call from Eleanor to the rector on the evening of the murders. Ignorance of the content of that conversation might sabotage Simpson's theory of the crime all right, but it spawned a gremlin of its own. If she had heard nothing on the phone at 7:00 p.m., how did she know—as she admitted knowing—that Edward's planned 8:15 p.m. meeting with Eleanor concerned the doctor's bill for her January operation? The easy answer is that Edward told her. Another answer was supplied by a few lines of direct testimony that introduced an unlikely and previously unmentioned phone call:

Q—During that afternoon [the day of the murders], and while Mr. Hall was out, ostensibly to go to the hospital as you thought, do you remember receiving a telephone call?

A—At some time in the afternoon I did—I do not know what time.

Q—Yes. Do you know from whom that telephone call was?

A—It was from Eleanor Mills.

Q—You recognized her voice?

A—Yes.

Q—And did you reply to the phone yourself?

A—I did.

Q—You heard what was said?

A—Yes.

Q—Please tell us.

A—She asked if Mr. Hall were home and I said no, and I said, "Do you want to leave any message?" and she said, "You tell him there is something about the doctor's bill I do not understand," and I said I would tell him. That is as much as I remember.[8]

In addition to this neat, unchallenged finesse of the evening phone call, Mrs. Hall made a few noteworthy changes from earlier statements. In 1922 Mrs. Hall and others reported that she took little interest in her husband's church, that he did his ministerial job, and she, by design, kept apart from it. She thought it best not to interfere. But four years later at the trial, for unknown reasons, she portrayed herself as busily engaged at St. John's. McCarter asked, "Did you or did you not, so far as you were able, enter into the church life." Mrs. Hall responded, "I did." He continued, "Did you endeavor to assist your husband in parish work?" Her answer: "In every way I could."[9]

In another switch, she now claimed to have returned home through the front door, not a rear or side door, presumably as a guiltless woman would.[10] But neither she nor McCarter could evade the fact that Mrs. Hall's first detailed account to Azariah Beekman and George D. Totten of her movements on the night of the murder made no mention of the nocturnal walk. Her first statement simply had her and Willie going to bed, sleeping through the night, and awakening the next morning to find the rector still unaccounted for. Only when Totten advised Mrs. Hall that she ("a woman in gray") had been seen hurrying back to her house in the early morning hours did she recall her walk with Willie in tow to St. John's and the Mills' home and back.[11]

Despite these apparent gaps and contradictions, Mrs. Hall remained calm and smiling not only during McCarter's direct examination but during most of Simpson's cross-examination as well. "With the very first question," the *New York Times* reported, "the prosecutor showed that he had abandoned the gentle method he employed in cross-examining her brothers Henry Stevens and Willie Stevens, co-defendants. The Senator's manner was a mixture of scornful disbelief and aggressiveness."[12]

He zeroed in on Mrs. Hall's actions after her husband's disappearance. Why hadn't she called area hospitals on Friday morning if she feared there might have been "casualties" the previous night? She had phoned the New Brunswick police station the next morning, and the police stenographer had recorded her use of the word *casualties*. Mrs. Hall had no recollection of using the word but persistently maintained that it was synonymous with "accident" and carried no implication of violent death. As for the two hospitals in town, she acknowledged that she had not called them.

Simpson struck on other fronts. Why, after the bodies were discovered, had she not offered a reward for the capture of the killer or killers? (To do so would have been "indecent," she replied.) Why hadn't she shown the least interest in her husband's body, refusing to view it at the funeral home and failing to choose the pallbearers? Mrs. Hall answered these questions coolly, picturing herself as a grief-stricken widow who did what she thought right under very trying circumstances.

Simpson found it odd that the first family members Mrs. Hall telephoned after her husband's disappearance were the rector's sisters, Mrs. Fannie Voorhees, of Jersey City, and Mrs. Theodora Bonner, of New York City. The prosecutor seemed to think the widow ought to have immediately phoned her brother Henry, not Edward's sisters.

A more fruitful avenue of inquiry for the prosecutor might have been what Mrs. Hall, Mrs. Voorhees, and Mrs. Bonner discussed on that Friday when the rector and his mistress lay undiscovered under a crab apple tree a couple of miles away. There was direct testimony on this matter. McCarter's questioning revealed that the three women had examined the missing Reverend Hall's checkbook to see "if any unusual sum of money had been drawn," in the words of the senior defense attorney. One might wonder why Mrs. Hall, Mrs. Voorhees, and Mrs. Bonner would be poring over the rector's checkbook if there wasn't at least a suspicion of elopement (money for a new life) or blackmail (money to keep someone quiet). The possibility of elopement or blackmail would hardly add luster to Mrs. Hall's portrait of her faithful and virtuous husband.

But Simpson dismissed the matter of the checkbook out of hand—no large sum had been drawn on the account. The significance of the search, rather than its outcome, seemed to elude him. Instead, he attempted to waylay Mrs. Hall on three issues that must have made the jury wonder more about his judgment than about the widow's carefully amended story.

In spite of having been embarrassed by Willie's sensible answer to the question of why he and Mrs. Hall had not awakened the Mills household at 2:15 in the morning to see if anyone there had news of Reverend Hall's whereabouts, the prosecutor began to harry Mrs. Hall on the same point. Why had she and Willie walked to 49 Carman Street and then, finding it dark, neglected to climb the outside stairs and pound on the door? Mrs. Hall handled the question as any rational person might: She thought her reluctance to rouse the Mills family in the middle of the night was no more "fishy" than her brother had viewed it.

Simpson also considered it highly suggestive that Mrs. Hall failed to give her name to the police when she phoned and asked them about "casualties" on the morning after the murders. But assuming Mrs. Hall to be innocent, assuming she knew nothing at all about her husband's whereabouts that morning, why on earth would she—one of the most respected citizens of New Brunswick—wish to report that her husband, the popular and prominent Reverend Edward W. Hall, had mysteriously disappeared overnight? It could well create a scandal where there was none. Or it could needlessly air a family scandal that might yet be concealed from the public.

The third double-edged question that Simpson pursued on cross-examination was why Mrs. Hall didn't get on the phone right away and tell her brother Henry Stevens that Edward Hall was missing. Simpson's strategy here was to stress his Henry-as-devoted-brother theme. But the more he pushed this line of inquiry, the more evident it became that Henry, notwithstanding his testimony about familial affection, had little contact with his New Brunswick brother and sister. The more obvious the estrangement between the Lavallette and New Brunswick Stevenses appeared, the more doubtful it seemed that Henry would have cranked up his Ford and raced over to New Brunswick to help his siblings confront the wayward minister—or to commit murder.

Only once during cross-examination did Mrs. Hall's instructions from her counsel lead her into a quagmire. The subject was the Friday morning conversation in the church study between Mrs. Hall and Jim Mills. After several unchallenging questions, Simpson, ever the showman, moved in close to her and declared in a somewhat menacing voice: "You said, 'They have met with foul play, they are together, they are dead.' Didn't you say that in the morning when you went to Mr. Mills?"[13]

Mrs. Hall did *not* say that. She may have implied it when she countered Jim Mills' suggestion of an elopement with, "I think they are dead and can't come home."[14] That remark was sufficiently intriguing by itself, but Simpson misquoted her, perhaps intentionally, perhaps not. Mrs. Hall could have denied making the self-incriminating comment offered by Simpson. Instead, she responded to the general tenor of the prosecutor's question: "I don't think I said so—no."

Simpson bored in, citing a prior witness, who, according to him, had quoted her as saying those words to Jim Mills. "I don't think I said that," Mrs. Hall repeated, her voice hesitant.

"You don't know whether you said it?" Simpson rasped.

"No, I don't think I said that," she replied, visibly shaken.

"Say you did not say it."

"I say I don't think I said it."

"Why can't you make a direct answer that you did say it, or did not say it?" asked Simpson.

"I don't think I said that."[15] Mrs. Hall's voice was now very low. Her lawyers had undoubtedly warned her not to indicate that she had suspected her missing husband to be dead. Instead, she was to use the familiar witness-stand hedge, which Willie had employed frequently and well: "I have no recollection of that." If Simpson had quoted her words to Jim Mills accurately, a sharp exchange might have occurred anyway. But with the prosecutor introducing an incorrect quote, Mrs. Hall could simply have denied making the statement. Instead, she followed the "no recollection" advice, and it gave Simpson one of his few small victories. When she hedged so doggedly, it made the widow, not the prosecutor, look like the one with the conveniently faulty memory.

The thrust and parry continued for a while longer. It ended when Simpson demanded, "Why can't you make a direct denial?" and Mrs. Hall answered resignedly, "If you have it down there, I must have said it, but I am quite sure that I did not say that."[16]

At which point Judge Parker adjourned court for the weekend. Mrs. Hall stepped briskly from the stand. Henry and Willie came over to her, smiling and whispering encouragement. Mrs. Elovine Carpender, Edwin's wife, patted the rector's widow cheerily on the back and laughed.

25 Summations

As the trial wound down, Alexander Simpson became increasingly wound up. Sensing an impending disaster—the jury was rumored to be eleven to one for acquittal—he put his detectives to work checking on the conduct of the jurors. On November 29, after finishing his cross-examination of Mrs. Hall, the special prosecutor threatened to demand a mistrial, saying his detectives had been obtaining affidavits "tending to show that several members of the jury have not been paying proper attention to the evidence in the case; that one or more have been asleep; that there has been laxity in guarding the jury; and that in some instances jurors have talked over the telephone with friends."[1]

Judge Frank L. Cleary received a cantankerous letter signed by seventy-seven-year-old Gilbert A. Van Doren, proprietor of Somerville's Colonial Hotel, where the jurors were housed. The letter set forth many complaints about the jurors' conduct, protesting at one point, "They sit there all evening [in a hotel room being used as their parlor] hollering about taxes. What has that to do with cleaning up a blot on our county? I'm one of the highest taxpayers in the county and I know that my share for the investigation and trial won't amount to more than $15 or $20. The way they talk about Simpson! Time and again I've heard them say, 'What has that guy got to do with Somerset County? Somerset doesn't go over and try to run Jersey City.'"[2]

Next day Simpson moved for a mistrial. In a letter to Governor A. Harry Moore he wrote, "I have reports that the jurors are so stupid and unintelligent—that is, one or two of them—that they have openly boasted they didn't care what the evidence was, but they would find against the State."[3] He backed his plea to the governor with thirteen affidavits to the court, detailing what he viewed as flagrant jury misconduct.

"You might just as well try this case before twelve trees," Simpson groused while arguing for his motion. He added that trees would be preferable, because "the trees in the course of time will bud, and blossom, and these jurors never will." Senator Case, arguing against the prosecution's motion for a mistrial, noted that the jurors were human, after all, to which Simpson barked, "Well, I'd like to have affidavits on that about a couple of them."[4] This acerbic dialogue occurred outside the hearing of the jury, but no doubt some of it filtered back to the twelve good men and true of Somerset County who would decide the fate of Mrs. Hall and her two brothers.

Nor did the fiery prosecutor spare the defendants and their attorneys as he pushed his request for the court to throw out the case. "Never was such a situation in the administration of justice or the trial of a homicide case," he railed. "Here is a social tea every day; port wine drunk; and these defendants surrounded by their relatives and snickering, sneering counsel."[5]

Early that afternoon Judge Charles W. Parker denied Simpson's motion for a mistrial. The jury returned and summations began.

First to speak was Robert H. McCarter, an impeccably turned out lawyer of the old school, a stout, balding gentleman, heavily jowled, whose spectacles rode precariously low on his nose. For two hours and fifteen minutes McCarter demonstrated his courtroom mastery, sometimes with soaring rhetoric, sometimes with mimicry, sometimes with a hearty "Ha! Ha!

Ha!," and once with a surprisingly nimble series of little dance steps. The "twelve trees" sat in rapt attention as the senior defense attorney unloaded his verbal heavy artillery at the testimony of one prosecution witness after another. A showman par excellence, one of the great trial lawyers of his day, he glowered in disbelief as he reviewed the evidence that Simpson purported to find persuasive.[6]

McCarter thundered that Edward A. Schwartz, a fingerprint expert for the prosecution, was a "fraud" and a "rascal" and that he, the distinguished founder of the McCarter & English law firm, would gladly meet the miscreant on the street and tell him so. Philip A. Payne, managing editor of the *Daily Mirror,* he excoriated as a Faustian devil. About Mrs. Marie Demarest, who claimed to have seen Henry Stevens in downtown New Brunswick when the defendant claimed he was in Lavallette, McCarter said he "was glad he didn't have that kind of a wife."[7] He charged that Henry L. Dickman ("out in Alcatraz prison in California") had been brought to Somerville without a scintilla of truth, honor, or useful information in his possession and that the only result was "to slander Azariah Beekman," Somerset County's recently deceased prosecutor. He dismissed James A. Faurot, the former Deputy Police Commissioner of New York City and a renowned fingerprint expert, as an egomaniac whose vanity cast doubt on his objectivity ("The greatest fingerprint man in the world. He admits it").[8]

Fingerprints were much on the mind of Robert H. McCarter that afternoon. He spent a major part of his two and a quarter hours insisting that (a) the fingerprint on Hall's calling card did not match the print of Willie Stevens' left index finger; (b) the print on the calling card, S-17, was a forgery; (c) the fly-specked calling card, despite George D. Totten's positive identification of it, was most likely not the fly-specked card that had been propped at or near the foot of the slain rector; and (d) the time elapsed and the journeys made by the calling card rendered it worthless as evidence anyway. Take your pick. What McCarter's oratory really seemed to show was that despite his drumbeat of scorn aimed at S-17, he took it seriously enough to believe that it had to be attacked from every angle, no matter how incompatible the angles.

Not surprisingly, he reserved his admiration mainly for his clients, Mrs. Hall and Willie Stevens—"refined, genteel, law-abiding persons, church-goers whose every tradition prohibited them from doing the acts charged against them." He praised Frances Noel Stevens Hall as "a devoted daughter to a fond mother and a devoted wife to what she supposed was a fond husband." William Stevens, he said, "does not have to work for a living, but is happy in his home, happy in his surroundings; has a hobby of running to fires, as a good many of us, as boys, have had, and is the idol of his sister with whom he is living and from whom he has never yet desired to separate, by marriage or otherwise."[9] Along the way he exclaimed, "Willie—God bless him!" at which Willie sat bolt upright and beamed.[10]

How seriously did the Million Dollar Defense take the Pig Woman's attempt to shatter this happy household? The answer would have to wait a bit, declared McCarter as he resumed his summation the next morning. Hoarse from his exertions the day before, he said he would leave the dissection of Mrs. Gibson's fanciful tale to his colleague, Clarence Case.[11] But McCarter was not quite finished. With theatrical vehemence he lit into the drab husband of Eleanor Mills.

"If knowledge of this affair is important, then what are you going to do with Jim Mills?" he roared, "a husband, a husband whose wife for two years had not shared his bed, a wife who had told him that she cared more for Dr. Hall's little finger than she did for his whole body: a wife who had told him that when Charlotte finished school she planned to go to Japan with Mr. Hall?"[12]

McCarter made it clear he thought the jury should take a long, hard look at the mild-mannered janitor as the possible killer. "I am not here to vindicate or to scold that dead couple," the jowly old attorney bellowed. "They have their account to make with their Creator, but I am here as a man with red blood in his veins, to question the innocence of a husband who placidly admits his wife to be absent for forty hours without raising a finger to find out where she is or what has happened to her, except to say to Mrs. Hall, 'Perhaps they have eloped.'"[13]

When McCarter finished his summation, Clarence E. Case stood to offer his own conclusions on the De Russey's Lane tragedy. Technically, Senator Case represented Henry Stevens, but his arguments, like McCarter's, usually applied to all three defendants. Case stood behind the defense table to deliver his summation. Ishbel Ross, describing his courtroom style, wrote in the *New York Herald Tribune,* "He had all the manner of speaking from the rostrum. He pounded with his fists, spread his arms, shouted at moments, then dropped his voice to a confidential pitch. As he warmed up to his subject he left his place behind the counsel table and moved back and forth before the jury—a tense and mobile figure."[14]

What did he think of the prosecution's case? He thought it was a shambles, not only for of its lack of credible evidence but also for its disjointed and unclear presentation. "Do we know yet, do you know yet," he asked the jury, "just what the prosecution in this case claims to have proved? Do you know how the thing was done? Do you know how they contend it was done? I do not." To him Simpson appeared to be rattling along "hit or miss, hit or miss."[15]

Case thought the special prosecutor, whom he claimed to like personally, had been positively "nos-tee" in his tweaking of the elderly McCarter about his age. He chided Simpson for putting on the witness stand such unsavory folk as a multiple deserter-from-the-ranks, Henry L. Dickman, and a convicted felon, Frank Caprio. At the same time, he asked why the prosecutor had not called as a witness the false accuser Raymond Schneider, who, along with Pearl Bahmer, had discovered the bodies. Case would have liked to cross-examine Schneider about his actions at the scene of the crime before the police arrived. Had the young man stolen the rector's gold watch? filched his money? toyed with the calling cards? disturbed the love letters? made off with other evidence unknown to the police or anyone else?[16]

Senator Case, who, as Damon Runyon remarked was "some pumpkins politically" in Somerset County, got in a few digs about Jersey City's ubiquitous presence in the case. Knowing that the Somerset County jurors had little affection for Hudson County and its abrasive Senator Simpson, he played up the Somerset-Hudson rivalry, partly, as McCarter had done, by defending the honor of Azariah Beekman, the recently deceased Somerset County prosecutor.[17]

He saved his strongest salvos for an attack on the character and credibility of the Pig Woman, the state's star witness. "She would have you believe, gentlemen," Case declared, "that as she on her mule was following this wagon out here, the wagon turned toward New Brunswick, that as it turned . . . while it was still in the lane, an automobile swung around in here, and threw the light on two people just ahead of her, here, on the right-hand side of the road, and the light that was thrown on them, she was able to identify them later as Mrs. Hall and William Stevens." Case recited several other improbabilities and flagrantly altered details that, in his judgment, made Mrs. Gibson's story "too grotesque to be believed."[18]

He pointed out the discrepancies in her testimony between the preliminary hearing and the trial, focusing a harsh light on the magical transformation of Henry Carpender into Henry Stevens: "My God, gentlemen! The prosecution [is] coming into court and asking you to convict that man [Henry Stevens] of murder on the testimony of a woman who in November says it was Henry Stevens, whom she now recognizes that she saw there, and in the month of August, two or three months ago here in this same courtroom, under the same solemn oath, she swore that Henry Carpender was the man that she saw there, and identified him as the man she saw there, and said that this was the only face she had seen there that night."[19]

The Pig Woman had also seen a "big white-haired woman" in De Russey's Lane, and Senator Case abruptly asked Mrs. Hall to stand, which she did, evidently taken by surprise and a bit embarrassed. "She is a short woman," reporter Runyon observed, "with a large head and face that suggests considerable size when she is seated."[20] Implicit in Case's demonstration was the message that Mrs. Hall might appear in photographs to be a "big" woman, as indeed she did—and Case was quite certain that the Pig Woman had gotten her initial description of Mrs. Hall from the newspapers.

Senator Case's most startling suggestion came late in his summation. After dismantling Mrs. Gibson's story—a story that was either intentional perjury, he said, or the "unsound and unbalanced" fabrications of "a rambling, dreaming, visionary mind"—he named a possible killer. It was not the meek, self-effacing James Mills whom McCarter had gone after in his impassioned summation, but rather the talky and quarrelsome Mrs. Gibson herself.[21] He could envision the Pig Woman, it seemed, as shooter, throat-slasher, accuser, and dying witness. He suggested that Mrs. Gibson was perhaps not, as many supposed, a cagey publicity seeker; she might be the actual killer, a mistress of deceit. It boggled the mind, but Case listed his reasons as if he meant them seriously. Mrs. Gibson owned guns, she had a violent temper, she had been at the scene of the crime (although the defense had labored mightily to prove otherwise), and she admitted to racing frantically home on her mule after the shots were fired.

Both Simpson and McCarter had been kind and thoughtful throughout the trial to the "not-quite-normal" defendant, Willie Stevens. Clarence Case went them one better. He described Willie as "a benign gentleman, well read, well poised, the essence of kindness, a soul of honor. Bubbling with good humor. The only witness in the trial, as one newspaperman put it, . . . who could 'high hat' Senator Simpson and get away with it."[22]

Case closed.

Case closed, that is, except for Simpson's summation, the judge's charge, and the jury's verdict. The special prosecutor put on quite a show. Although he was badly disadvantaged by his lack of credible evidence—physical, eyewitness, or circumstantial—and by the seven-lawyer Million Dollar Defense, no one could accuse him of being anything but a game fighter. He had accepted the role of special prosecutor in a four-year-old case in which the original county investigators had come up with virtually no useful evidence, a case in which the most likely

Jim Mills at the trial. In his summation, Robert McCarter pointed the finger of suspicion at the mild-mannered janitor–the betrayed husband– as the possible killer. (photo 1926)

Felix B. De Martini. A private investigator hired by the defense, De Martini was thought by Alexander Simpson to have bribed and threatened potential witnesses. (photo 1926) perpetrators were wealthy, philanthropic, socially prominent, and politically connected residents of a distant, semirural county. He had failed, but he had put on a gutsy (if ethically questionable) performance. Now it was time for the "little man with oily gray hair and a very blade of a voice" to wrap it up. His summation took five hours.[23]

He spoke his mind, sometimes aiming his remarks at individual jurors. "I know that Mr. [John W.] Young's son works for an intimate friend of Senator Case, his political buddy, but that should not sway him. . . . His personal dislike of me may grow into an idea that he should weigh the evidence."[24] Young had allegedly commented that the jury would "kick this case out in twenty minutes."[25]

Simpson pointed to another juror, Samuel B. Hope, a clerk from Raritan, and called him "a great friend of Mr. Case," but trusted the gentleman to respect his oath and decide the case on the facts presented. He objected to Senator Case's references to members of the jury as "men of my county," saying sarcastically, "I thought you were the crowd that held the pass at Thermopylae, the way he addressed you—'men of my county.' It doesn't make any difference what county you are in. You are human beings with a human being's sense of justice."[26]

But it did make a difference what county they were in, and Simpson knew it. He reviled "the cheap politicians" of Somerset County, saying, truthfully but unhelpfully for his own cause, that the prosecution of the Hall-Mills case "was murdered [by the inept investigation in 1922] and that is the first murder you have got to deal with." He also took a few potshots at Middlesex County, commenting at one point, "Wonderful New Brunswick. The home of the mustard plaster."[27]

If the locals detested him, if the men on the jury despised

him, so be it: "I am not trying to get in your good graces. . . .
I am speaking for the great State of New Jersey in this abomi-
nable murder. . . . We are not pleading for a verdict. We are
not smooching for a verdict." He moved in close to the jurors,
almost stepping on the toes of those in the front row.[28] Simpson was nothing if not aggressive. He must have known his efforts were in vain, but he presented a clear and spirited summation of the state's case.

He reserved his most scathing remarks for Mrs. Hall and the
role he thought she had played in the murders. "Then this
woman—look at her eyes if you want to know the truth about
this thing. . . . 'Hell hath no fury like a woman's scorn,' Byron
says, and the fires of hate and jealousy are raging in this woman's heart. The Bible says the coals of jealousy have a most
vehement flame. Jealousy is one of the most terrible things.
Here is this woman who bought and paid for her husband, who
sees him dead before her [supposedly shot by Henry Stevens
while she looked on]. Of course, she is jealous of the other
woman. Why shouldn't she be? She was full of jealous hate.
Look at her eyes."[29]

Simpson did not maintain that Mrs. Hall had cut Eleanor
Mills' throat, only that she knew who had done it.

He tried to show that Henry Stevens' Lavallette diary, a key
element in the eldest brother's alibi, had been crudely altered to
save his skin. He suggested that since Henry had been an exhibition marksman his claim of never having fired a handgun
was ludicrous. Yet the sharp-tongued little prosecutor showed
none of the animosity toward Henry Stevens, the supposed
shooter, that he did toward Mrs. Hall, "this Christian lady,"
proud, self-righteous, cruel, and "cold-blooded."[30]

As for Willie Stevens, he had "been taught a story," Simpson declared. "Senator Case said he 'high-hatted' me. I don't know what he means by that. William Stevens has got the mind of a child, and he has been taught a story and has gone over and over it until I think he really believes that story now. He has not got a man's mind. I am not criticizing him, but it is a fact. He has a trust fund set apart for him. He does not follow any occupation. He plays with a revolver with .32-caliber bullets; and he knows the difference between Union Metallic cartridges and a Peters shell, which I showed him. What was the use of trying to harass William, antagonize William? Why go over that story?"

Surely Simpson knew the meaning of the verb *high-hatted*—"patronized or condescended to." In quoting Case (who had been quoting a newspaperman) Simpson was trying to disparage Willie's testimony by making it sound snobbish. In fact, Willie had been polite and effective as a witness. Simpson may have *expected* him to testify like a person "with the mind of a child," but on the witness stand he had proved more than a match for the special prosecutor. While some, if not all, of Willie's *bon mots* may have been suggested to him by counsel, he delivered them with considerable skill.[31]

No one will ever know whether Alexander Simpson believed in his heart that he had the killers in the dock. He must have known that his case against the three Stevenses was fatally weak. Nevertheless, he played to the hilt the part of society's outraged avenger.

"You may kick this case out in twenty minutes," he said, glaring at John W. Young, the juror who had supposedly made that remark, "but if you do you may kick yourselves out."

It took the all-male jury five hours and eight minutes to kick the case out.[32]

26 Money Can Buy Anything

Justice Charles W. Parker gave a concise and simple charge to the jury, stressing the concept of reasonable doubt. He pointed out that "The defendants are indicted jointly. It may be that you will find only one or more of them is guilty and the remainder not guilty. In that event you should return a verdict of guilt against such as you find guilty, and not guilty as to the other or others." He emphasized that a guilty verdict was justified only if the defendant "was there and participated in the killing as a principal and not as an innocent onlooker." Parker's charge took thirty-five minutes.[1]

Despite Alexander Simpson's vocal contempt for the Somerset County jury, the "twelve trees" deliberated earnestly and at length, going over the testimony of each of the main witnesses. They took three ballots before reaching a verdict. At first the vote was ten to two for the acquittal of all three defendants. On the second try it widened to eleven to one, which was the rumored split prior to deliberations. On the third ballot the lone holdout joined the majority, and at 6:38 p.m. on Friday, December 3, 1926, white-haired old Bill Pangborn, a custodian of the jury and Somerville's only surviving Civil War veteran, poked his head in at the door to the court-room. He signaled that the jury was ready to return.[2]

Justices Charles W. Parker and Frank L. Cleary arrived from their chambers within a few minutes. Two McCarter assistants, left behind as observers, summoned the chief defense counsel from his South Somerville headquarters. Clarence Case, caught in the middle of dinner at a nearby restaurant, raced up Main Street on foot, reaching the courtroom just as members of the jury filed in, where, according to New Jersey custom, they formed a straight line facing the bench. Alexander Simpson was not in court, having left for the day immediately after the judge's charge to the jury. He knew well enough what was coming and preferred to be elsewhere. On hand in his place, representing the state, was Francis L. Bergen, the young Somerset County prosecutor.[3]

The jury foreman, Frank A. Dunster, a man of sixty with a florid face, led the solemn twelve-man procession to the front of the courtroom. The members of the jury were mostly old men, snowy-haired and weather-beaten, six of them farmers, three of them walking with canes.[4]

"Gentlemen of the jury, have you agreed upon your verdict?" the clerk asked.

"We have," they said in unison.

"Who shall say for you?"

"The foreman," replied the panel.

"Mr. Foreman"—Dunster's face blanched as his big moment neared—"how do you say you find the defendant Henry Stevens, guilty or not guilty?"

The square-shouldered sportsman from Lavallette strained forward in his chair. Dunster hesitated for a moment before answering.

"Not guilty," he said firmly.

Tears came to Henry's eyes, as they had occasionally during the trial. He slumped back in his chair, then sat upright, wiping his eyes with a handkerchief. His hand sought that of his wife Ethel, who had moved in behind him. She patted him on the shoulder. He smiled broadly.

"Mr. Foreman," the clerk said again, "what do you find as

to William Stevens, guilty or not guilty?"

Once again Dunster's voice was emphatic. "Not guilty."

Although Willie had entered the courtroom with a blank expression, his face now lit up with joy. He glanced around the courtroom, his broad smile conveying unbounded delight. He shook the hands of all the attorneys who had played a part in his defense.

"Mr. Foreman," said the clerk, "what do you find as to Frances N. Hall, guilty or not guilty?"

There was little doubt as to the answer. "Not guilty."[5]

Mrs. Hall, whose faint and familiar smile had touched her lips even before the verdicts were announced, looked directly at the jury and smiled more openly. The ordeal was over.

Justice Parker dismissed the jury, expressing his appreciation for their efforts. About half the spectators had remained in the courtroom for the entire five hours, awaiting the verdict. The others, including many reporters, had drifted away as time passed. Some made it back in time; others did not. When the acquittals were announced, nearly everyone present seemed to approve. Relatives, friends, and spectators showered Mrs. Hall, Henry, Willie, and the legal defense team with congratulations. A few expressed annoyance that Simpson had failed to stay for the outcome, thereby missing a chance to "get a dose of his own medicine," as Henry Stevens' wife noted acidly.

Early reports from the jurors suggested that they had discussed the fingerprint evidence in some detail and, in the end, rejected it. None of the jurors, not even the two initial holdouts, put any credence in Mrs. Gibson's story about Jenny and the corn thieves. They found the colorful tale of her nocturnal wanderings "illogical" and not quite "real." On the other hand, they were much impressed by the testimony and demeanor of

Charlotte Mills. Alert and attractive, the daughter of the slain choir singer was sixteen at the time of the murders, twenty at the time of the trial. Charlotte thought a woman with "terrifying eyes" had killed her mother. (photo 1920s)

Mrs. Hall. They found the story of *her* nocturnal wanderings to be reasonable and believable. In general, the jurors viewed the arguments of defense counsel as being far more credible than those of the prosecution. Some jurors praised Simpson for doing the best he could with the evidence he had, but they thought his evidence was weak and unconvincing.

During deliberations, one of the jurors reportedly had said he would "remain here thirty years rather than vote a verdict of guilty on such evidence."[6]

At her home on Nichol Avenue, Mrs. Hall told a group of reporters, "I am happy, so happy. I cannot tell you how happy I am." She still hated being photographed, but on this cold evening in early December she endured it willingly.

Alexander Simpson received the news of the verdict at his office in Jersey City. He was not at all happy. "It is just what I expected," he snapped, reiterating his displeasure with the jury and stressing the need for a foreign jury in a future trial, if there was to be one, of the three defendants on the still unresolved charge of having murdered Reverend Edward W. Hall. Down in Trenton, Governor A. Harry Moore expressed doubt about a second trial for these three defendants. "I think the state has gone far enough," he said. "It's prosecution, not persecution, we want." But the governor promised to consult with Senator Simpson before deciding how to proceed.[7]

Jane Gibson, the Pig Woman, lay seriously ill back in Jersey City Hospital, from whence she had begun her trip to Somerville just a couple of weeks earlier, expecting to become "the Babe Ruth of the trial." Upon learning that the twelve jurors had disbelieved her story and found the defendants not guilty, she seemed astonished. "Acquitted?" she exclaimed. "Well, can you beat that!"[8]

The usually mild-mannered James Mills displayed unwonted anger at the news of the acquittals, even though he had often said he doubted that Mrs. Hall had anything to do with the murder of his wife. "I ain't letting no reporters beyond the door," he growled to them at his Carman Street home. "I'm acting on advice of counsel now. I've had legal advice, and I ain't talking to nobody."[9]

His daughter Charlotte, appearing less upset than her father, admitted that, like Simpson, she wasn't surprised at the outcome. She added tartly, "Money can buy anything."[10]

The next day all charges against the three defendants were dismissed—*nolle prossed.* So were the charges against Henry Carpender, who, like Henry and Willie Stevens, had spent the previous four months in jail. The Stevens brothers appeared pleased and relieved upon their release. Henry Carpender did not share their joy. When he stepped into the brisk December air on the morning of his release, he was irate. A respected New York stockbroker, he was not about to let his torment in Somerville's yellow-brick jail pass unremarked. As he left the building, he made a caustic statement to reporters:

"I was indicted solely on the lying story and false identification of Jane Gibson and have spent four months in jail without a trial because of the crooked tactics of Simpson. However, the world now knows the truth about both Jane and Simpson, and no trial of my own is necessary to clear my name. I took the stand in my cousins' trial, denied any knowledge of the murder, and was cross-examined. The pitiless logic of Senator Case in his summation tore Jane's story so completely to pieces that the jury's verdict shows there is nothing of it left. No more could be done to clear my name at any other time."[11]

He had every reason to be distraught. An imaginative liar

like Jane Gibson can wreak havoc. So can a mercilessly ambitious politician like Alexander Simpson. The Pig Woman and Simpson joined forces in the Hall-Mills case to try to impose what they must have seen as a kind of common-sense but unobtainable justice on those they supposed to be guilty.

Simpson was neither contrite nor discreet after the trial. Without consulting Governor Moore, he resigned abruptly as special prosecutor on the morning following the verdicts. He may truly have believed that justice had been thwarted. In his letter of resignation to Governor Moore he wrote, "I respectfully suggest to you as Chief Executive of the State that you embalm 'Jersey Justice' and send her to the British Museum."[12]

Simpson's wrath was as misplaced as was his faith in the Pig Woman's veracity. Justice *had* triumphed at the trial, not because the three acquitted defendants were all necessarily innocent but because the state offered insufficient evidence to convict them. The special prosecutor from Hudson County was on firmer ground when he complained during the trial that justice had been "murdered" in 1922 at the investigative stage.

In any event, the trial of the decade was over, the great crime of the Roaring Twenties unsolved. No one else would ever be charged with the murders.

When Willie Stevens emerged from jail on the morning after the verdicts, he noticed Frank Dunster, the jury foreman, in the crowd waiting outside. Willie, beaming, went over to him, extended his hand, and said, "You were the foreman. God bless you!"

Dunster, an aging teamster unaccustomed to such flattery, looked abashed. "I only did my duty," he said.[13]

27   Stranger than Fiction

The prosecution failed to make a cogent case against the three Stevenses for several reasons. One was its inability to explain, or its lack of interest in explaining, the most striking aspect of the crime scene. Words like *brutal, gruesome,* and *savage* were bandied about by the tabloid press and, to some extent, by investigators and prosecutors. The reading public knew all about the bizarre scene under the crab apple tree. The actual murders were quick and unexceptional—one shot to Reverend Hall's head, three shots to Mrs. Mills' head. Only the aftermath of the slayings—the belated throat-cutting, the showy arrangement of the bodies—justified the colorful adjectives. Simpson, to no avail, paid a great deal of attention to Eleanor's slashed throat, but he focused little attention on the unusual tableau the killer or killers had created. That tableau cried out for intelligent analysis by the prosecution, for surely it meant something to somebody. But what, and to whom?

William M. Kunstler suggests in his book that the tableau points to the culpability of the Ku Klux Klan, and indeed that would be so if the killer or killers had left behind a specific, credited KKK warning of some kind.[1] But the tableau, in the absence of any such signpost, points to a couple of other possibilities.

The first of these is that it represented the fairly common practice of perpetrators (especially common in domestic homicides) of tidying up the scene of the crime. According to a standard textbook on crime scene investigation, "Such persons would like everything to be in proper order when the police arrive, or they may be trying to conceal something, or simply out of psychological need they desire to put everything back in order."[2]

The second possibility is that the careful arrangement of the slain pair under the crab apple tree was a somewhat childish expression of anger at the lovers' illicit relationship, which was conveyed more vengefully by the throat-cutting. The tableau was also a whimsical rationale of the crime to those who would eventually find the bodies.

Since the arrangement of the corpses was so integral a part of the crime, and since the killer or killers surely meant to send a message with the tableau, one would expect the prosecution to offer a detailed analysis of it at the trial. None was forthcoming. Perhaps Simpson believed that his pillorying of Mrs. Hall on the witness stand gave an implied explanation of the crime's brutal-tender aftermath, but that was clearly insufficient. No jury, particularly one composed of "twelve trees," should be expected to draw such subtle inferences. A careful prosecutor would have spelled out everything for even the most sharp-witted jurors.[3]

Major murder cases always seem to attract charlatans—would-be witnesses willing to testify to almost anything. These are men or women whose only real relation to the crime is their desire to join in the public spectacle. The Hall-Mills murder case was extraordinary in this regard, with an almost comedic cast of characters relating improbable tales—of jabbering strangers on doorsteps, of phantom corn thieves, of guns glittering in automobile headlights—so that the complete story is still shrouded in mystery. Nearly all of the main actors in the Hall-Mills drama seemed to have a reason to avoid the truth, stretch the truth, shade the truth, or deny the truth. Indeed, one is hard-pressed to think of anyone except the two judges and a few minor witnesses who would pass the Diogenes lantern test for honesty when it came to answering questions. Small wonder that the journalists and the jury both had a difficult time in sorting fact from fiction with so much misinformation rolling in like a miasma.

This is not to exempt the press from criticism. Tabloids like the New York *Daily Mirror* were no doubt irresponsible, as tabloids often are. But even the *New York Times,* with its voluminous coverage of the case, made avoidable factual errors. When Adolph S. Ochs, publisher of the *Times,* was asked why his newspaper was devoting as much space as the *Daily News* to the Hall-Mills case, he replied, "When the *Daily News* prints it, it is sex; when *we* print it, it is sociology."[4] Unfortunately, it was somewhat tainted sociology, not only because of the pressure of daily deadlines but also because of the reporters' frequent carelessness. James Thurber wrote an essay for the *New Yorker* in which he remarked, "If the story [of the Hall-Mills case] is vague in your mind, it is partly because its edges, even under the harsh glare of investigation, remained curiously obscure and fuzzy."[5] More incisive daily journalism could have clarified it somewhat, even in the face of the rampant fibbing that was occurring on the banks of the Raritan.

Many people in the New Brunswick area did not lie, of course. They simply refused to divulge anything. One reason for their not leaping at the chance to help punish the guilty was that, in their eyes, the guiltiest of all were the two victims. Adultery was bad enough, but to have in their midst the scandal of a married Episcopal minister cavorting with a married choir singer, and then to have the wanton couple die by gunfire practically in each other's arms, was intolerable. Even Jane Gibson, who did speak out, said that Edward W. Hall and Eleanor Mills "got their just deserts."[6]

It is telling that two county officials, legally charged with handling corpses properly, felt constrained to slice open Eleanor Mills' womb to see whether her rumored adultery had borne fruit.

The decade of flappers and bathtub gin may have roared, but there were plenty of Puritans left in central New Jersey, plenty of vexed traditionalists who saw sexual license "as the most powerful bogeyman" of the day.[7] James Truslow Adams, writing in the *Atlantic Monthly* for November 1926, the month of the trial, lamented "Our Dissolving Ethics." He saw youth ethically adrift and doubted the moral stature of Protestant ministers, noting, "It is my experience that many boys and girls who cannot be induced to go to church are more genuinely religious than the clergyman who bewails the fact that they do not come to hear him preach."[8] Commenting on the Hall-Mills trial for the *Evening Graphic,* Aimee Semple MacPherson, founder of the International Church of the Foursquare Gospel, called on God "to teach young men to say as a lesson from the case, 'I want a wife like Mother—not a Red Hot Cutie.'"[9]

Attempts by investigators in 1922 and 1926 to establish a circumstantial case against any or all of the Stevenses required shrewd questions and honest answers. There may have been a host of searching questions asked, but what the detectives got in return was a barrage of falsehoods and half-truths. Some of these were based on a desire to protect the greatly respected Mrs. Hall. It is hard to overstate the esteem in which the rector's widow was held by those who knew her. She was trusted and admired. Many people, women especially, viewed her as the only true victim in the case.

As noted before, seventy-six women, none of them members of the St. John's congregation, signed their names in 1922 to a letter of support for the beleaguered widow. The women, many of them prominent in New Brunswick society, were effusive in their praise—"a woman of the highest type, above suspicion and above reproach, incapable of thinking, much less doing, evil."[10] By 1926 the number of local women signing a similar letter had risen to one hundred and ninety-four.[11] Sally Peters, Frances' childhood friend and maid of honor at her wedding, rushed to the widow's side from New York City in 1922 and again in 1926, staying with her until each crisis had passed. All these estimable folk and many more considered it unthinkable that Mrs. Hall could participate in the murder of her husband and Eleanor Mills.

Several witnesses had transgressions of their own to hide, some of them tied directly to the scandalous behavior of the rector of the Church of St. John the Evangelist. In the mystery fiction of the 1920s, in the novels of Agatha Christie, S. S. Van Dine, and Dorothy L. Sayers, the reader often encounters a drawing room full of suspects, all with dark secrets that force them to avoid or alter the truth under questioning. Few readers would have expected to meet up with such a case in real life. Then came Hall-Mills. When the secrets of New Brunswick started tumbling out of the closets of next-door neighbors, it was apparent that life could imitate art. For example:

• Jim Mills claimed to know nothing of an affair between his wife and Reverend Hall, when in fact he knew plenty.

• Ralph V. Gorsline and Catherine Rastall insisted they had never been near De Russey's Lane on the night of the murders, when in fact they were parked in a lovers' lane next to the murder scene.

• Ray Schneider accused his best friend, Clifford Hayes, of killing Edward Hall and Eleanor Mills in a tragicomedy of mistaken identity, an accusation he quickly and tearfully withdrew.

• Minnie Clark, caught in a scandal she was trying to expose, not participate in, hit on the idea of pretending to investigators that she was sick in bed, when, on at least one occasion, she was fully dressed under the covers and obviously trying to avoid answering their questions.[12]

There were other reasons for people connected with the case to lie or plead ignorance. Some wanted to downplay the disgrace, as they saw it, to the church.[13] Some feared offending the wealthy and powerful in Middlesex or Somerset County.[14] Some had guilty knowledge of the crime.[15] Some were threatened or bribed by persons working for the prosecution or the defense.[16] Some were congenital liars, or publicity seekers, or both.[17] Some were unobservant and got things wrong; they were not so much liars as reckless endangerers.[18] Some were lawyers—adversarial hired guns who shaded or withheld the truth.[19]

Perhaps the most egregious error made by both the prosecution and the press lay in their seeming inability to understand the individual characters and personalities of the main players in the drama. Said Alexander Simpson about his star witness, "I am absolutely convinced that Jane Gibson tells a truthful story."[20] Concerning Mrs. Hall, he declared in his summation, "Messalina, Lucretia Borgia, Bloody Queen Mary ... there are lots of cruel women in history. But what is crueler than a woman who is older than her husband and who knows that he is being taken away by a younger woman and sees him slain at her feet? What is crueler than that?"[21] Toward Willie

Stevens he was compassionate. In the midst of cross-examining Willie, he said, "I have no desire unnecessarily to harass or annoy the witness, nor have I any desire to make it hard for him."[22]

It is impossible to escape the conclusion that Simpson's legal acumen was sharply limited by his lack of insight into living, breathing human beings. Jane Gibson, the Pig Woman, played Scheherazade, spinning a thousand tales which, alas for the prosecution, were variations on fabrications. Mrs. Hall was a proud, reserved, but inherently decent person, sternly moral by her own standards—not quite Messalina or Lucretia Borgia. Even the special prosecutor never thought that Frances Hall had personally murdered her husband. Simpson treated Willie on the stand as if he were a simpleminded child with a fragile ego, yet Willie, under cross-examination, proved with answer after answer to be a canny, composed, assured witness who knew what to say and how to say it. He knew what to admit, what to fudge, and what not to recall. He was anything but the rote-mouthing automaton that Simpson at first supposed and later insisted he was.

With character judgments of this caliber, it is hardly surprising that the special prosecutor from Jersey City was unable to construct a plausible scenario for the murders. A prosecutor has to have some notion of what people are really like and how they might actually act if he or she hopes to get the story right, to persuade the members of a jury that he or she has gotten it right, to win at least their grudging respect and trust, and to remove reasonable doubt from their minds.

To praise an apparently psychopathic liar, who continues to change her story as often as a new mother changes her baby's diapers; to mercilessly assail a widow who he does not believe

Catherine Rastall on the witness stand. She was in a lovers' lane with Ralph V. Gorsline near the murder scene when the shots were fired. But, like Gorsline, she claimed to have seen nothing that night. (photo 1926)

for a single moment fired the fatal shots—and almost certainly did not *want* the shots to be fired; to try to elicit admissions of familial devotion from a distant brother whose every response shows him to care very little about his younger sister and brother;[23] and to coddle and defer to a verbally resourceful, if eccentric, stay-at-home bachelor brother who the widow admits accompanied her on a predawn stroll in New Brunswick on the night of the murders—all these misreadings of people and events contributed in part to making Simpson's case look even flimsier than it was.

For Alexander Simpson was basically on the right track, just as Wilbur A. Mott had been four years earlier. Like Mott, Simpson strongly suspected that the Stevens family bore some sort of responsibility for the murders. He could not figure out precisely what it was, and with Mrs. Gibson writing her own script, he found himself, because of a lack of physical evidence, building his shaky story around the Pig Woman's blend of fact (from the newspapers) and fantasy (from her own fertile imagination). Had he flung Mrs. Gibson and her story out the front door of the Somerset County Courthouse, he probably would have gotten the fundamental outline of events right. The scenario would not have incriminated Henry Stevens or Henry Carpender. Nor would it have won Simpson any indictments, because he would have had nothing to put before a grand jury except a questionable fingerprint on the rector's calling card and a couple of witnesses who had seen a Dodge sedan out near De Russey's Lane more than an hour and a half after the murders.

One of the most helpful witnesses in the investigation was perhaps the most mysterious. In 1922 detectives had learned as early as October 7 that a vestryman and a woman parishioner of the church had been seen near the Phillips farm on the night of the murders, and "it was understood that the officials had obtained the names of the man and woman."[24] When investigators began intensive questioning of the named individuals, Ralph Gorsline and Catherine Rastall, the couple stubbornly denied being anywhere near the scene of the crime. The name of the informer was not made public.

Four years later a different account conveyed the same information. This time it was attributed to a person Simpson listed as a witness for the prosecution but who never took the stand. He was Jacob Van Pelt, a garage mechanic in New Brunswick at the time of the slayings. According to Van Pelt, Gorsline came to his garage on September 15, 1922, the morning after hearing the four shots fired and said "something to the effect that he had been near a murder the night before."[25] Whether Van Pelt was the same person who spoke up in 1922 is unknown. The two stories are different in certain respects. But something convinced Simpson's investigators to lean heavily on Gorsline (twenty-one hours of questioning) and Rastall (nine hours of questioning) until one or the other of them broke.[26]

Even so, Simpson could never conclusively pin down the role of Gorsline in the events leading up to and following the fatal shots. As a consequence, the special prosecutor did not present a plausible or even a very coherent scenario of the murders to the skeptical jurors. The supposed presence at the crime scene of Henry Stevens was a serious drawback, and so was the real but unexplained presence of Ralph V. Gorsline. Simpson allowed the lanky vestryman's trip to De Russey's Lane with Miss Rastall to pass as a pure, remarkable coincidence. Almost certainly it was not.

28   Theories of the Crime

When the state dropped all charges against the Stevenses and Henry Carpender, there was general agreement that the killer or killers would never be punished. The *New Yorker* took a satiric view of the matter: "After reading pages of testimony as voluminous as Wanamaker's advertisements, everyone has voiced an opinion on the Hall-Mills case. Of all the theories advanced to date our favorite follows: Senator Simpson was carrying the 'Pig Woman's' rifle when Willie threw a bluefish at him and the gun went off, leaving a fingerprint on the defendant's calling card."[1] Typical of the more sober reactions was a comment in the Morristown *Daily Record* of December 4, 1926, pointing to "every indication that the Hall-Mills murder case has passed into the long list of unsolved crimes."[2]

It had, but speculation about it remained. Even during the trial, members of the press and public were trying to outguess Alexander Simpson, the special prosecutor, whose theory of the crime was widely doubted. In November 1926, just before the Pig Woman told her story in court, journalist Elizabeth Meriwether Gilmer, known to millions under the byline Dorothy Dix, wrote a piece for the *New York Evening Post* titled "A Nation of Detectives." She pictured the impact of the trial on the reading public: "In business houses, on the street corners, in the lobbies of hotels, in drawing rooms, in kitchens, it is practically the sole topic of conversation. For the time being every man, woman, and child in the land is turned into a temporary detective, and each individual has his own private solution of the mystery, which he defends with all the logic at his command."[3]   Dorothy Dix offered eight solutions that she had heard people discuss.

(1) *Mrs. Frances Noel Stevens Hall alone committed the murders.* Mrs. Hall had a powerful motive—revenge—and the slashed throat of Eleanor Mills argued strongly that the killer despised the pretty choir singer. Mrs. Hall was the only person that William Phillips, the night watchman, had seen returning to the Hall mansion after 2:00 a.m. on the night of the murders. She was a frequent and enthusiastic motorist and could easily have driven out past the Parker Home to do the deed. At least two witnesses claimed to have seen a Dodge sedan parked on Easton Avenue, although nearer to midnight than 10:20 p.m. Still, Dorothy Dix—and nearly everyone else—dismissed the likelihood of the widow being the sole killer. Mrs. Hall, declared Dix, was "particularly repressed, unemotional, reserved, and proud . . . a woman of fifty . . . far more apt to forgive an erring husband, as if he were a bad little boy, than . . . to slay him."[4] More persuasive than the widow's steely reserve, however, and more compelling than her supposed lack of physical strength, was this: The very last thing Mrs. Hall wanted was publicity about her husband's adultery. The gruesome murder of Reverend Hall and his mistress was guaranteed to generate a blizzard of publicity and a chorus of embarrassing tongue-wagging. Why would she invite such humiliation?

(2) *James Mills was the killer.* Like Mrs. Hall, Jim Mills had a strong and obvious motive. He also had a strong and obvious alibi. He was at home working on window boxes at the time of the slayings. Several people, including Mrs. Elizabeth Kelly, who lived downstairs, saw him there. One neighbor even complained about the noise he was making. Later, at about the time he would have been cutting his wife's throat, Jim walked

to the corner grocery store, Blitz's, for a soda. Jim Mills could neither drive a car nor shoot a pistol. He owned neither. He was also a milquetoast. Dorothy Dix's dismissal of him as a suspect was based solely on his meekness and patience—"Have you seen Jimmy Mills?"[5] But that perception in itself seems inadequate to clear the sexton. Plenty of meek and patient men have murdered their wives. The senior defense attorney, Robert McCarter, knowing full well that spouses are the most obvious suspects in slayings such as this one, attempted throughout the trial to implicate James Mills.[6] When, in 1994, Nick Pelino, Jr., wrote a play based on the Hall-Mills case, he fastened on Jim as the probable killer.[7] But detectives in 1922 and again in 1926 were unable to crack the mild sexton's alibi, no matter how much they may have wanted to, and there is no reason to think it could ever have been cracked. The poor fellow was manifestly at home at the time his straying wife hurried to her final, fatal rendezvous with the rector.

(3) *Simpson got it right. The three culprits in De Russey's Lane were Mrs. Hall, Willie Stevens, and Henry Stevens.* This is the scenario that the special prosecutor, with little physical evidence except the disputed fingerprint, pursued but never managed to explain clearly. He persisted in spite of a great deal of story-changing by his star witness. Wilbur A. Mott, the special prosecutor in 1922, had (like Simpson and the New York *Daily Mirror* four years later) riveted his attention on Mrs. Hall as the likely instigator of the confrontation that led to murder. Mott obtained no indictments, his efforts failing for essentially the same reasons that Simpson's case misfired. The physical evidence was inadequate, and his eyewitness was un-trustworthy. Mrs. Gibson's "Oh, Henry" recollection forced Mott (and later Simpson) to try to implicate somebody named

Henry. Mott chose a neighborhood cousin of Frances Hall, Henry Carpender, as the likely accomplice. Simpson first chose him too, then switched to Henry Stevens. This other Henry, the gun-savvy older brother of Mrs. Hall, insisted he was fifty miles away at Lavallette on the night of the murders. And a few days after Dix wrote her article, Henry Stevens' defense lawyers hammered home Henry's angling-for-bluefish alibi with a phalanx of exemplary witnesses and a diary.

(4) *An unnamed "other woman" did the deed.* What other woman? Undoubtedly Mrs. Minnie Clark, Eleanor Mills' presumed rival for the affections of the popular Episcopal minister, the woman who had to be "contented with crumbs, in Eleanor Mills' acerbic remark."[8] Dix mentions that a "couple of names are whispered," but the only one whispered recurrently was that of Minnie Clark, the plump Sunday school teacher. In this unlikely other-woman scenario, Ralph V. Gorsline, the "Iago in the vestry," while not cited by Dix, usually played a supporting role. There are indications that Gorsline and Mrs. Clark did participate in bringing one or more of the Eleanor-Edward love letters to Mrs. Hall's attention. But neither of them had a motive for murder. Gorsline was at the epicenter of the crime, but only as a spectator, with the lovely young Catherine Rastall at his side in the Apperson. As for Mrs. Clark, there was no evidence to suggest her involvement in anything other than amateur spying and possible letter-filching.

(5) *The Ku Klux Klan administered vigilante justice.* Incensed over the open adultery of a man of God, the KKK decided to make an example of Reverend Hall and his choirgirl sweetheart. Dorothy Dix noted this possibility in 1926,[9] and William M. Kunstler argued for it at some length in *The Minister and the Choir Singer* in 1964. Kunstler states in his book

that the only possibility "with any claim to logic and reason" is that the trysting couple were "victims of vigilante action," specifically the murderous act of one of the New Jersey branches of the Second Invisible Empire, Knights of the Ku Klux Klan. He goes into a history of the KKK, noting its particular aversion to sexual transgressions and its dislike of the Protestant Episcopal Church. He argues that the "elaborate positioning of the bodies was wholly in keeping with Klan practices. The placing of Mrs. Mills' head on her lover's arm was a graphic demonstration of the couple's adulterous relationship. The calling card propped against Hall's left leg dramatized the fact that the murdered man was an Episcopal clergyman. The scattering of the love notes around the two corpses emphasized the fiery nature of the love affair that undoubtedly led to the murders."[10]   As Kunstler contends, the tableau certainly did accomplish those purposes, but the Klan was hardly alone in wanting to send the two adulterers a posthumous message. Anyone who figured to make the same accusatory points could have prepared the tableau.

Dorothy Dix rejected the Klan argument in her 1926 column. She could not grasp why a vigilante group would "blame Mrs. Mills more than Mr. Hall," as the killer or killers clearly did. "Surely he was more at fault than she, seeing that he was older than she, that he was rich and highly placed in the world, and that she was a poor and humble woman, easily flattered, easily tempted by his lovemaking."[11]   Kunstler thought that Eleanor's "German extraction" helped to explain the Klan's supposed hatred of her, a none-too-convincing argument.[12] Writing about the case in 1992, nearly three decades after the appearance of Kunstler's book, Marc Mappen found the KKK theory improbable. Mappen wrote, "Although estimates place

New Jersey membership in the Klan at 60,000 at the time, the historical record shows that the activities of the hooded order in the Garden State were nonviolent. Instead, Jersey Klan members devoted themselves to activities such as protesting the showing of movies on Sunday."[13]

It should also be pointed out that the KKK typically took pains to make certain the public knew who was responsible for its actions. The Klan did not try to create mysteries of the Hall-Mills type. Just the opposite. It boldly advertised what it was doing and trumpeted its intention to treat similar wrongdoers in an equally unpleasant way.[14] It is almost unimaginable that every participant in a highly publicized group murder by the Ku Klux Klan went to his grave without uttering a word about the Klan's involvement, if only to clear the names of those falsely accused and prosecuted. The KKK was a bad outfit, to be sure, but in their own minds the Klansmen were moralists. They were not out to frame widows, eccentrics, sportsmen, and stock-brokers. The unbroken silence of New Jersey Klan members for the rest of the century is fairly conclusive proof of their lack of participation.[15]

(6) *Willie Stevens fired the shots, slit Eleanor's throat, and arranged the corpses.* Dorothy Dix argues that this would suggest "a dual personality . . . at times the gentle-kindly child-man, interested in little-boy games and amusements. . .; at other times a fierce beast, lusting for blood, committing abnormal crimes." That is sob-sister writing at its melodramatic peak.[16] But Kunstler too, a hard-headed defense attorney, found the Willie-as-killer idea absurd. It is inconceivable, he suggests, that Willie "could have been involved in a brutal slaying. The Stevenses were hardly the types to solve their problems with blood." *Noblesse oblige* and all that. Earlier, on the same page

of his book, Kunstler makes the point that Mrs. Hall could not have committed the murders because "she was neither an impulsive fool nor a naive simpleton."[17]

(7) *Frances Hall, using previously unrecognized hypnotic powers, caused Willie to commit the crime and then forget about it afterward.* Having "no memory of it whatever," the fifty-year-old simpleton was able to withstand "the long grilling at the hands of the police without breaking down."[18] But Willie Stevens was not the tomfool that the Million Dollar Defense hoped the public, the press, and the jury would suppose him to be. Willie in real life was much as Dr. Lawrence Runyon, the Hall family physician, characterized him during Simpson's cross-examination—"brighter than the average person" but "not absolutely normal." Willie "was able to take care of himself." He had "never advanced as far in school learning as some others," but he enjoyed reading "heavy books." To suggest that Willie could not have stood up to lengthy and intense grilling by the police unless hypnotized is a rather patronizing surmise. He held up brilliantly on the witness stand, much to Alexander Simpson's consternation. (In fairness to Dorothy Dix, it should be noted that Willie's superb courtroom performance lay two weeks in the future.)

(8) *The unfortunate couple were done in by thugs and footpads.* This had been Mrs. Hall's first reaction. Her faithful husband (forget Eleanor Mills for the moment, as the widow tended to do) was murdered for his money, fifty dollars or so, and his gold watch. But Mrs. Mills, whom Dorothy Dix did not so readily forget, had suffered a cruel fate indeed if she was murdered just for her male companion's cash, what with three bullet holes in her head and her throat cut from ear to ear. Robbery may have occurred in the thirty-six hours between the

slayings and the discovery of the bodies, but no one, not even Mrs. Hall, argued for very long that the motive in the murder of the minister and his mistress had been robbery. A corollary to the thugs-and-footpads theory, one also voiced for a time by the Hall-Stevens contingent, held that blackmail was the motive for the murders. This theory also ran aground on the rock of logic, for the two victims under the crab apple tree were not the blackmail*ers*, as one would expect, but the blackmail*ees*. Talk about killing the goose. . . .[19]

Those eight possibilities exhaust Dorothy Dix's list, but other theories made the rounds too, then and later. William M. Kunstler added four:

(9) *Assassins hired by Mrs. Hall carried out her detailed instructions.* Actually, Kunstler states it somewhat differently, putting Mrs. Hall under the crab apple tree in the company of her bravos. But since he insists elsewhere that she was at home when the murders occurred, why not leave Mrs. Hall in her Nichol Avenue mansion and permit the hired assassins to do their work unsupervised? This explanation is an intriguing one. When Julius Bolyog, a one-time friend of Willie Stevens, came forward with his belated account of having been recruited by Willie to carry two envelopes containing six thousand dollars in cash from Mrs. Hall to two young men in a New Brunswick alley on the day after the murders, the suspicion arose once again that hired assassins had committed the murders. Rumors of money being paid for silence, if not for murder, had surfaced during the initial investigation. Paid assassins were not unknown in the 1920s. Still, it is hard to believe that the principled and strait-laced Mrs. Hall would have hired a couple of gunsels, low-lifes and strangers to the family, to murder her husband and the married woman who had beguiled him, thus

opening the floodgates to humiliating publicity, the very kind of public scandal she wanted to avoid.[20]

(10) *Jane Gibson shot the two lovers and cut Eleanor's throat.* Senator Clarence E. Case made this outlandish suggestion in his summation for the defense—"somewhat facetiously," according to Kunstler.[21] "Oh, gentlemen," Case told the jury, "I don't say it is so, but I do say to you that it is within the realm of possibility." No, it isn't. It was refuted by the entire thrust of the defense arguments.[22] The Pig Woman had no motive, no pistol, and, according to the defense team prior to this headline-producing insinuation, no knowledge at all of the events that night on the Phillips farm. Perhaps, in his summation, Republican Senator Case was being a wee bit nos-tee toward Democrat Senator Simpson and Mrs. Gibson, the recently and thoroughly discredited star witness for the prosecution.

(11) *Ray Schneider mistook the victims for Nicholas Bahmer and his incorrigible daughter.* This theory stands the Clifford Hayes theory on its head. It presumes that Raymond Schneider, Hayes' buddy and later his accuser, was angry at Nick Bahmer for having an incestuous relationship with his teenage daughter, Pearl, the girl Ray loved. Schneider followed Bahmer and Pearl to the Phillips farm and in a fit of rage he, not Clifford Hayes, shot them dead—or so he thought in the dark of night. In reality he had killed Reverend Hall and Mrs. Mills. This theory is almost as absurd as the Mrs. Hall-as-hypnotist idea or the Pig Woman as executioner proposal. Whoever murdered the minister and the choir singer did so at close range with a flashlight pointed at their faces. There was no possibility of mistaken identity. Ray Schneider may have stolen Hall's money and his watch on the morning he and Pearl

Bahmer discovered the bodies, although he was never charged with the theft.

(12) *A lunatic committed the murders.* When all else fails, blame a madman. Had the murders occurred several decades later, a quartet of drug-crazed hippies might have filled the bill, as Captain Jeffrey MacDonald tried to make them do in the 1970 slaughter of his wife and two daughters. A lunatic in the 1920s, or a strung-out druggie later on, is always a remote possibility in any homicide with less than a cut-and-dried solution. But the nature of the Hall-Mills crime scene—the well-placed bullets, the carefully arranged bodies, the scattered love letters, the propped-up calling card—refutes the notion of a deranged killer. Whoever did away with Edward W. Hall and Eleanor Mills knew what he, or she, or they were doing, why they were doing it, and what message the tableau would convey to those who discovered it.

Obviously, some of the twelve theories of the crime are more plausible than others. The reader will notice that five of the theories implicate members of the Stevens family, which is hardly surprising, since both investigations, 1922 and 1926, centered on the perceived role of the Stevenses, a family whose local prominence seemed to make homegrown justice impossible and special prosecutors imperative. Yet Kunstler, after analyzing the evidence, states in *The Minister and the Choir Singer* that "In all likelihood, Mrs. Hall had nothing whatever to do with the crimes," and "It is also equally clear that her brothers were not involved."

Kunstler's dismissal of Willie Stevens as a suspect takes two sentences: "The testimony placing Willie in [North] Plainfield on Thursday night is . . , to say the least, incredible." That is quite true. "There was also evidence that Willie was in his bedroom shortly before the time the murders took place."[23] That is not true. There is no such evidence except in the testimony of Willie himself.

Other than Mrs. Hall, the only witnesses who could provide Willie with an alibi for the time of the murders were the two live-in maids, Barbara Tough and Louise Geist. Neither did so. On the witness stand both denied knowledge of where anyone else in the household was between the hours of ten o'clock and two o'clock on the fatal night.[24] The murders occurred at or around 10:20 p.m. The drive from 23 Nichol Avenue to the Phillips farm in Mrs. Hall's Dodge would have taken perhaps ten minutes.[25]

The Minister and the Choir Singer is a worthwhile book, well written, exhaustive in its coverage of the case, and difficult to fault on the facts. But its final chapter, "One Man's Solution," strays from the objectivity of the rest of the book and enters the arena of advocacy. It is engaging advocacy, for William M. Kunstler was a formidable trial lawyer. His long and particularized exploration of the iniquities of the Ku Klux Klan, thirteen pages long as opposed to two dismissive sentences on Willie Stevens, persuaded a few reviewers at the time of publication, including Rex Stout, that the white-hooded order was probably responsible for the deaths of Edward W. Hall and Eleanor Reinhardt Mills.

Advocacy, however, does not have to be scrupulously fair—witness Alexander Simpson's antics in 1926. And Kunstler's Ku Klux Klan argument in "One Man's Solution" is neither impartial nor persuasive. It is slanted toward his own preoccupations. The lawyer-author presents no evidence to support his thesis; he perpetuates the baffling-mystery view of the case. To name the Klan as the only reasonable instrument of murder and to glide past Willie Stevens, or even Mrs. Hall, as a legitimate suspect is to make the "capital mistake," commented on by Sir Arthur Conan Doyle and others, of twisting the "facts to suit theories, instead of theories to fit facts."[26]

Members of the Hall-Mills jury. The jury consisted entirely of men, several of them elderly. Eight of the twelve jurors are shown here as they approach the entrance to the Somerset County Courthouse. (photo 1926)

29   No Fierce Beast

Of the eight theories of the crime on Dorothy Dix's 1926 list, theory number six—Willie Stevens as shooter, throat-cutter, and tableau-arranger—is the most plausible. The Hall-Mills murder case was a domestic homicide. The murders were not premeditated in the usual sense, although the killer carried a gun to the scene of the crime. The true nature of what happened under the crab apple tree may have been suggested by Clarence Case in a surprising slip of the tongue as he began his cross-examination of Somerset County detective George Totten. "What time did you get to the place of the accident?" he asked.[1]

The *accident?* Why would the junior defense attorney, as Simpson liked to call him, refer to the murders as an accident? The autopsy reports made them look like cold-blooded executions. It is more likely, however, that they were hot-blooded, spur-of-the-moment acts. Yet Willie Stevens was not the "fierce beast" of Dorothy Dix's imagination.[2]

In fact, the crime was almost as mindless as the subsequent investigation. The cover-up that followed was efficient and thorough, but it would have stood little chance of success if the physical evidence at the crime scene and elsewhere had been properly collected, evaluated, stored, and presented in court. As it was, the person who fired the fatal shots got away with murder, although not without a trial.

What follows in this chapter is conjecture, based primarily on the mass of material that was written and published on the case in 1922 and 1926. It attempts to weave together what seems to be unquestionably true with a number of inferences about what must have happened if the known events and times on the night of September 14, 1922, and the morning after are to be satisfactorily explained.

To begin at the beginning: The Reverend Edward W. Hall and Eleanor Mills had been having a love affair for at least four years. Countless people knew it or suspected it, including Jim Mills and Frances Hall. Although Jim was aware of the liaison and had grudgingly accepted his cuckoldry, Mrs. Hall insisted on maintaining that the affair was platonic. But even if it was physical, she doubted that her husband would abandon his comfortable lifestyle at 23 Nichol Avenue and go sailing off to Japan with the wife of a school janitor.

There were those in the St. John's congregation who were not so sure. One of them was Mrs. Minnie Clark, active in the Sunday school and half in love with the minister herself. Another was Ralph V. Gorsline, vestryman and man-about-town, who had complained to members of the vestry about the rector's sexual misconduct.[3] The love affair between the rector and the choir singer was not a well-kept secret, partly because Eleanor Mills was so openly pleased with her part in it. At some point Gorsline or Clark learned that the married lovers were clandestinely exchanging notes. One of these amateur sleuths presumably ferreted out the location of the lovers' post office in the church study, a discovery that set in motion the series of occurrences that culminated in murder. Gorsline and Clark also appear to have spied on the minister and the choir singer in and about Buccleuch Park, across Easton Avenue from the Phillips farm.[4]

Either Gorsline or Clark, or perhaps both, suggested to Mrs. Hall that the affair was reaching scandalous proportions and that she must confront her husband for the good of the church and for the sake of her own reputation. She must demand that he break off the love affair. She may well have replied that she had already done so, but that Edward had merely laughed and said she was too suspicious. The closeness between him and the choir signer, he said, was not romantic; it was ministerial. Mrs. Hall doubted that to be true—too many ugly rumors were in the air—but she had no tangible proof of his infidelity. Gorsline, or Clark, or both offered to provide some.

On the afternoon of September 14, 1922, Minnie Clark visited the home of Mrs. Hall, accompanied by a niece who was to be photographed in the picturesque Hall flower garden. While Minnie was there, she showed Mrs. Hall at least one of Eleanor's love letters to the rector, perhaps the Lake Hopatcong letter that had been written and "mailed" in the church study that morning. It began, "Do I love you too much?" It spoke of her willingness to leave his "physical presence, and go into a convent," arguably as a preface to elopement or to the rector's divorce. It is the letter with the oft-quoted line, "Oh, my darling babykins, what a muddle we are in!"[5] Minnie Clark probably returned this letter to its hiding place in the rector's study, but in the interim its absence may have been noticed.

On the day of the murders something—whether the missing letter, or letters, or some other telltale sign—alerted either the minister or his mistress, or both, to impending trouble. Reverend Hall phoned Eleanor at about 3:00 in the afternoon, but Millie Opie, who took the call, was unable to rouse her napping neighbor. According to Mrs. Hall's trial testimony, Eleanor made a phone call to 23 Nichol Avenue during that afternoon, hoping to speak to Edward, who was out.[6]

Later, at about 7:00 p.m., came the critical phone call of the day and of the trial—the call whose message Mrs. Hall may or may not have heard. Eleanor was on the line, calling Edward, and the rector, after listening to her on the upstairs phone for a moment, murmured, "That is too bad." They arranged a meeting for 8:15 that night.[7]

Whether or not Mrs. Hall heard the whole conversation on a downstairs extension is an issue much argued about at the trial. Important as it seemed to Simpson, it may not have been especially significant. The usual meeting place for the minister and his mistress was the Phillips farm, located on "our Easton Avenue road."[8] Ralph V. Gorsline, who, along with Minnie Clark, had been shadowing the couple for quite a while and in all likelihood had been reading their love notes, presumably knew about their trysting place, the unnamed lovers' lane with the scraggly crab apple tree not far from the Parker Home.[9] If so, Gorsline and Clark may have conveyed the information to Mrs. Hall as part of their ongoing espionage.

Here was an ideal opportunity for a confrontation between the betrayed Mrs. Hall and the clandestine lovers. If Edward and Eleanor were on their way to the Phillips farm, and if Mrs. Hall was to go to there later, after the servants had retired for the night, she could stand accusingly before them in their out-of-the-way love nest. Perhaps such an encounter would bring Edward to his senses. At the very least it would prove conclusively what Frances bitterly suspected. It would make it impossible for her husband to insist in the future that his association with Eleanor was nothing more than a minister-assistant relationship.

The difficulty from Mrs. Hall's standpoint was that while Gorsline knew the terrain in and around De Russey's Lane, she did not. She may have asked Barbara Tough, the upstairs maid, to go to the Parker Home that afternoon to scout the area. Certainly, Barbara Tough did go there, a trip that seems too handily timed for coincidence. Nevertheless, if Mrs. Hall hoped to find the exact trysting place of her husband and his inamorata—a narrow dirt lane off another narrow lane off Easton Avenue at the far end of town—she would need some specific on-site guidance. Why not enlist the prying Ralph V. Gorsline, with that green Apperson of his, to help out? Since Gorsline was one of the church leaders calling for a showdown, he might be more than willing to lead Mrs. Hall to the secluded locus of sin. Indeed, Gorsline, not Mrs. Hall, may have suggested the idea. The arrangement was made.

Timing would be important. The Hall household seemed to have had an informal 10:00 p.m. curfew. If the bribery charges had any substance, then Louise Geist and Barbara Tough were flatly, stubbornly going to deny any knowledge of what happened after ten that night. In any case, the tragic adventure began a few minutes after ten o'clock at the Hall mansion on Nichol Avenue. Almost simultaneously, Ralph V. Gorsline swung into action at the New Brunswick YMCA, downtown on George Street.

Mrs. Hall asked Willie to accompany her on the unpleasant journey. Understandably, she did not want to ask either of the maids, or the gardener-handyman Peter Tumulty, or even one of the sympathetic Carpender cousins to go along on this embarrassing trip. But Willie she trusted. Willie was loyal. Willie adored her. Willie was a powerfully built man, though clumsy. He would be a reassuring presence to have beside her. She needed no chauffeur, being a capable driver herself. All she needed, besides the stout and kind-hearted Willie, was a clear marker showing where to find her husband and the woman people were saying had stolen him. The green Apperson touring car would serve that purpose.

Unbeknownst to Mrs. Hall, there was a terrible flaw in her plan. Willie, taking his responsibility all too seriously, decided to carry a concealed weapon with him. It was probably not his old Iver-Johnson revolver.[10] Possibly it was the rector's gun, the one seen by several people at the Point Pleasant campground, a .32-caliber Colt semiautomatic pistol, the gun Louise Geist said was kept in a drawer in the Halls' library.[11] And it was loaded. It seems reasonable to speculate that Willie did not intend to shoot the pistol that night. He was enthusiastically playing the role of bodyguard, much as he had played the role of fireman for so many years. Willie was not a killer, although he knew how to shoot.[12] In a childlike way he felt protective toward his sister, even though Frances, who was two years younger than he, had spend a lifetime mothering him.

While Mrs. Hall and her brother were leaving Nichol Avenue in the Dodge sedan, Ralph V. Gorsline was picking up Catherine Rastall on George Street. This development was not part of Mrs. Hall's plan. It was not something she anticipated. But for the gaunt vestryman it was too good a chance to pass up. Miss Rastall was in the choir, knew of the Hall-Mills affair, was pretty as all get-out, and would be titillated to observe the confrontation between one of the city's toniest matrons and her caught-in-the-act clergyman husband. He invited her to join him. Off they sped in the open-top Apperson with Gorsline at the wheel and Rastall at his side. They parked in a brushy, unnamed lovers' lane, one lane away from where the Reverend Edward Wheeler Hall and Eleanor Mills, his "red-hot cutie," were communing under a crab apple tree.

Mrs. Hall parked her Dodge on Easton Avenue near De Russey's Lane. The sedan was probably pointed toward New

Brunswick, because that side of the road would put it adjacent to the Phillips farm and would not require Willie and her to cross Easton Avenue on foot.[13] Mrs. Hall and Willie walked down De Russey's Lane, evidently talking, since Gorsline and Rastall testified to hearing "mumbling" voices behind them.[14] Upon seeing Gorsline's green Apperson parked in the first unmarked lane to their left, they knew they were approaching the site. Mrs. Hall and Willie kept walking, reaching the second unnamed lane within moments. They turned in.

What they saw when they aimed their flashlights toward the crab apple tree is impossible to know. It may be, though it seems unlikely, that Edward and Eleanor, or both, were in some state of undress. More likely, they were kissing and caressing. Or they may just have been sitting there, holding hands, discussing the latest novel they had read or talking about the purloined letters they might have to explain. There is no way to tell. What does seem clear is that their pose and their position, rather than any angry dialogue or furious struggle, prompted the next act.

As the testimony of Gorsline and Rastall confirms, the sound of gunfire erupted almost immediately. Whatever Willie saw, whatever Edward or Eleanor may have exclaimed in astonishment, the quick-tempered bachelor brother lost control. He was not thinking, he was acting. He pulled the Colt pistol from his jacket or under his belt and fired one shot into the head of the Reverend Edward Wheeler Hall. As the angle of the first bullet suggests, the rector was seated when he died. Since the Colt semiautomatic may have been no more than a foot from Hall's face when Willie pulled the trigger, he did not have to be an accomplished marksman.

The act shocked Mrs. Hall. It terrified Eleanor. One or

both of them screamed.

Willie, realizing in his fury and befuddlement that in a way he had shot the wrong person, aimed the pistol at the head of Eleanor Reinhardt Mills, who had probably risen to her feet. He fired three more times. Again, he held the pistol at close range to the victim, as the autopsy reports showed.[15]

Few reporters who covered the case could imagine the big galoot Willie Stevens as the killer. Yet many of them had seen him become enraged in an instant, his body tensing, his face reddening, his eyes popping, his teeth suddenly bared.[16] Some of them undoubtedly recalled a statement made early in the investigation, when detectives were asking questions about the disabled Iver-Johnson revolver. It was reported that some time before the De Russey's Lane crime Edward and Frances Hall had decided that "a person of Willie's excitable temperament should not have a weapon."[17]

Mrs. Hall, stunned and dismayed, now faced the dilemma of her life. What could she do? One thing she could not do was panic. Journalists would later picture her as the Iron Widow, stiffly stoical. Although those who knew her well saw her in a much different light, there is no question that she drew upon remarkable reserves of self-reliance and strength in adversity. She seems to have made two decisions almost immediately. One was that Willie Stevens would not suffer the legal consequences for his act, thereby embarrassing the Stevens and Carpender families. Another was that the crime scene had to tidied up. She would not let the authorities find her dead husband in such a disgraceful posture, whatever that posture may have been.

She made several other quick decisions. She needed to speak immediately to Ralph Gorsline, and she did. Either she went to his car, or he, hearing the shots, came to investigate. Whichever way it was, Mrs. Hall learned to her vexation that a young lady, Catherine Rastall, was occupying the front seat of the vestryman's car. Mrs. Hall, adjusting her plan to the circumstances, asked Gorsline, perhaps pleaded with him, to take Miss Rastall home and then to come straight back to the Phillips farm, pick up Willie, and drive him home. In the meantime, Willie had an important job to do. Like any naughty but properly disciplined child, he would have to clean up his own mess. He would have to make the corpses presentable.

Mrs. Hall, leaving Willie to his grisly task, made a few crucial moves of her own. First, she got rid of the murder weapon. If it were found at the scene, or in her car, or back at the house, all would be lost. As far as she knew, the gun was the only piece of physical evidence that could point to her and Willie. After disposing of the pistol, possibly in the nearby Raritan River but more likely at a more remote and less predictable location, she sought counsel—legal, personal, or both. Mrs. Hall, given her position in society, had several people to whom she could turn for advice and assistance. There is no way to speculate which choice or choices she made, but given the magnitude and pressing nature of her problem, it is certainly conceivable that before she returned home at 2:30 or so in the morning, she had already spoken to a New Brunswick lawyer.

One observation: It might seem that Frances, Willie, Ralph, and Catherine would have fled like startled deer once the sound of gunfire died away. That would have been a natural reaction, and the thought must have occurred to all four. But the Phillips farm was in a semirural area, not overrun with spooning couples late on this Thursday night. It was unlikely that anyone would rush to the scene. Gunfire, as Mrs. Anna L. Hoag, who lived on Easton Avenue near the Phillips farm, told reporters, was a fairly common event in the area.[18] Shooting was the pastime of those detested "foreigners," according to Mrs. Gibson.[19] In any case, a frantic dash from the area, on foot by Mrs. Hall and Willie, in the Apperson by Gorsline and Rastall, might attract more attention than a calm and measured departure. Mrs. Hall, unlike her eccentric brother, was nothing if not rational in dicey situations. Also, there was work to do: clean up the scene, get rid of the gun, begin to explore alibis, and seek legal advice.

Ralph Gorsline drove Catherine Rastall back to her home on Senior Street not long after the shootings. In her trial testimony Rastall said they left the scene immediately. Gorsline said they waited three to six minutes, but could not explain why. More likely they were on the Phillips property somewhat longer than that, although perhaps not much longer.

After Gorsline left, so did Mrs. Hall, giving stern instructions to the chastened, if confused, Willie to make sure that Mr. Hall and even the deplorable Mrs. Mills looked respectable in death. Willie would have half an hour or so to accomplish this chore, while Gorsline was making his trip to New Brunswick and back. When the accommodating but by now rattled vestryman returned to the scene, watchful for the police or any other snoopers, he picked up Willie Stevens and drove him home. Gorsline probably dropped Willie off some distance from the Nichol Street mansion so that his flashy Apperson would not be noticed and so that Willie could enter the mansion with the needed stealth. Willie made it home, unnoticed, some time before his sister.

Mrs. Hall's whereabouts between 10:30 p.m. and 2:30 a.m. are unknown. There is some evidence that she returned to the

ACCUSING FINGERS

Story on Page 3

Daily Mirror **headline and illustration**. The New York *Daily Mirror* was instrumental in reopening the unsolved Hall-Mills murder case four years after the crime. Its coverage was sensational and libelous. This 1926 front-page illustration shows Willie Stevens propping Reverend Hall's calling card against the slain rector's foot. As in most sketches of the crime scene, the details are inaccurate. (photo 1998) crime scene at least once—probably only once, around midnight, possibly with one of her male cousins—to check on Willie's handiwork.[20] It is impossible to speculate on her reaction to Willie's tableau. If she noticed her brother's final touch, Eleanor's slashed throat, a grim flourish added after the bodies had been clothed and arranged, even she, cool as she always was, must have been unnerved for a moment. But with the scarf covering Eleanor's neck, Mrs. Hall may not have noticed Willie's postmortem throat surgery. When she did learn of it, then or later, she would have made sure that Willie's bloody pocket knife was as efficiently hidden as the pistol.[21]

Although Mrs. Hall handled the immediate aftermath of the crime with calm efficiency, problems arose. The first stemmed from the sighting by night watchman William Phillips of Mrs. Hall darting into her house in the small hours of the morning. That necessitated the apocryphal predawn stroll that Mrs. Hall claimed to have taken with her brother Willie. Phillips said he saw no one with Mrs. Hall when she entered the side door of her home, and he was correct. No one was with her. Willie had already returned to his bedroom.

The second problem had to do with the sighting of Ralph V. Gorsline's car near the scene of the murders. Fortunately for Mrs. Hall and Willie, the Apperson was sighted while Catherine Rastall, not Willie, was the passenger. Of course, Willie was probably not sitting upright in the seat when Gorsline drove him from the Phillips farm to New Brunswick. Common sense suggests that he was hunkered down out of sight for the potentially perilous return home.

A third problem grew out of Willie's ride in the Apperson. The gunshots may have left traces of blood on Willie's person or clothes. Then when Willie was arranging the bodies and cutting Eleanor's throat, he surely must have splashed blood on himself and his clothes. It is unlikely that Gorsline concerned himself with the possibility of bloodstains at the time. He may not even have seen the blood in the darkness.

On the evening after the bodies were discovered, Austin Grealis, the Stevens' dry cleaner and older brother of William Grealis, noticed what he thought might be bloodstains on a suit Willie had sent him for cleaning. He public-spiritedly turned the garment over to investigators, who somehow managed to lose it before the 1926 trial. As a consequence, the stains were dismissed by the defense as gravy stains, and Simpson could do little to prove otherwise.[22]

If there was any blood on Willie's body when he got home, he promptly washed it off. But, sadly for Gorsline, there must have been bloodstains on the floor or upholstery of the Apperson that would not wash off. The next day after the Middlesex County prosecutor questioned Gorsline about his whereabouts on the night of the murders, the lanky vestryman suffered a major loss. So did the prosecution. Gorsline's expensive green touring car went up in flames, damaged beyond repair. The fire started under the seat and spread so fast that there was no time to use the car's fire extinguisher.[23]

The love letters found between the bodies are one of the most puzzling aspects of the case. Simpson believed the letters were taken there by Mrs. Hall to bolster her case in the lovers'-lane confrontation. That could have happened, but probably didn't. If Mrs. Hall had all those letters in her possession at one time, she might well have avoided the confrontation altogether. The letters by themselves were sufficiently damning. The defense team claimed the letters were carried to the scene, for whatever reason, by Eleanor Mills. And they probably were.

Two witnesses for the defense, Mrs. Agnes Blust and Mrs. Alameda Harkins, New Brunswick housewives, testified that Eleanor was carrying "a brown scarf" that may have held a sheaf of letters as she walked toward the Phillips farm.[24] Jim Mills had acknowledged this probability at the very outset.[25] The minister and the choir singer never mailed their local love letters, exchanging them instead. They also seem to have read them aloud to each other when they met.[26]

There was conflicting testimony as to whether the letters, when first seen by detectives, were scattered about or were in a packet.[27] Given the many crime-scene foul-ups in the case, it is within the realm of possibility that the letters were strewn about as they were being read by fascinated investigators. Some people believed they were scattered by Ray Schneider as he searched the bodies for valuables. Others assumed that the person who straightened the victims' clothes and arranged their bodies found the letters and distributed them between the bodies as a part of the tableau. It is an intriguing question, but it makes no real difference who did the scattering. It could even have been the wind. The salient point is that the letters, being there, confirmed what many people knew anyway, that Edward and Eleanor were lovers.

The mystery, posed in part by Mrs. Hall's maneuvers after the murders (or the "accident," to use Senator Case's word), was not beyond human solution. It was, however, beyond the capacities of the original investigators. Alexander Simpson realized from the beginning that he was facing a nearly impossible task. "Any reasonable murderer ought to be satisfied with four years in which to get away," he said in August 1926, soon after accepting the assignment as special prosecutor. In the same statement he listed five blunders made by the 1922 investigators.

"1. Took the eyeglasses of the murdered man which were found in the position on his face after the murder, where they must have been handled by the person who did the killing, and wiped the glasses so that any fingerprints would be obliterated and there [would] be no possibility of taking them and comparing them with fingerprints of persons under suspicion.

"2. Left the place of the murder open to the public for days so that no trace of automobiles or markings of any kind would be discerned because of the press of people at the spot.

"3. Avoided any search for fingerprints on the clothes and bodies of the murdered persons so the same might be taken and compared with fingerprints of suspected persons.

"4. Avoided holding a Coroner's inquest at which witnesses could immediately after the event be publicly examined, which would tend to bring to the notice of the State authorities evidence in the case which would be suggested by those publicly examined.

"5. Treated witnesses who volunteered to give evidence which might implicate persons in a manner to make such witnesses hostile."[28]

Simpson might have added that in 1922 the authorities failed to order autopsies before the bodies were buried and never took the fingerprints of Mrs. Hall and Willie Stevens. Small wonder that in 1926 the prosecution could not meet its burden of proof.

30 Ever After

The press soon lost interest in the Hall-Mills case. All those millions upon millions of words, having entertained the multitudes before being used to wrap fish, seemed after the trial to have been a wasted if not a tawdry effort. The mystery remained unsolved. Many of those who wrote about it later regarded it, like Alexander Woollcott, as a "farrago of transparent nonsense, when contrasted with the engaging candor and obvious honesty of Willie Stevens on the stand."[1] Frederick Lewis Allen in his book *Only Yesterday* interpreted the acquittals to mean absolute innocence and maintained that "the reputation of the Stevens family had been butchered to make a Roman holiday of the first magnitude for newspaper readers."[2] It was generally believed that none of the defendants had played a part in the De Russey's Lane murders. William M. Kunstler echoed that belief in *The Minister and the Choir Singer*.[3]

But an acquittal in a criminal trial, no matter how justified—and the acquittals in the Hall-Mills case were surely justified—does not mean that the person or persons indicted and tried have been proved innocent of the crime. In the epilogue to his book about the O. J. Simpson trial, Vincent Bugliosi, prosecutor in the Manson murder case, makes this point with some vehemence. "In many people's minds," he writes "the term 'not guilty' is often considered to be synonymous with 'innocent.' In American criminal jurisprudence, however, the terms are not synonymous. 'Not guilty' is simply a legal finding by the jury that the prosecution has not met its burden of proof, not that the defendant is innocent."[4] Bugliosi stresses his belief that O. J. Simpson, despite having been acquitted in the criminal trial, did in fact kill Nicole Brown Simpson and Ron Goldman.

The acquittals of Frances Hall, Henry Stevens, and Willie Stevens left the defendants free to resume their normal lives, but it did not remove all doubts about their involvement in the sudden leave-taking of the rector and his mistress. Henry Stevens returned to his sportsman's life in Lavallette. Mrs. Hall and Willie Stevens continued to live in the mansion at 23 Nichol Avenue. Between trips abroad the widow pursued her various church and welfare activities in New Brunswick, but after the trial she took little part in the social life of the community.[5] Willie "tried to pick up the old routine of life where he had left it, but people turned to stare after him in the street, and boys were forever at his heels, shouting, 'Look out, Willie, Simpson is after you!'" His visits to the firehouse became less and less frequent, sometimes months apart. He complained of headaches, suffered from a heart ailment, and, as he got older, lost a great deal of weight.[6]

In March 1927 Mrs. Hall, through her attorney, Martin Conboy, began an action for libel against William Randolph Hearst's Public Press Corporation, publisher of the New York *Daily Mirror*.[7] A similar lawsuit was filed five months later against Hearst and the *New York Evening Journal*. The plaintiffs in both cases were Frances Hall, William Stevens, and Henry Carpender.[8] Henry Stevens did not join in. One year before these lawsuits were settled, Philip A. Payne, the leading ogre of the press in many people's eyes, was killed in an accident that made front-page headlines across the country. Payne, managing editor of the *Daily Mirror* and chief instigator in the reopening of the Hall-Mills case, died when *Old Glory,* the single-engine airplane in which he was a passenger, crashed at sea on an attempted transatlantic flight.[9]

The libel suits were settled out of court. Each plaintiff had asked for $500,000, and, although the amount of the settlement was not immediately disclosed, it may have totaled $50,000.[10] Since the tabloid coverage had been plainly defamatory, the award was not unreasonable. But one purpose of the lawsuits, aside from the money, may have been the plaintiffs' desire to inhibit other writers from delving further into the case and coming up with a scenario that made more sense than the Pig Woman's. If so, it worked. No one wrote a nonfiction book about the case until 1953.[11]

And what of the Pig Woman? Despite Simpson's fear that she might die before testifying, Mrs. Jane Gibson proved tougher than her mule; the famed Jenny died two years before her owner. The cancer-ridden Pig Woman remained a patient in Jersey City Hospital for nearly a year after the trial, and then in 1928 was able to return to her farm. She later had to be re-admitted to the hospital for treatment, but soon went home once more. In late January 1930 her son, William Easton, Jr., carried her into the hospital for her final stay. She passed away on February 7, 1930, without delivering any quotable exit line, as the *Daily Home News* dutifully reported. It was just as well. She had said quite enough. Her husband, William Easton, upon being informed of her death, said, "She's gone, eh? There was a right smart, honest little woman—a hard-working woman she was, too."[12] Three days later a small, inconspicuous funeral procession made its way through Jersey City to Holy Cross Cemetery in North Arlington, where Jane Gibson, or, legally, Jane Easton, was laid to rest.[13]

Alexander Simpson did not attend the funeral. No doubt he

was too busy pursuing his political career to bid farewell to the woman who had given him name recognition throughout the state and nation. Of course, not all the notice he got was favorable. Less than a month after the trial the Hudson County Bar Association passed a resolution asking the State Bar Association to look into the prosecution of the Hall-Mills case.[14] Nothing came of the probe. This was Frank Hague's New Jersey, after all, and Simpson, like Hague, was a Hudson County Democrat.

The ex-special prosecutor remained in the New Jersey Senate until 1930, when he resigned to run for the United States Senate against Dwight W. Morrow, a lawyer, banker, and diplomat from Englewood. The stock market had crashed the previous year, and Morrow, a Republican, was forced to concede that the country was in the midst of a depression, but said he expected "employers and others" to lead the nation "to a new and better prosperity."[15] Simpson assailed his opponent's rosy view of the situation. He charged Morrow with endorsing the supposed sins of the Republican President: "You [Dwight Morrow] stand for everything Mr. [Herbert] Hoover stands for," Simpson told an enthusiastic audience in Jersey City, "—high, destructive tariff; unemployment, bread lines, oppressed farmers, depressed industry . . . and Wall Street."[16]

When Simpson lost resoundingly to Morrow, despite a Democratic landslide across the nation, he abandoned politics, gave up the brightly colored shirts he wore on the campaign trail, and settled down to the practice of law, mainly as a criminal defense attorney.[17] He was not a great success in the role. As his *New York Times* obituary stated, "He took on some difficult cases . . . in several of which his clients, despite his flair for the dramatic, were convicted."[18]

After the Hall-Mills trial Simpson had nothing but praise for Charles W. Parker of Morristown, the presiding judge—"beyond reproach," said the senator from Hudson County while flailing away at the tactics of the Million Dollar Defense attorneys.[19] Parker served as a justice of the Supreme Court of New Jersey from 1907 until his retirement in 1947. The Hall-Mills case was his most highly publicized trial, although in 1935 he again made national headlines when he wrote the unanimous opinion of the State Court of Errors and Appeals, upholding the conviction of Bruno Richard Hauptmann for the kidnap-murder of Charles A. Lindbergh, Jr. Justice Parker's 14,000-word decision in effect sent Hauptmann to the electric chair.[20]

All three of the principal defense lawyers in the Hall-Mills case enjoyed distinguished careers. Timothy N. Pfeiffer, Mrs. Hall's personal attorney in 1922, and 1926, became a partner in the New York City law firm of Milbank, Tweed, Hadley & McCloy, where he served for more than forty years. In 1950 he helped to found the Legal Aid Society and was its president from 1950 to 1955. A relatively young man at the time of the Hall-Mills case, he lived in Princeton in his later years, dying there in 1971 at the age of eighty-four.[21]

Robert H. McCarter, senior defense attorney in the Hall-Mills trial, had achieved noteworthy success in law long before 1926. Founder of the Newark law firm of McCarter & English, McCarter was primarily a corporation lawyer. He accepted very few criminal cases, and those only out of friendship. When he was questioned years after the Hall-Mills case by one of his law partners, he replied that he "always had a little suspicion that Eleanor Mills' husband Jim was involved in the killings, although there was no evidence against him at all, and he was never considered a suspect."[22] It beggars belief to suppose that

DAILY NEWS

FINAL EDITION

NEW YORK'S PICTURE NEWSPAPER

Average net paid circulation
of THE NEWS, Nov., 1926:
Sunday 1,426,685
Daily--1,164,542

Vol. 8. No. 139. 32 Pages   New York, Saturday, December 4, 1926   2 Cents

NOT GUILTY!

—Story on Page 3.

Relief spread over face of Henry Stevens (above) as he heard verdict. Arthur Applegate's bluefish had saved him.

Mrs. Hall didn't exhibit a trace of worry over what her fate would be. This is the broad smile she wore while the jury was deliberating. She listened to reading of verdict with same stoicism she has shown all through the great trial.
NOT GUILTY! SIMPSON WILL ASK NEW TRIAL.—Mrs. Frances Stevens Hall, Willie and Henry Stevens, her brothers, were found not guilty of Hall-Mills murders yesterday. The jury deliberated Prosecutor Simpson will seek new trial.

Willie Stevens grinned and chuckled with d-

Jim Mills was too clever for McCarter and the Million Dollar Defense.

At the time of the Hall-Mills trial Clarence E. Case and Alexander Simpson were both state senators with higher ambitions. During the trial Simpson delighted in twitting Case as "junior counsel," which technically he was, since the older McCarter was the senior attorney on the defense team. After the trial, at a time when Senator Simpson was preparing to run for a U.S. Senate seat, Senator Case was named to the Supreme Court of New Jersey. The year was 1929. Case became chief justice in 1945, serving in that position until 1948, when, owing to a reorganization of the court, he became senior associate justice. A long-time resident of Somerville, he died in 1961 at the age of eighty-three.[23]

The man whom McCarter thought deserved a closer look as a murder suspect also lived well into his eighties. He was James Mills, the long-suffering husband of crazy-cat Eleanor. During the trial the *New York American* hired Jim as a reporter, but his dispatches were apologetic and often ridiculous: "If my wife had only told me! If she had come to me and said: 'Jim, I have had an affair with Mr. Hall. I have been untrue to you. Can you forgive me?'"[24]

Jim stayed on as sexton of the Church of St. John the Evangelist long after the murders. If he knew anything about the identity of the killer or killers, besides what he hinted vaguely at now and then, he never revealed it. When Mills was eighty-five years old, Arthur Sutphen Meredith, a superior court judge who had become fascinated by the Hall-Mills case, set up an interview with him to try to learn anything he could from the elderly widower. "It was a rather unsatisfactory interview," Meredith recalled. "He was stone deaf and I had to shout my questions." Jim, it seemed to Meredith, knew no more in 1963 about the murders under the crab apple tree than he had known in 1922.[25] The church sexton died two years later.

Charlotte Mills, Jim's daughter, was deeply affected by Eleanor's murder, although her pert flapper image helped to hide the pain. Eleanor and Charlotte were basically roommates in their upstairs 49 Carman Street flat. They shared some confidences, although Charlotte did not know the whole story, or did not acknowledge it. She insisted that the relationship between her mother and the rector was "quite proper." In 1922 Charlotte was a high school senior; by 1926 she was employed in the office of the International Motor Company in New Brunswick.[26] A favorite of the reporters in 1922 and 1926— and briefly a journalist herself, writing commentary for a news syndicate during the trial—she soon faded into obscurity. In later years she lived in self-imposed anonymity in New York City, working as a records supervisor in a savings bank. She never married. Diagnosed with cancer in early 1952, she entered a nursing home in Metuchen, New Jersey, where she died on February 1, two days after unsuccessful surgery. She was forty-five years old.[27]

Another person whose life was permanently scarred by the Hall-Mills affair was Henry de la Bruyère Carpender. A real-life victim of the imaginary voices in the Pig Woman's head, Carpender spent four months in the Somerset County jail, awaiting a trial that never came. The indictment against him was dismissed after the not-guilty verdicts in the trial of his cousins. Nonetheless, his arrest and confinement shattered his health, not to mention his faith in the criminal justice system as represented by Alexander Simpson. A suave and dignified New York City stockbroker, Carpender suffered a paralytic stroke at the age of forty-eight. Unable to move his right arm and leg, he retired from business in January 1930 and lived quietly in South Somerville until his death four years later at the age of fifty-two.[28]

Henry Stevens, the other Henry who was swept into the Hall-Mills vortex, seemed to take his misfortune less to heart. He returned to Lavallette immediately after being acquitted, accompanied by his spirited wife Ethel. Within a month he began serving his second term on the village council. The people of Lavallette had never believed in his guilt, and it was the testimony of several of them that tore a gaping hole in the state's case. After his return to the Jersey shore, Henry Stevens resumed his favorite pastimes, fishing and hunting. At the time of his death, on December 3, 1939, he was preparing to leave on his annual winter trip to Florida. He was seventy years old.[29]

Not long before the Hall-Mills trial began in Somerville in 1926, Mrs. Frances Stevens Hall, the main defendant in many people's minds, told a group of reporters, "I have just about reached the conclusion that New Jersey is not a fit place for decent people to live in."[30] But after it was all over, after the acquittals, she decided to remain in her mansion on Nichol Avenue, the home in which she had lived since 1890. She devoted herself to tending her tranquil garden and to community service—to the New Brunswick Chapter of the American Red Cross, Middlesex General Hospital, the Visiting Nurses' Association, the Episcopal Evergreens Home in Bound Brook, and Christ Church Home for Girls in Helmetta.[31]

One of her final contributions was to the war effort. In response to a scrap metal drive in 1942, the first full year of World War II, she donated the four-foot-high iron fence that surrounded the extensive grounds of her home.[32]

Mrs. Hall died at 23 Nichol Avenue on December 19, 1942, at the age of sixty-eight. Her health had been failing for some time, and she had suffered several heart attacks in the final years of her life.

Funeral services for Mrs. Hall were held at the Protestant Episcopal Church of St. John the Evangelist, attended by a small group of relatives and friends. Willie Stevens, in very poor health, took his place among the mourners. The services were conducted by the Reverend Horace E. Perrett, rector of the ivy-covered church that Edward W. Hall had once served in the same capacity. Eight or ten people accompanied the body to Green-Wood Cemetery, Brooklyn, where Mrs. Hall was laid to rest beside her murdered husband. In the twenty years after the tragedy, the self-possessed widow never publicly deviated from the sentiment she expressed to journalists in October 1922: "I lived for him and he lived for me."[33]

Yet that statement made far more sense when applied to her faithful brother Willie than to her straying husband Edward. It was Willie, not the rector, who had truly loved, honored, and obeyed Frances Hall.

Just nine days after Mrs. Hall's funeral, Willie Stevens died at the family home on Nichol Avenue. Seventy years old, he had been under a nurse's care for many years, suffering, like his sister, from a serious heart condition. He had seldom ventured outside the shaded grounds of the mansion in more than a decade, and then only in a chauffeured automobile.

All his life Willie had wanted to be a fireman. When New Brunswick's Engine Company No. 3 was the volunteer Phoenix Engine Company, he had been a proud honorary member. But when the city's firefighters turned professional, he could not make the grade. Despite Willie's wealth and family connections, the new city fire department did not offer to hire him. Firefighting was his obsession, though, and he stayed on at Engine Company No. 3 as a kind of mascot, a hanger-on, a big, goofy guy who played cards, polished the brass, and, with his forty-dollar-a-week allowance, bought steaks and other treats for the firemen.

In 1922, when Willie was fifty years old, a crisis arose, not at the firehouse on Dennis Street but at his own house on Nichol Avenue. His beloved sister Frances was being betrayed by her husband of eleven years, a minister of God, a man who ought to have known better, a man who ought to have acted honorably. On the night of September 14, Frances asked her bachelor brother to accompany her on a drive to the Phillips farm, out by the Parker Home, across from Buccleuch Park. Their mission was to confront the faithless rector and his married girlfriend at their trysting place and demand an end to the affair. Frances would do the talking. Willie accepted the role of guardian. He decided to take along a pistol.

It is doubtful that Willie Stevens was aware of the love letters that had been passing between his sister's husband and Eleanor Mills, even though he may have delivered some of them himself. He had certainly not read Eleanor's fervent line, "I am fiery today," or known of the rector's desire to place "a long burning kiss on your dear lips—liquid fire into your very soul."

Willie Stevens knew only that his adored sister was being hurt, deeply and callously, by Edward Wheeler Hall, her husband, the man who had promised to cleave to her unto death. Willie accompanied his sister in the family Dodge, his temper seemingly well under control. He could not tell Frances about the gun, but he felt that taking it with him was a wise precaution.

Under the crab apple tree, in the focused beam of his flashlight, he saw something unexpected, something obscene, something outrageous. His temper flared. He fired once, then three times. The terrible affair was over.

Willie had put out the fire.

Willie Stevens after his acquittal. An inept investigation, a protective sister, the Million Dollar Defense, and an impressive performance on the witness stand got Willie out of deep trouble. (original sketch based on photos)

Source Notes and Commentary

Preface (pages 9-15)

1. *New York Times,* September 21, 1922.
2. Frederick Lewis Allen, *Only Yesterday* (1931), 213.
3. *New York Times,* editorial, September 26, 1922.
4. *New York Times,* August 26, 1926.
5. *Ibid.,* December 2, 1926 ("twelve trees" quote) and December 4, 1926 (verdict)
6. William M. Kunstler, *The Minister and the Choir Singer* (1964), 317-334. Among the many who have expressed doubts about the KKK theory are Mary S. Hartman, Dean of Douglass College, Rutgers University, in "The Hall-Mills Murder Case: The Most Fascinating Unsolved Homicide in America," *The Journal of the Rutgers University Libraries* (June 1984), 13; novelist Stephen Longstreet, quoted in a feature article by Jennifer Judd in the New Brunswick *Home News,* April 10, 1986; Somerset County (NJ) Judge Arthur Meredith, quoted in a feature article in the Newark *Star-Ledger,* September 13, 1992; and New Jersey archivist-author Donald W. Sinclair, cited in Gerald Tomlinson, "Under a Crab Apple Tree," *Murdered in Jersey* (1994), 10.
7. Wendy Kaminer, "The Latest Fad in Irrationality" (a review of popular books about angels), *The Atlantic Monthly* (July 1996), 105.

1 Tableau in Lovers' Lane (pages 16-20)

1. The three phrases are from Jane Spangler's "Murder for the Minister," *Central Jersey Monthly* (November 1979), 7; Marc Mappen's "Passion in the Parish," *Rutgers Magazine* (Winter 1992), 18; and Christopher Hann's "A Dangerous Affair," *New Jersey Monthly* (September 1995), 57.
2. Early newspaper reports sometimes claimed that a struggle had taken place. On September 19, 1922, the *New York Times* headline read "Rector and Choir Singer Clawed by Woman Before the

Murder"; a subhead read: "Scratches on Mrs. Mills's Face and Hall's Hands Indicate Furious Attack." And two weeks later: "Hall Put Up Fight, Autopsy Indicates, *New York Times,* October 6, 1922--a headline that is not supported by the text of the article. See Chapter 10, "Burial Now, Autopsy Later."

3. This description of the murder scene is based on several sources, including the New Brunswick *Daily Home News,* September 16, 1922, and the trial testimony, particularly that of George D. Totten, *New York Times,* November 7, 1926.

4. *New York Times,* November 21, 1922.

5. New Brunswick *Daily Home News,* September 16, 1922. Although Cardinal was the first journalist on the scene, he was not the only one to arrive from the *Daily Home News.* By noon he had been joined by city editor Daniel Wray and, as noted in the text, reporter Frank Deiner.

6. *New York Times,* September 19, 1922.

7. New Brunswick *Daily Home News,* September 16, 1922 ("scarcely decomposed"); *New York Times,* November 25, 1926 ("in bad shape"). The latter was the recollection of Edwin R. Carpender, the widow's cousin, who reached the scene around noon.

8. The events involving Raymond Schneider occurred in early October 1922. They are covered in this book in Chapter 11, "Bizarre Interlude."

9. Damon Runyon, "The Hall-Mills Case," *Trials and Other Tribulations* (1946), 51.

10. *New York Times,* October 18 and 19, 1922; several of Eleanor Mills' letters were introduced as evidence at the trial, *New York Times,* November 16, 1926.

2 Characters and Setting (pages 21-34)

1. William M. Kunstler, *The Minister and the Choir Singer* (1964), 335-344.

2. Hall's life is summarized in many news and feature articles. Among the most complete and apparently accurate sketches, although no sources are given, is the one in Charles Boswell and Lewis Thompson, *The Girl in Lover's Lane* (1953), 14-15.

3. *New York Times,* October 29, 1922.

4. New Brunswick *Daily Home News,* September 18, 1922.
5. *New York Times,* November 23, 1926. When Willie Stevens died, sixteen years after the trial, the *New York Times* obituary noted that the quirky, lifelong bachelor "wore loose, baggy clothes, and the world swam happily before his eyes through thick-lensed spectacles." *New York Times,* December 31, 1942.
6. Mrs. Gibson's quote about having "heard the name 'Henry' called out by a woman at the scene of the tragedy" first appeared in the *New York Times* of October 27, 1922. The distance that the fatal shots traveled, a critical bit of evidence, is contained in the autopsy reports, chronicled in the *New York Times* of September 30, 1922, and October 6, 1922, and in testimony at the trial, particularly that of Dr. Otto H. Schultze, reported in the *New York Times* of November 10, 1926.
7. Mrs. Gibson's hard-to-pin-down life story emerged, albeit confusingly in the direct examination and cross-examination at the trial, as reported in the *New York Times,* November 19, 1926. The *Times* article contains the complete text of her testimony. Two weeks earlier Mrs. Gibson's mother, Salome Cerenner, had questioned the truthfulness of her daughter's statements, primarily those of the details of her life as they had been reported in the press. See Morristown *Daily Record,* November 5, 1926.
8. Simpson's obituary appears in the *New York Times,* July 21, 1953.
9. The obituary of Timothy N. Pfeiffer, *New York Times,* February 13, 1971, contains no reference to the Hall-Mills case.
10. Damon Runyon, "The Hall-Mills Case," *Trials and Other Tribulations* (1946), 83.
11. The population of New Brunswick in 1920 is from the U.S. Census report, New Brunswick Public Library. The titles of the movies being shown on the night of the murders come from the *Daily Home News,* September 14, 1922.
12. *The City of New Brunswick: Its History, Its Homes, & Its Industries,* published by the New Brunswick Times (1908); see also Lawrence G. Foster, *A Company That Cares: Johnson & Johnson* (1986).
13. *New York Times,* November 16, 1926.
14. *The City of New Brunswick,* 23, and *Heidingsfeld's General Directory of New Brunswick, 1921-1922.*
15. *New York Times,* September 29, 1926, contains a vivid description of Mrs. Hall at the wheel of her car. While being interviewed by

two reporters of her choice, she drove them from Somerville to New Brunswick. This photo op and reportorial coup for these two journalists came two weeks after her indictment. Its importance lies less in what she said to them than in the reporters' account of her driving. For some reason both special prosecutors seemed to assume that Mrs. Hall needed a chauffeur to transport her from place to place. This 1926 incident and the accounts of her several motor trips to Point Pleasant in the summer of 1922 show her to have been perfectly capable of driving her Dodge wherever and whenever she wished.

16. *Ibid.*, November 22, 1922; November 25, 1926.
17. *Ibid.*, August 10, 1926.
18. *Ibid.*, October 19, 1926.
19. *Ibid.*, September 20, 1922; *Daily Home News,* September 21, 1922. These two articles go into some detail about the Phillips farm and farmhouse. The caption under the *Daily Home News* photo reads, "In this, the living room of the Phillips farmhouse, near spot where bodies were found, there were signs of recent occupancy. On the ash tray on table, cigar ashes were found."
20. *New York Times,* September 22, 1922.
21. *Ibid.*, November 12, 1922.

3 Mrs. Hall's Ordeal (pages 35-44)

1. *New York Times,* November 28, 1926. The complete text of Mrs. Hall's trial testimony gives many factual details of her life.
2. This part of Mrs. Hall's story is covered in Chapter 7, "The Woman in Gray." The widow admitted almost immediately to having been out with her brother Willie in the early morning hours following the murders. The *Daily Home News* of September 18, 1922, reports her statement to that effect.
3. *New York Times,* September 24, 1922.
4. *Ibid.*, October 19, 1922.
5. *Ibid.*, June 9, 1925 (obituary of Fanny Hall); *New York Times,* November 28, 1926 (Mrs. Hall's trial testimony); and *Heidingsfeld's General Directory of New Brunswick, 1921-1922.*
6. *New York Times,* October 18, 1922.
7. *Ibid.*, November 23, 1926.

8. *The City of New Brunswick: Its History, Its Homes & Its Industries,* published by the New Brunswick Times (1908), 124; also Lawrence G. Foster, *A Company That Cares: Johnson & Johnson* (1986) , 9.

9. Charles Boswell and Lewis Thompson, *The Girl in Lover's Lane* (1953), 12.

10. Quoted in Frances Hall's obituary, *New York Times,* December 20, 1942.

11. *New York Times,* June 8, 1914.

12. *Ibid.,* September 24, 1922. At the time Mrs. Hall's statement was prepared, a New Brunswick attorney, W. Edwin Florance, represented her. Within three days he was replaced by Timothy Newell Pfeiffer.

13. *Ibid.,* September 18, 1922. These remarks, like several others, are quoted somewhat differently in different sources. The *Daily Home News* of this date quotes Bishop Knight as saying, "From my knowledge, I cannot believe Rev. Mr. Hall guilty of anything wrong. His life has been exemplary, and I have found his home to be one of the most Christian I have ever been in."

14. *Ibid.,* November 10, 1922.

15. *Ibid.,* November 11, 1922.

16. New Brunswick *Daily Home News,* November 10, 1922.

17. *New York Times,* August 12, 1926. Mrs. Hall's attorneys began using anonymous sources such as this to get their side across to the public, since they were convinced that the prosecution was attempting to try the case in the press.

18. *Ibid.,* November 9, 1922.

4 Babykins and Wonder Heart (pages 45-54)

1. William M. Kunstler, *The Minister and the Choir Singer* (1964), 9-10; Charles Boswell and Lewis Thompson, *The Girl in Lover's Lane* (1953), 14-15; New Brunswick *Daily Home News,* September 18, 1922.

2. Jennifer Judd, New Brunswick *Home News,* April 10, 1986.

3. *Heidingsfeld's General Directory of New Brunswick, 1921-1922.*

4. *New York Times,* October 20, 1922.

5. *Ibid.,* September 25, 1922.

6. *Ibid.*
7. *Ibid.*, October 19, 1922. Here as elsewhere in the *Times* coverage, reporters often seem to be using the words *pistol* and *revolver* interchangeably, as if there were no differences between the two types of weapons. Although the .32 caliber cartridges found at the scene could have been used in either a pistol or a revolver, they were most likely used in an automatic (or, strictly speaking, a semiautomatic) pistol.
8. This Point Pleasant incident is described in many sources but most fully in the *New York Times* of September 25, 1922, and October 20, 1922.
9. Letters from Hugh L. Dwelley, president of the Islesford Historical Society, July 3 and 21, 1997. At the Islesford Historical Museum, open in July and August, the old Register of the Woodlawn House shows that "Mr. & Mrs. Edw. W. Hall, New Brunswick, N.J." checked in on August 2. The handwriting is that of the rector.
10. *New York Times,* October 20, 1922, and in trial testimony, November 4, 1926. "D.T.L." explained, *New York Times,* November 14, 1926 (letters).
11. Typed transcripts of diary and letters in Rutgers' Special Collections and University Archives; also, in slightly different form and without underlined emphasis in trial transcripts, *New York Times,* November 14, 1926 (letters) , and November 17, 1926 (diary).
12. *New York Times,* October 20, 1922. The content of this letter, which reportedly was written at Islesford about August 20, was provided to journalists by Florence North, attorney for Charlotte Mills.
13. Kunstler, 11.
14. *New York Times,* September 24, 1922.
15. *Ibid.*, November 9, 1922. This lack of cooperation from the people in New Brunswick who presumably knew something about the crime was the subject of an editorial in the *Daily Home News* of November 16, 1922. Four years later Alexander Simpson's investigators noted a similar chill in the air when they tried to interview these people and others. *New York Times,* August 3, 4, and 5, 1926.
16. *Ibid.*, October 22, 1922. See also Kunstler, 65.
17. *Ibid.*, November 30, 1922.
18. *Newark Evening News,* September 23, 1922.
19. *Ibid.*, October 24, 1922; also November 23, 1922.

5 Willie the Fireman (pages 55-64)

1. *New York Times*, September 18, 1922.
2. There was never any mention, before or after the trial, of Willie's having held a job. His obituary in the New Brunswick *Daily Home News*, December 31, 1942, stated that "He had never had an occupation." However, in response to a question from Simpson on cross-examination at the trial, Willie said, "For about four or five years I was employed by Mr. Siebold, a contractor." When Simpson paused, taken aback by this unexpected answer, Willie added, "Do you wish his address?" *New York Times*, November 24, 1926. James Thurber wrote, "He [Willie] did this in good faith, but the spectators took it for what the *Times* called a "sally." James Thurber, "A Sort of Genius," *Hanging by a Thread* (1969), 458-459. Here as elsewhere in his essay Thurber seems to believe that Willie took the witness stand without having received any preparation from his attorneys.
3. Charles Boswell and Lewis Thompson, *The Girl in Lover's Lane* (1953), 13-14; *Heidingsfeld's General Directory of New Brunswick, 1921-1922;* New Brunswick *Daily Home News*, September 18, 1922; *New York Times*, September 19, 1922.
4. New Brunswick *Daily Home News*, September 22, 1922.
5. Damon Runyon, "The Hall-Mills Case," *Trials and Other Tribulations* (1946), 16-17.
6. New Brunswick *Daily Home News*, September 21, 1922.
7. This is not to say that Willie memorized his story word for word. He knew the basic outline and was easily able to fill in the details in his own words. Willie had considerable verbal facility, as he would demonstrate in his trial testimony.
8. *New York Times*, October 8, 1922. The attorney quoted is Timothy N. Pfeiffer, introduced in Chapter 2, "Characters and Setting."
9. Boswell and Thompson, 17.
10. *Ibid.*
11. Thurber, 455.
12. *Ibid.*, 462.
13. *Ibid.*
14. Lawrence G. Foster, *A Company That Cares: Johnson & Johnson* (1986), 70.

15. *New York Times,* August 13, 1926.
16. *Ibid.,* November 1, 1926; see also Willie Stevens' trial testimony, November 24, 1926.
17. *Ibid.,* November 4, 1922. There was much speculation about the Iver-Johnson revolver. Some experts said it could have fired the .32 caliber short ammunition the murderer used. Investigators also speculated that the firing pin might have been removed after the crime was committed. But Willie said the gun had not been used in years, an assertion easily verified or disproved.
18. *Ibid.,* September 18, 1922. As with numerous other quotations in news articles about the Hall-Mills case, different reporters heard different words. The *Daily Home News,* September 18, 1922, had Willie telling the firemen, "There's going to be a big explosion in this case soon." Asked by newsmen to explain the statement, according to the *Daily Home News,* he "refused to state what he meant by it. The *Times* reported his reply as, "I did say something like that, but I meant nothing by it."
19. *Ibid.*
20. *Ibid.*
21. *Ibid.* September 19, 1922.
22. *Ibid.* November 16, 1922.
23. Obituary of Timothy N. Pfeiffer, *New York Times,* February 13, 1971.
24. *New York Times,* November 29, 1922.
25. *Ibid.*
26. The complete Bolyog story appears in the New Brunswick *Home News,* September 14, 1972, the fiftieth anniversary of the crime. The timing seems almost too perfect, but Reginald Kavanaugh, a *Home News* staff writer, points out that Bolyog, fearing he was about to die, had first spoken out two years earlier, telling his story to George Saloom and then to the *Home News.*
27. *New York Times,* November 5, 1922.
28. *Ibid.,* October 20 and 21, 1922.

6 Carman Street (pages 65-75)

1. Charles Boswell and Lewis Thompson, *The Girl in Lover's Lane* (1953), 18-20.

2. *New York Times,* November 23, 1922.
3. Damon Runyon, "The Hall-Mills Case," *Trials and Other Tribulations* (1946), 20-21.
4. *New York Times,* October 29, 1922.
5. Boswell and Thompson, 19.
6. *New York Times,* October 19, 1922.
7. *Ibid.,* November 12, 1922. Charlotte told reporters that her mother's affair with Gorsline lasted about two years and that Mrs. Mills was the one who put an end to it. Gorsline continued to pay attention to Eleanor, according to Charlotte, but she "expressed contempt for him."
8. Typed transcript in Rutgers' Special Collections and University Archives; also in trial proceedings, *New York Times,* November 14, 1926.
9. *New York Times,* September 27, 1922.
10. *Ibid.,* November 16, 1926. Mrs. Elsie P. Barnhardt, a sister of Eleanor Mills, testified at the trial that Eleanor "said numerous times" that "she cared more for Mr. Hall's little finger than she did for her husband's whole body." When asked if Eleanor made the remark to her husband, Mrs. Barnhardt replied, "She made it to several people." On at least one occasion Charlotte and Daniel were present.
11. *Ibid.,* September 27, 1922.
12. Boswell and Thompson, 19.
13. *New York Times,* September 18, 1922. The suggestion that Eleanor Mills carried the love letters with her on the fatal night fit the defense theory of the crime better than the prosecution theory, particularly in view of the timing: Jim Mills admitted seeing the letters in his wife's scarf after her return from Lake Hopatcong-- one day before the murders.
14. *Ibid.,* November 6, 1926.
15. *Ibid.,* September 27, 1922.
16. *Ibid.,* November 28, 1926. Mrs. Hall did not mention this afternoon phone call in her detailed statement of September 23, 1922.
17. William M.Kunstler, *The Minister and the Choir Singer* (1964), 12.
18. *New York Times,* November 28, 1926. The afternoon phone call to Mrs. Hall *may* have occurred, particularly if Eleanor had found her morning letter missing or misplaced in the lovers' "post office."

19. *Ibid.,* August 12, 1926.
20. *Ibid.,* August 17, 1926.
21. *Ibid.,* November 6, 1926.
22. Kunstler, 17-18. But see also Jim Mills' trial testimony, *New York Times,* November 6, 1926, which touches on Daniel's but not Charlotte's whereabouts.
23. *New York Times,* November 6, 1926.
24. *Ibid.,* October 22, 1922. If Jim Mills actually said this, it would obviously clear him of any complicity in the murders. But Charlotte Mills' recollections cannot always be trusted. Even though Millie Opie was undoubtedly right about Charlotte's knowing a good deal about the affair between her mother and the rector, that knowledge did not translate directly into reliable testimony. Charlotte seems to have been inventive in some of her memories.
25. *Ibid.,* November 6, 1922.

7 The Woman in Gray (pages 76-86)

1. *New York Times,* September 24, 1922; November 2, 1922; November 16, 1926; and November 26, 1926.
2. *Ibid.,* September 24, 1922; November 28, 1926.
3. *Ibid.,* November 2, 1922; November 16, 1926. Minnie Clark was also called Minna. The two names appear almost interchangeably in newspaper accounts of the day. The confusion has persisted. Boswell and Thompson use Minna throughout the text of *The Girl in Lover's Lane.* Kunstler uses Minnie in *The Minister and the Choir Singer.* In addition to the Minnie-Minna question, there is a Clark-Clarke question. Several 1920s issues of *Heidingsfeld's General Directory of New Brunswick* (a useful but not wholly reliable publication) show Clarke as the spelling. The 1921-1922 issue, however, has it as Clark. Boswell-Thompson and Kunstler both spell it without the *e.*
4. *Ibid.,* November 16, 1926.
5. *Ibid.,* November 2, 1922.
6. New Brunswick *Daily Home News,* October 18, 1922; *New York Times,* October 19, 1922.
7. *New York Times,* September 18, 1922.
8. *Ibid.,* October 29, 1922. Mrs. Hall's statements throughout the

case stressed her belief in the rector's faithfulness. She never admitted there was any conflict or tension between her and her husband. When she died in 1942 she was buried beside him in the Stevens family vault in Green-Wood Cemetery, Brooklyn.

9. *Ibid.,* November 28, 1926.

10. *Ibid.,* November 13, 1926.

11. Damon Runyon, "The Hall-Mills Case," *Trials and Other Tribulations* (1946), 41.

12. *New York Times,* August 7, 1926.

13. *Ibid.,* August 14, 1926. George D. Totten was the best of the early investigators, but Francis L. Bergen, the Somerset County prosecutor for four years, fired the long-time detective during the 1926 investigation, after which Philip Payne, managing editor of the New York *Daily Mirror,* personally recruited Totten to join the staff of his newspaper.

14. *Ibid.,* October 7, 1922.

15. What Phillips actually told investigators in September 1922 and July 1926 is hard to piece together. Reports in the New Brunswick *Daily Home News* and *New York Times* vary widely from paper to paper and issue to issue. In 1922 the time of Phillips' sighting of the woman in gray varies between 2:10 a.m. and 2:45 a.m. See the *New York Times* of September 18, 1922; October 7, 1922; and November 2, 1922; and the *Daily Home News* of September 18, 1922. In 1926 it is uniformly reported as being 2:10 a.m. See the *New York Times* of July 30 and 31, 1926. On the witness stand at the trial his memory had faded in most respects, but as to the time of sighting, it had improved. He said, "I can fix it within five minutes. It was either 2:40 a.m. or 2:45 a.m." *New York Times,* November 7, 1926.

16. New Brunswick *Daily Home News,* September 18, 1922; *New York Times,* October 7, 1922, and November 28, 1926.

17. *New York Times,* November 9, 1926.

18. Mrs. Hall's timetable, like William Phillips', was muddled in the newspapers. Early reports had her and Willie leaving the house at 2:00 a.m. and returning at 3:00 a.m. *New York Times,* September 18, 1922. That soon changed to leaving at 2:30 a.m. and coming "directly home with my brother William" (her signed statement for public release). *New York Times,* September 24, 1922. But in her interview with twenty-five members of the press on November 1,

1922, in response to the question, "About how long were you absent from your home?" she answered, "It was about half-past two when I dressed and got up, and I was back here about half-past three." *New York Times,* November 2, 1922. Since Timothy N. Pfeiffer prepared Mrs. Hall for this press conference, and the transcript of it was made public, it seems clear that 3:30 a.m. was the agreed-upon time for her having returned home from the walk with Willie.

19. New Brunswick *Daily Home News,* September 18, 1922. Also *New York Times,* September 18, 1922.

20. *New York Times,* July 30, 1926.

21. *Ibid.,* November 7, 1926. Prosecutor Simpson often complained about the outside pressure being exerted on witnesses whose testimony might benefit the prosecution. Phillips' lack of recall at the trial suggests that something besides time had made the night watchman, potentially one of the state's most important witnesses, uneasy and uncooperative.

8 Collecting Evidence (pages 87-96)

1. William M. Kunstler, *The Minister and the Choir Singer* (1964), 4.

2. The information on Edward Stryker and Grace Edwards comes from *Heidingsfeld's General Directory of New Brunswick, 1921-1922.*

3. The strange events involving Raymond Schneider, Pearl Bahmer, and their friends and relatives are the subject of Chapter 11, "Bizarre Interlude."

4. Kunstler, 4.

5. New Brunswick *Daily Home News,* September 16, 1922. In this, the first news article about the murders, Albert J. Cardinal reported that the letters were scattered between the bodies. But Bogart Conkling, Somerset County sheriff, insisted that when he arrived, later than Cardinal, the letters were neatly stacked. *New York Times,* August 6, 1926.

6. *New York Times,* August 17, 1926. Garrigan's and Curran's roles are well described by Kunstler, 4-6.

7. *New York Times,* August 14, 1926; November 5, 7, and 11, 1926 (Totten); November 14, 1926 (Conkling); August 18, 1926 (Long).

Dr. William H. Long testified only at the preliminary hearing, not at the trial.

8. *Ibid.*, November 5, 7, and 11, 1926. This is Totten's trial testimony.

9. The "piece of steel . . . running board" quote is from the *New York Times,* September 17, 1922. The fact that the cartridge case, or shell casing, was manufactured by Peters appears in Totten's trial testimony. *New York Times,* November 7, 1926.

10. *New York Times,* November 16, 1926. This is Dr. Loblein's trial testimony.

11. *Ibid.*, November 7, 1926.

12. *Ibid.*, November 25, 1926.

13. Stricker is quoted in the *Daily Home News,* September 18, 1922.

14. *New York Times,* October 5 and 19, 1922. The front-page, three-column headline in the *Times* for October 19 reads, "New Evidence Places Hall-Mills Murder Five Miles from the Phillips Farm and the Time at 8:30 p.m. September 14." But the E. R. Squibb report, cited in the same article, states: "Nor is it likely that we would have found 0.08 of a pint of blood in the soil if the bodies had been brought to the spot after the murder." In other words, the conclusion of the Squibb chemists is diametrically opposed to the suggestion made in the *Times* headline.

15. Leo J. Coakley, *Jersey Troopers* (1971), 59-65. According to the author, the State Police played an even smaller role in the 1926 investigation than they had in 1922.

16. The Somerset County taxpayers had a point. After the failure of the special prosecutor from Essex County to get indictments in 1922, Somerset County taxpayers wound up paying most of the bill. They had not expected it, thinking there was a kind of gentlemen's agreement between them and the taxpayers of Middlesex County to share expenses. *Daily Home News,* December 14, 1922; *New York Times,* December 15, 1922.

17. *New York Times,* October 23, 1922.

18. *Ibid.*, November 6, 1922.

19. *Ibid.*, November 2, 1922. The *Times* discreetly left out the name of the family but noted that "it is one of the richest and most influential in New Brunswick."

20. *Ibid.*, November 17, 1922.

21. *Ibid.*, November 19, 1922.

22. *Ibid.*

9 A Crackerjack Idea! (pages 97-106)

1. *New York Times,* November 30, 1922.
2. Barry A. J. Fisher, Arne Svenson, and Otto Wendel, *Techniques of Crime Scene Investigation, 4th ed.* (1987), 18-19. There is no question that members of the general public, not just law enforcement officials, know more about crime-scene investigation today than the Middlesex and Somerset investigators did at the time of the Hall-Mills murders. Television, with its relentless focus on murder and mayhem, both factual and fictional, has educated even casual viewers about the need to secure the crime scene, collect fingerprints, maintain an unbroken chain of custody, and so on.
3. *New York Times,* October 1, 1922. These troopers were Sergeant John J. Lamb, Corporal F. P. Spearman, and Henry L. Dickman. See Leo J. Coakley, *Jersey Troopers* (1971), 59-65.
4. *New York Times,* October 5, 1922.
5. *Ibid.,* October 3, 1922.
6. De Martini is described in Damon Runyon, "The Hall-Mills Case," *Trials and Other Tribulations* (1946), 73-75, and in Charles Boswell and Lewis Thompson, The Girl in Lover's Lane (1953), 141.
7. See De Martini's trial testimony, *New York Times,* November 27 and 28, 1926.
8. *New York Times,* November 7, 1926. Defense attorney Clarence E. Case pressed hard on Totten's uncertainty about the chain of custody of the state's exhibits. At one point Simpson admonished the court to remember that "this murder is four years old, and we will have a little trouble" [proving that the bullets introduced into evidence actually came from the body of Eleanor Mills]. Judge Parker replied, "We are quite aware that it is four years old, but that does not seem a good reason for disregarding the rules of evidence."
9. *Ibid.,* November 11, 1922.
10. *Ibid.,* November 13, 1922.
11. *Ibid.,* August 27, 1926.
12. It is worth noting that no matter how often the card had been handled by the police and the press, no matter how many unwarranted trips it had made, if Willie Stevens' fingerprint was undeniably on it, the only critical question--really the only question--would be how his fingerprint got there.

13. Fisher *et al.*, 14.
14. *New York Times Book Review,* February 2, 1964.
15. *New York Times,* November 14, 1926.
16. *Ibid.,* November 11, 1926.
17. *Identification Wanted: Development of the American Criminal Identification System, 1893-1943* (1977), 100-104.
18. *Ibid.,* 131, 138-139, 166-167.
19. Alexander Woollcott, *Long, Long Ago* (1943), 114-115.

10 Burial Now, Autopsy Later (pages 107-116)

1. *New York Times,* September 29, 1922. Dr. Long was also quoted as saying later in regard to Reverend Hall that "the cause of death was apparent and an autopsy was unnecessary." *New York Times,* September 30, 1922.
2. *Ibid.,* August 5, 7, and 11, 1926.
3. *Ibid.,* August 14, 1926.
4. William M. Kunstler, *The Minister and the Choir Singer* (1964), 8.
5. *New York Times,* October 1, 1922.
6. New Brunswick *Daily Home News,* September 21, 1922.
7. *New York Times,* November 7, 1922.
8. *Ibid.,* November 13, 1926.
9. *Ibid.,* November 11, 1926.
10. *Ibid.*
11. *Ibid.*
12. *Ibid.,* September 19, 1922.
13. *Ibid.,* September 20, 1922.
14. This is the same Dr. Smith who performed the operation on Mrs. Mills in January 1922, for which the church, through Reverend Hall, was gradually paying the bill.
15. *New York Times,* September 30, 1926.
16. *Ibid.,* November 10, 1926. For Dr. Hegeman's recollections more than half a century later, see Jane Spangler, "Murder for the Minister," *Central Jersey Monthly* (November 1979), 6-10. Dr. Hegeman concluded, "Someone really hated her. She was actually killed four times."
17. *Ibid.,* September 30, 1922.
18. *Ibid.,* November 11, 1926.

19. *Ibid.,* October 6, 1922.
20. *Ibid.* The abrasions could also have been caused when the killer or killers dragged the rector's body into its tableau position. Although he and the choir singer were murdered under the crab apple tree, their bodies were undoubtedly moved about somewhat to create the eerie scene.
21. *Ibid.,* September 19, 1922.
22. *Ibid.*
23. *Ibid.,* November 11, 1926.
24. *Ibid.,* October 6, 1922.
25. *Ibid.,* November 10, 1926. Dr. Otto H. Schultze, "a tall, well-built man in a double-breasted blue serge suit," made quite an impression on the jurors, defendants, and spectators at the trial. Even the stoic Mrs. Hall was shaken when, taking the witness stand, Dr. Schultze unveiled a rather gruesome-looking "mannikin." It was "a model of a head, neck, and the beginning of a shoulder of a human subject" brought in to represent the deceased Mrs. Mills. Dr. Schultze proceeded to trace the path of each bullet with a red crayon. For a detailed account of his testimony, see Kunstler, quoted above, 214-217.
26. Alexander Simpson's question came during his cross-examination of defendant Henry Stevens on November 20, 1926, as reported in the *New York Times,* November 21, 1926. The curious exchange between the two is covered in more detail in Chapter 17, "Like a Small Town Sport."

11 Bizarre Interlude (pages 117-125)

1. *New York Times,* October 10, 1922. For Nicholas Bahmer's purported occupation, see *Heidingsfeld's General Directory of New Brunswick, 1921-1922.*
2. *New York Times,* October 11, 1922. News accounts published on this date show how quickly the authorities could move when those being investigated were not prominent in local society. Nearly everything significant about the Schneider-Bahmer-Hayes fiasco was reported on this one date. The contrast with the real Hall-Mills investigation--slow, reluctant, and fumbling--is striking.
3. *Ibid.*

Panama hat that covered the rector's face. Except for the ardent love letters and Reverend Hall's fingerprint-enhanced calling card, much of the physical evidence in the Hall-Mills case was more sartorial than incriminating. (photo 1998)

Edward W. Hall's shoes. A box of trial evidence in Rutgers University's Special Collections and University Archives at Alexander Library contains Reverend Hall's shoes and other items of his and Mrs. Mills' clothing. (photo 1998)

4. *Ibid.*, November 21, 1926. This brief article concerning the rector's watch, which appeared during the trial, states that the amount of money stolen was twenty dollars. In fact, there is no way of knowing how much it was.

5. *Ibid.*, October 10, 1922.

6. *Ibid.*, October 11, 1922.

7. *Ibid.*

8. *Ibid.*

9. *Ibid.*, October 10 and 11, 1922.

10. *Ibid.*, October 11, 1922.

11. *Ibid.*, October 10, 1922.

12. *Ibid.*, October 11, 1922.

13. *Ibid.*

14. *Ibid.*

15. *Ibid.* Toolan termed it "utterly improbable that either Mrs. Mills or Hall would stay out until midnight unless something had already happened to them." Boswell and Thompson, *The Girl in Lover's Lane* (1953), 27.

16. William M. Kunstler, *The Minister and the Choir Singer* (1964), 50.

17. *New York Times*, October 11, 1922. The general theory of mistaken identity as an explanation for the murders was first voiced by Sally Peters, Mrs. Hall's confidante and frequent spokesperson. But nothing about the crime scene suggested mistaken identity. *Newark Evening News*, October 12, 1922.

18. *Ibid.*, October 11, 1922.

19. *Trenton Times*, October 11, 1922.

20. New Brunswick *Daily Home News*, October 11, 1922.

21. *New York Times*, October 11, 1922.

22. *Ibid.*, December 5, 9, and 16, 1922.

23. *Ibid.*, October 25, 1922. Pearl Bahmer recanted her accusation of incest against her father. In doing so, she said she had made the complaint against him because she feared he would have her sent to a correctional institution. Nick understandably disapproved of her relations with the married Raymond Schneider and had threatened to take action.

24. *Ibid.*, October 25, 1922, and November 21, 1922.

25. *Ibid.*, October 15 and 24, 1922.

26. *Ibid.*, October 18, 1922.

12 The Witness from Hell (pages 126-137)

1. *New York Times,* November 9, 1926.
2. *Ibid.,* October 18, 1922.
3. *New York Times,* editorial, October 11, 1922. The Hall-Mills case, said the *Times* editorial writer, "has been all along bungled. If the prosecutor of Somerset County has not made another mistake [in arresting Clifford Hayes], he will have to be congratulated upon a remarkable piece of detective work. But New Brunswick is thoroughly skeptical." So was the press in New Jersey and elsewhere.
4. *New York Times,* August 14, 1926. Ferd David is not mentioned by name as the person obliterating fingerprints in this pre-trial exchange between Simpson and George D. Totten. David is identified as the culprit four days later. *New York Times,* August 18, 1926. See also the *New York Times,* August 3 and 4, 1926, regarding the alleged wiping away of fingerprint evidence on the rector's eyeglasses.
5. *Ibid.,* October 3, 1926. The timing of Stricker's death led to rumors of suicide or some other misadventure, but there was no substance to the speculation. The ex-prosecutor died of natural causes in plain view of doctors and staff at Monmouth Memorial Hospital.
6. *Ibid.,* August 18, 1926.
7. *Ibid.,* August 31, 1926. William Fitzpatrick was dead by 1926, and this assertion comes from Jersey City detective John J. Underwood, whose dim view of the 1922 investigation can hardly be exaggerated. Whether Stricker gave such an order cannot now (and could not then) be determined. It is consistent with the Middlesex County prosecutor's reticence to do anything that might point the finger of guilt in an unwanted direction.
8. *Ibid.,* October 21, 1922.
9. *Ibid.,* February 7, 1930. For the text of Clarence Case's withering cross-examination regarding Mrs. Gibson's name, background, marriages, and so on, see the *New York Times* of November 19, 1926.
10. *Ibid.,* October 25, 1922.
11. *Ibid.,* October 31, 1922.
12. Diary-calendar page in Rutgers' Special Collections and University Archives. William M. Kunstler included a photograph of this page

in *The Minister and the Choir Singer,* pointing out that the prosecution had not introduced the page into evidence at the trial. His implication is that Mrs. Gibson's jottings all but destroy her credibility as an eyewitness. In a sense they do, but they also suggest that she was at or near the scene when the shots were fired, something the defense attorneys in 1926 vehemently denied.

13. *Ibid.* The last line of this entry reads "Willie [her son} 1.00," which has no apparent relevance to the murders.

14. *New York Times Book Review,* "Letters to the Editor" (March 1, 1964), 34.

15. *New York Times,* November 15, 1922. There was never any serious doubt about the authenticity of Mrs. Gibson's calendar-diary. The *Times* article states that detectives "found that the pencil marks with which the Sept. 9 notation had been made were covered with flyspecks and smudges, convincing them that the entry had been made on the date given and that it was not a fraudulent attempt to offset Mrs. Russell's story." William M. Kunstler, who fastens so firmly on Mrs. Gibson's calendar entries of September 14 and 17, ignores the entry of September 9, which shows that the conversation Nellie Lo Russell thought she had with Mrs. Gibson on the night of the murders actually took place a week earlier. By disregarding the Pig Woman's September 9 entry, Kunstler does precisely what he accuses Alexander Simpson of having done. When Timothy N. Pfeiffer learned of this diary (as it was being used in 1922 to refute Nellie Lo Russell's story), he naturally asked about the entry for September 14. When no one on the prosecution team would tell him what it said, he complained to the press: "It seems strange that this calendar-diary of Mrs. Gibson's was not mentioned before, when it might have given the authorities such valuable information as to just what did happen the night of September 14." At this juncture Pfeiffer must have realized that the Pig Woman's diary entry for September 14 did not adequately corroborate her baroque tale.

16. *Ibid.,* October 26 and 27, 1922. In late October 1922 Mrs. Gibson consistently stated that she saw two men and two women.

17. *Ibid.,* Mrs. Gibson told reporters, "I am positive that I could identify the murderer, even though there was no moon and the stars were dim." A reporter was prompted to ask, "Did you have a flashlight with you?" to which she replied, "No."

18. *Ibid.,* October 27, 1922.

19. *Ibid.,* November 8, 1922.
20. *Ibid.,* Mrs. Gibson did not claim to have seen these faces clearly under the crab apple tree, only at the intersection of Easton Avenue and De Russey's Lane.
21. *Ibid.,* November 1, 1922.
22. *Ibid.,* November 5, 1922.
23. *Ibid.,* November 29, 1922.

13 Two Henrys (pages 138-147)

1. *New York Times,* December 14, 1922.
2. Justice Parker's obituary in the *New York Times,* January 24, 1948, stresses his role in the Hall-Mills case and notes the high praise he received for his conduct of the trial. In his younger days Parker practiced law in Newark, Bayonne, and Jersey City. Appointed to the Supreme Court of New Jersey in 1907, he served on the state's highest court for forty years, retiring in 1947.
3. *New York Times,* October 28, 1922.
4. *Ibid.,* November 25, 1926.
5. *Ibid.*
6. *Ibid.*
7. Damon Runyon, "The Hall-Mills Case," *Trials and Other Tribulations* (1946), 46.
8. *New York Times,* October 28, 1922.
9. *Ibid.*
10. Rutgers' Special Collections and University Archives. A photograph of this diary entry appears in William M. Kunstler's *The Hall-Mills Murder Case* (1980), a Rutgers University Press reissue (with several new photographs) of *The Minister and the Choir Singer* (1964).
11. *New York Times,* October 22, 1922.
12. *Ibid.,* October 27, 1922.
13. The unpremeditated nature of the crime is a recurring theme in the investigations of both 1922 and 1926. For a typical expression of this theme, see the *New York Times,* November 8, 1922.
14. Biographical facts are from the obituary of Henry de la Bruyère Carpender, *New York Times,* May 27, 1934.
15. *New York Times,* November 12, 1922.

16. *Ibid.*
17. *Ibid.,* November 9, 1922.   On Sunday, November 12, Henry
    Carpender suffered an attack of acute appendicitis and was taken to
    Middlesex County Hospital, where his appendix was removed the
    next day.   His recovery from the operation extended through the
    end of the grand jury hearing, November 28, and he was not ques-
    tioned between those dates.
18. *Ibid.,* November 19, 1922.   Mott declared, "I do not say now, and I
    have never said, that I am confident of getting an indictment.   I
    shall simply do my duty by presenting my case to the grand jury."
19. *Ibid.*

14 Iago in the Vestry (pages 148-160)

1. Damon Runyon, "The Hall-Mills Case," *Trials and Other Tribula-
    tions (1946), 20, 21.*   Ralph V. Gorsline's obituary in the *New York
    Times,* September 29, 1945, provides some of the biographical
    information included in this chapter.
2. *New York Times,* November 7, 1926.   The only significant coat in
    the case is the one Mrs. Hall was wearing on the night of the mur-
    ders.   Early reports referred to it as gray, but Mrs. Hall called it
    "khaki-colored."   In view of the uncertainty, it seems puzzling that
    Simpson made no effort at the trial to clarify the shade of brown in
    this coat sent out for dyeing--was it tan?   fawn?   dark brown?
    Without knowing the answer to this question, the jury may well
    have viewed Mrs. Bearman's testimony as superfluous.
3. Runyon, 30.
4. *New York Times,* September 18, 1922.
5. *Ibid.,* November 12, 1922.   This article includes Charlotte Mills'
    tale of a two-year affair between her mother and Gorsline.
6. *Ibid.,* October 8, 1922.
7. *Ibid.,* October 17, 1922.
8. *Ibid.,* September 11, 1926.   This is an estimated distance from the
    Apperson to the crab apple tree made by the *New York Times* re-
    porter.   Gorsline is quoted by Catherine Rastall as having said to
    her on Saturday, September 17, 1922, when he and she, along with
    Gorline's daughter, Jean, and a Mr. Fick, visited the scene of the
    murders, "See how close we were.   If I had turned my spotlight on,

we could have seen what happened over this way." At the trial, however, both Gorsline and Rastall estimated the distance from the car to the crab apple tree at seven hundred feet. *New York Times*, November 5, 1926. One problem in estimating the distance accurately is that by 1926 De Russey's Lane had become Franklin Boulevard and the Phillips farm had become a housing development. The lovers' lanes were entirely obliterated.

9. *Ibid.*, November 9, 1922. Without naming names, the *Times* article outlines in detail the facts and inferences that special prosecutor Wilbur A. Mott would present to the grand jury.

10. The man was Jacob Van Pelt. See Chapter 27, "Stranger Than Fiction."

11. *New York Times*, November 5, 1926.

12. *Ibid.*, September 14, 1926.

13. *Ibid.*, September 29, 1945.

14. *Ibid.*, November 4, 1926.

15. *Ibid.*, October 19, 1922, and November 16, 1926. Eleanor's comments, along with the arrangement for exchanging letters, suggest that one letter at a time, not a collection of letters, went into the book.

16. *Ibid.*, November 9, 1922, and August 7, 1926.

17. *Ibid.*, October 13, 1922.

18. *Ibid.*, November 9, 1926.

19. *Ibid.*

15 A Tabloid Crusade (pages 161-170)

1. *New York Times*, September 16, 1924. When questioned by reporters in 1922, James Mills sometimes intimated that he knew who the culprit or culprits were and at other times insisted that he had no idea.

2. *Ibid.*, December 1, 1922. Pfeiffer's private investigator, Felix De Martini, did continue working on the case until March 1923, but it is hard to know what he was trying to accomplish. At the trial four years later, Simpson suggested that De Martini's four months of work had turned up nothing and implied that the main purpose of the probe was to try to implicate James Mills in the murders. "Q– You [De Martini] worked then, as far as I can learn from you,

those 121 days on Jimmy Mills. **A**--No, I would not say that--no."
New York Times, November 27, 1926. Despite this disclaimer, the
Million Dollar Defense, led by Robert H. McCarter, leaned heavily
(and unconvincingly) on the Jim Mills-as-killer theory.

3. *Ibid.,* December 5, 1922.
4. *Ibid.,* April 16, 1924.
5. *Ibid.,* November 7, 1926.
6. *Ibid.,* February 8, 1923.
7. *Ibid.,* April 16, 1924.
8. Another so-called "crime of the century" occurred in May 1924,
    the Leopold-Loeb thrill-killing of fourteen-year old Bobby Franks.
    Nathan Leopold and Richard Loeb, tried in Chicago, were sen-
    tenced to life imprisonment on September 10, 1924. See Edward
    W. Knappman, ed., *Great American Trials* (1994), 307-311.
9. Payne's career is traced in the *New York Times,* September 7, 1927,
    as a consequence of the crash of the monoplane *Old Glory* off the
    coast of Newfoundland in which Payne died, along with the pilot
    and navigator.
10. *New York Times,* July 17, 1926.
11. *Ibid.,* July 17, 1926. Notice that once again an alleged eyewitness,
    Louise Geist, deemed it necessary to provide Mrs. Hall with a
    driver to convey her to De Russey's Lane.
12. *Ibid.,* July 18, 1926. The judge was Peter F. Daly.
13. *Ibid.,* November 14, 1926.
14. *Ibid.*
15. *Ibid.,* July 29, 1926.
16. *Ibid.,* July 17 and 18, 1926.
17. *Ibid.,* June 8, 1927, and August 26, 1927.
18. Damon Runyon, "The Hall-Mills Case, *Trials and Other Tribula-
    tions* (1946), 84.
19. *New York Times,* November 13, 1926.
20. Bruce Bliven, "The Hall-Press-Mills Case," *The New Republic*
    (December 1, 1926), 39-40.
21. Calvin H. Goddard, a partner of Charles E. Waite, took the stand in
    Waite's place. His main contribution to the prosecution's case was
    to identify the fatal bullets as .32 caliber Peters, probably fired
    from a Colt automatic pistol, although Goddard qualified his testi-
    mony on that score because of the poor condition of the bullets.
    For Goddard's testimony see the *New York Times,* November 20,
    1926. Another of the witnesses who died between the date of the

murders and the date of the trial was Captain Michael Regan of Engine Company No. 3. Captain Regan knew Willie Stevens well, conversed with him frequently, and was more willing than many others in New Brunswick to try to assist in the investigation.
22. New Brunswick *Daily Home News,* July 21, 1953.

16 Jail for the Widow (pages 171-178)

1. *New York Times,* July 29, 1926.
2. *Ibid.* In 1922 Captain Lamb, then a sergeant, had been assigned to the case, and Mrs. Hall and Willie Stevens may have remembered him from that time.
3. *Ibid.* Researchers are indebted to Captain Harry Walsh for keeping a large collection of original news photos of the Hall-Mills trial. Walsh donated the album containing his collection to Rutgers University, where it is in the Special Collections and University Archives at Alexander Library. Most of the photos in this book are from Captain Walsh's collection.
4. Francis L. Bergen had replaced Azariah Beekman as Somerset County prosecutor after Beekman's death in 1926.
5. William M. Kunstler, *The Minister and the Choir Singer* (1964), 119.
6. *New York Times,* July 30, 1926.
7. *Ibid.* According to the *Times,* Judge Sutphen said the warrant had been issued after 10:00 p.m., rather than earlier in the day. But whenever the warrant was issued, the midnight arrest was unfortunate. The timing of it appeared to the public to be both pointless and callous. Not surprisingly, it evoked a good deal of sympathy for Mrs. Hall.
8. An article in *Time* magazine, November 15, 1926, reported, "Editor Payne had everything in the *Mirror* office for a story of the arrest of Mrs. Hall. He went to New Brunswick on July 28, accompanied by Captain Lamb of the State troopers, who arrested Mrs. Hall and hurried her away to Somerville, N.J."
9. *New York Times,* July 30, 1926.
10. *Ibid.*
11. *Ibid.* November 25, 1926. One of the two pasteboard boxes that Edwin R. Carpender carried from the Hall home and put in his

olive green Mercer contained clothes in which the rector was to have been buried. The other box was empty. Carpender went to the church and put Reverend Hall's vestments in the empty box. He then took both boxes to Hubbard's funeral home.

12. *Ibid.,* August 14, 1926; September 16, 1926.

13. *Ibid.,* November 4, 1926. A photo shows Mrs. Hall arriving at the courthouse accompanied by Commander Carpender. Biographical information on Arthur S. Carpender is from *Who Was Who in America,* Vol. 3.

14. *Ibid.,* July 30, 1926.

15. *Ibid.,* August 1, 1926.

16. *Ibid.,* July 31 and August 1, 1926.

17. *Ibid.*

18. New Brunswick *Daily Home News,* November 21, 1922.

19. *New York Times,* November 22, 1922.

20. Emily Post, whose book *Etiquette* has been continuously in print since 1922, was a year older than Frances Hall. She came from a wealthy and socially prominent family in Baltimore, Maryland. Her father was the architect who designed Quebec's famous Chateau Frontenac. See *Current Biography, 1941.*

21. *New York Times,* July 30, 1926.

22. *Ibid.,* July 31, 1926.

17 Like a Small Town Sport (pages 179-191)

1. Damon Runyon, "The Hall-Mills Case," *Trials and Other Tribulations* (1946), 13.

2. Somerville *Unionist-Gazette,* August 5, 1926.

3. Somerset *Democrat,* August 6, 1926.

4. *New York Times,* July 30, 1926.

5. This biographical information comes mainly from the Simpson obituaries in the New Brunswick *Daily Home News* of July 21, 1953, and the *New York Times* of the same date.

6. *Legislative Manual, State of New Jersey, 1922.*

7. *New York Times,* March 19, 1922, and July 31, 1926.

8. The trial testimony of Captain Walsh and Chief Hayes appears in the *New York Times,* November 17, 1926. Detective Underwood's testimony is in the *Times* of November 20, 1926.

9. *New York Times,* August 3, 1926.
10. William M. Kunstler, *The Minister and the Choir Singer* (1964), 129.
11. *New York Times,* August 3, 1926.
12. *Ibid.*
13. *Ibid.,* November 13, 14, 15, and 23, 1922. Nellie Lo Russell signed an affidavit on November 10, 1922, that, as William M. Kunstler says in his book, "completely contradicted [Mrs. Gibson's] story of what happened on the night of the murders." And so it did--but Mrs. Russell had gotten the date wrong. According to Mrs. Gibson's calendar-diary, the conversation about the missing dog had occurred the previous week. Since Kunstler presents the calendar-diary as "suppressed evidence uncovered by author" in regard to the entries of September 14 and 17, he should hardly dismiss it in regard to the entry of September 9.
14. Erling's testimony at the preliminary hearing is quoted at length in the *New York Times,* August 17, 1926. A brief excerpt of his trial testimony appears in the *New York Times* of November 9, 1926. The testimony of Jenny Lemford Wahler, a witness for the defense, is quoted in the *New York Times,* November 25, 1926.
15. *New York Times,* August 18, 1926. The affidavit was dated August 2, 1926.
16. *Ibid.,* November 25, 1926.
17. *Ibid.,* August 2, 1926.
18. See Mrs. Gibson's calendar-diary in Rutgers University's Special Collections and University Archives.
19. In 1922 Nellie Lo Russell had testified before the grand jury for twenty-five minutes, nearly as long as Charlotte Mills. Mrs. Russell emerged from the jury room wearing a broad smile, *New York Times,* November 23, 1922.   The press reported later that Mrs. Russell's testimony was a significant factor in the grand jury's refusal to indict.
20. *New York Times,* October 18, 1922.
21. See, for example, the *New York Times,* November 3, 1922. "There may have been a friendship between them," Jim allowed, "but it was a friendship of the mind. Rector Hall was a fine man. I know that my wife would never have done anything wrong."
22. *New York Times,* August 10, 1926.
23. *Ibid.,* November 11, 1926. The *Times* reporter saw Alpaugh as "an earnest, convincing witness."

24. *Ibid.*, November 14, 1926. Defense attorney Clarence E. Case asked on cross-examination why the Randalls had bothered to pay any attention to the parked Dodge. William F. Randall replied that his wife had said, "I wonder what is going on here?" and that both of them had looked closely at the car to see if they could find out.

25. Curiously enough, six weeks after the murders, special prosecutor Wilbur A. Mott stated in an interview that he had the probable murder weapon in his possession: "Q—Have you a pistol or revolver believed to have been the murder weapon? A—Yes. Q—Have you traced its ownership? A—I do not care to answer that." It is difficult to fathom why Mott responded as he did. The only weapon the prosecutor had in his possession was Willie Stevens' supposedly disabled .32 caliber revolver (later returned); but if that was the weapon that killed Reverend Hall and Eleanor Mills, surely Mott would have sought an indictment against Willie, and just as surely the grand jury would have regarded this gun as significant evidence.

26. The travels of the calling card and its much-disputed Willie Stevens fingerprint (genuine? forged? misidentified?) are covered in Chapter 9, "A Crackerjack Idea." The fate of the fingerprint evidence at the trial is dealt with in Chapter 20, "Simpson at Apogee."

27. This is an interpretation, of course. St. John's vestryman Gorsline and choir singer Rastall may have been a few hundred feet from the crime scene at the time of the murders by pure chance, but that seems more like the plot fabrication of a mystery novel than it does real life. For Gorsline's and Rastall's long withheld but still guarded disclosures, the see *New York Times*, September 11, 1926. It is worth noting that only Gorsline and Rastall, the Pig Woman, and Erling claim to have been in De Russey's Lane on the fateful night. The other witnesses, among them Alpaugh and Randall, were on Easton Avenue, some distance from where the murders occurred.

28. *New York Times*, September 18, 1926, and November 14, 1926.

18 Hippodroming (pages 192-203)

1. Somerville *Unionist-Gazette*, August 5, 1926. The *Unionist-Gazette*'s editorial was headlined "Bungled," a word used repeatedly in regard to the Hall-Mills case.

2. New Brunswick *Daily Home News,* September 18, 1922; July 31 and August 1 and 2, 1926.
3. *New York Times,* August 2, 1926.
4. *Ibid.,* August 3, 1926.
5. *Ibid.,* August 5 and 6, 1926.
6. *Ibid.,* August 6 and 7, 1926. Neither Mrs. Gildea nor Peter Tumulty lived in the Hall mansion. Mrs. Gildea's remarks about murder were allegedly overheard by Louis Geist, but during the 1926 investigation, Geist (by then Mrs. Riehl) denied hearing or quoting them.
7. *Hudson Dispatch,* August 9, 1926.
8. *Jersey Journal,* August 9, 1926.
9. *New York Times,* August 18, 1926. This is from the pretrial testimony of John J. Underwood, one of Simpson's Hudson County detectives. An earlier account had Willie saying exactly the opposite: "My God, I didn't expect this!" *New York Times,* August 13, 1926.
10. *Ibid.,* August 13, 1926. J. K. Rice, Jr., of Highland Park, a broker with whom Henry Carpender and his wife had had dinner on the night of the murders said, "It is a mystery to me why the authorities in the present and in the past investigations never in any way sought to get the story from me, my wife, or my son."
11. *Ibid.*
12. *Ibid.,* August 14, 1926. Since Jim Mills is on everyone's short list as the possible killer, it is useful to look at his reactions to events as they unfolded in 1922 and 1926. There is not the slightest hint of artifice. Jim was a simpleton in a way Willie Stevens never was.
13. *Ibid.,* November 18, 1922.
14. *Ibid.* The statement had a blank in place of Henry Stevens' name, but when an interrogator pressed Hamborszky, "I asked him who -- was, Hall answered ' * * * .'" The asterisks in the published statement of 1922 were filled in as "Henry Stevens" by Alexander Simpson four years later, *New York Times,* August 20, 1926.
15. *Ibid.* September 1, 1926.
16. *Ibid.,* August 20, 1926.
17. *Ibid.,* November 2 and 3, 1926.
18. *Ibid.,* September 3, 1926.
19. *Ibid.,* September 2, 1926. A speedometer was a factory option on Fords in those days. In Simpson's view, the lack of a speedometer,

Somerset County Courthouse today. Several famous trials have taken place here, but none with press coverage equal to that of the Hall-Mills trial. A play based on the case premiered in the upstairs courtroom in 1997. (photo 1997)

or odometer, merely meant that Stevens couldn't prove he *hadn't* driven 150 miles that night.

20. *Ibid.,* September 4, 1926.
21. *Ibid.,* September 16, 1926.
22. *Ibid.,* October 3, 1926.
23. Somerset *Unionist-Gazette,* August 19, 1926.
24. This claim, like so many others by Mrs. Gibson, was almost certainly false. A detailed sketch of Jane Gibson's life, with no mention of bareback riding, appears in the *New York Times,* August 14, 1926.

19 The Prosecution Begins (pages 204-217)

1. *New York Times,* November 4 through 20, 1926. Several of the witnesses were called to the stand more than once. Two of the prosecution's fingerprint experts, Edward A. Schwartz and Joseph A. Faurot, each made four appearances.
2. Morristown *Daily Record,* November 3, 1926.
3. Bruce Bliven, "The Hall-Press-Mills Case," *The New Republic,* December 1, 1926.
4. *New York Times,* January 24, 1948.
5. *Ibid.,* November 2 and 16, 1926.
6. Morris Markey, "A Reporter at Large: The Somerville Follies," *New Yorker* (November 20, 1926), 38. Major renovations of the Somerset County Courthouse occurred in the 1940s and again in the late 1990s. Inside the rotunda is a leaded glass oculus that has been there since 1909 when the courthouse was dedicated. The renovation of the 1990s included installing two clear sections of glass in the oculus. Contrasting noticeably with the surrounding colored glass, these two panes mark an incident that happened during the Hall-Mills trial, when an overzealous photographer tried to photograph the proceedings from the very top of the courthouse. His foot slipped through the glass, much to the annoyance of the presiding judge, Charles W. Parker. This incident is described in the playbill for *The Hall-Mills Murder Trial,* presented in November 1997 by the Somerset County Cultural & Heritage Commission.
7. *New York Times,* November 4, 1926.

8. *Ibid.*, November 23 and 24, 1926.

9. Charles Boswell and Lewis Thompson, *The Girl in Lover's Lane* (1953), 19.

10. *New York Times,* September 23, 1922.

11. *Ibid.* It may not be accurate to conclude that Charlotte was thinking only of Mrs. Hall as the jealous woman who wanted revenge. Reverend Hall, although married, attracted a small group of female admirers in his congregation besides Eleanor Mills, most notably Minnie Clark, who was active in the Sunday school. Investigators seemed to regard Mrs. Clark primarily as a busybody intent on exposing the sexual scandal involving Edward and Eleanor. Even so, just before the trial began, Alexander Simpson had Minnie Clark arrested as an accessory to the murders. What she was supposed to have done, other than spy on the lovestruck couple, remained hazy. At the time of the trial, to which her testimony contributed nothing, she was free on bail. *New York Times,* October 23 and November 17, 1926.

12. New Brunswick *Daily Home News,* August 5 and 27, 1926.

13. *New York Times,* August 11, 1926.

14. *Ibid.*, November 4, 1926. Charlotte's recollections were not always accurate. Timothy N. Pfeiffer would not have been at the Hall mansion this soon after the events at the Phillips farm. He was retained by Mrs. Hall ten days after the discovery of the bodies.

15. *Ibid.*, November 2, 1922. Mrs. Hall made this statement at a meeting for twenty-five newspaper reporters and four photographers arranged by her attorney, Timothy N. Pfeiffer. At one point in the interview a reporter quoted a remark that Mrs. Hall had supposedly made in reference to the murders--"This is an awful mistake." The widow said she had no recollection of having made such a remark.

16. *Ibid.*, November 13, 1926.

17. *Ibid.*, November 16, 1926.

18. *Ibid.*

19. *Ibid.*

20. *Ibid.* Questions still remained about the lovers' use of the Phillips farmhouse for their assignations, but there was never a suggestion that the couple used the house for overnight stays.

21. *Ibid.*, November 11, 1926. The emphasis in Case's tag line could have been on the word *you,* or it could have been on the word *know.* The *Times* transcript does not indicate the emphasis.

22. *Ibid.*
23. *Ibid.*
24. *Ibid.*, November 13, 1926.
25. Runyon, 40-41.
26. *New York Times,* November 13, 1926.
27. *Ibid.* The word *katzenjammer* comes from the German words for "cat" and "discomfort." Signifying "anguish" or "distress" as Louise Geist Riehl may have used it, the word had been popularized by the comic strip *The Katzenjammer Kids,* which first appeared in 1897.

20 Simpson at Apogee (pages 218-227)

1. *New York Times,* November 16, 1926.
2. *Ibid.* Soper's failure to identify the passengers in the touring car must have disappointed Simpson, who was sure they were Mrs. Hall, Willie Stevens, and Henry Stevens.
3. *Ibid.* It seems possible that Soper, in casual conversation, did tell Nixon that the three people in the car were Mrs. Hall and her two brothers, without actually knowing it to be true, and was therefore unwilling to make the same statement under oath.
4. *Ibid.*, November 14, 1926.
5. *Ibid.* This throwaway exchange gives a glimpse of the kind of clever, sarcastic questioning of which Simpson was a master. It probably went over better with juries in urban Hudson County than it did with the Hall-Mills jury in rural Somerset County.
6. Damon Runyon, "The Hall-Mills Case," *Trials and Other Tribulations* (1946), 90.
7. The reference to Case as "junior counsel" was not an isolated affront. Simpson used the term frequently.
8. *New York Times,* November 16, 1926.
9. Runyon, 51.
10. *New York Times,* November 24, 27, and 30, and December 2, 1926.
11. *Ibid.*, November 5, 1926.
12. *Ibid.*
13. Runyon, 19.
14. *New York Times,* November 5 and 7, 1926.

15. *Ibid.,* November 5, 1926.
16. James Mills had been fingerprinted in February 1923, on the very day the unindicted Mrs. Hall sailed for Europe. Mills was resentful that the Middlesex authorities, and those of Somerset to a lesser degree, had treated him as a bona fide suspect throughout the investigation while trying hard not to inconvenience or annoy the wealthy and socially prominent Hall-Stevens-Carpender families.
17. *New York Times,* November 30, 1926.
18. The text of the transcript in the *New York Times* shows the exhibit number as 37. It should be 17, for the reference is clearly to S-17, the fly-specked calling card of Reverend Hall.
19. *New York Times,* November 24, 1926.
20. *Ibid.,* November 30, 1926.
21. *Ibid.,* November 24, 1926.

21 A Liar, Liar, Liar! (pages 228-238)

1. *New York Times,* November 19, 1926.
2. *Ibid.* Although the *Times* articles of that period did not carry bylines, there is general agreement that Bruce Rae wrote this lead story. See Barbara Belford below.
3. Quoted in Barbara Belford, "Ishbel Ross," *Brilliant Bylines* (1986), 232.
4. Simpson's question seems contradictory. What he meant is that Mrs. Gibson had testified earlier to having seen Mrs. Hall and Willie Stevens in the glare of headlights as they entered De Russey's Lane on foot from Easton Avenue. According to her trial testimony, she did not see Willie under the crab apple tree.
5. *New York Times,* November 19, 1926.
6. *Ibid.*
7. Morristown *Daily Record,* November 5, 1926.
8. *New York Times,* November 19, 1926.
9. *Ibid.*
10. *Ibid.*
11. Jane Spangler, "Murder for the Minister," *Central Jersey Monthly* (November 1979), 10.
12. Damon Runyon, "The Hall-Mills Case," *Trials and Other Tribulations* (1946), 60.

13. *Random House Webster's College Dictionary* (1996), 1090.

14. Dr. Robert D. Hare, *Without Conscience: The Disturbing World of the Psychopaths Among Us* (1993), 33-70. The analysis in this chapter is based primarily on Dr. Hare's book. As he points out, the terms *psychopath* and *sociopath* are sometimes used interchangeably. When a distinction is drawn, it usually focuses on the determinants of antisocial behavior. Those who use the term *psychopath* consider the determinants to be psychological, biological, and genetic, while those using *sociopath* tend to emphasize social forces and early experiences. Some avoid using the word *psychopath* because they think many people mistakenly equate it with *psychotic*. The great majority of psychopaths are legally sane, while psychotics are not.

15. Hare, 34-35, 38, 59.

16. *Ibid.*, 40, 44, 46.

17. *Ibid.*, 58, 61, 62, 64, 148-149.

18. *Ibid.*, 34-35, 38, 44, 46, 58, 61, 64.

19. *New York Times,* December 3, 1926. "I don't know who committed this crime," Clarence Case said in his summation. "All that we know is that a crime was committed, but I lay before you for your consideration that this crime may have been committed by Mrs. Gibson herself." (See Chapter 24, "The State's Case Collapses.")

22 The Million Dollar Defense (pages 239-249)

1. *New York Times,* July 29, 1926.

2. *Ibid.*, May 31, 1941. See also *Who Was Who in America,* Vol. 1, 798.

3. *Ibid.*, September 4, 1961. This obituary noted that Case "splintered many a lance against civic wickedness in Hudson County in the days of Frank Hague, but he never succeeded in unseating the Jersey City political leader, although evidence adduced before the so-called Case committee in 1928 was sensational."

4. Damon Runyon, "The Hall-Mills Case," *Trials and Other Tribulations* (1946), 90.

5. *New York Times,* December 4, 1926. The lead article in the *Times* contains a photograph of the seven attorneys.

6. It should be noted that the widespread expectation among press and public that Willie Stevens would fall apart on the witness stand and thus rescue the prosecution's case was based on the tacit assumption that Willie had guilty knowledge of the crime. Had he known nothing, he could have revealed nothing.

7. Runyon, 61. See also *New York Times,* November 21, 1926.

8. *New York Times,* November 21, 1926.

9. Runyon, 65.

10. *New York Times,* November 21, 1926.

11. *Ibid.* Henry Stevens wife Ethel had a gear-shift Chandler, a seven-passenger touring car that Henry claimed he couldn't drive. According to him, both the Chandler and the Ford were in the Stevens' garage at Lavallette when the murders were committed.

12. *Ibid.*

13. *Ibid.* The New Brunswick *Daily Home News,* September 16, 1922, identifies the female victim only as "Mrs. James Mills," wife of the "assistant janitor of the Lord Stirling School and . . . sexton of the Church of St. John the Evangelist."

14. *Ibid.*

15. *Ibid.,* September 20, 1926.

16. *Ibid.,* November 11, 1926.

17. Runyon, 51.

18. *New York Times,* August 27, 1926.

19. James Thurber, "A Sort of Genius," *Hanging by a Thread* (1969), 456.

20. Runyon, 64.

21. *New York Times,* November 21, 1926. This talk of shots in the dark is apparently based on the Pig Woman's recollection that "the light went out." See her testimony, page 231. But surely the shooter would not switch off the flashlight before firing. And the three shots to Eleanor Mills' head could hardly have been fired blindly.

22. *Ibid.*

23. *Ibid.,* November 21 and 23, 1926.

23 Willie Comes Through (pages 250-262)

1. *New York Times,* November 24, 1926. Damon Runyon watched Willie carefully throughout the trial, commenting frequently on his

appearance and conduct. When the rector's love letters to Eleanor were being read into the record, "Willie Stevens listened with his head up. Willie misses very little that goes on in court, but his interest is that of a child. I am not so sure that Willie comprehends the gravity of this matter. His demeanor in court would indicate no great sense of responsibility." Damon Runyon, "The Hall-Mills Case," *Trials and Other Tribulations* (1946), 46.

2. *Ibid.*
3. See Chapter 5, "Willie the Fireman."
4. *New York Times,* September 18, 1926.
5. Henry B. Rothblatt, *Successful Techniques in the Trial of Criminal Cases* (1961), 82.
6. *New York Times,* November 24, 1926.
7. *Ibid.*
8. *Ibid.*
9. See James Thurber, "A Sort of Genius," *Hanging by a Thread* (1969), 459. Thurber seems to admire the mentally abnormal Willie for his clever sallies on the witness stand, yet he never mentions the Million Dollar Defense. He appears to think that Willie Stevens routed Alexander Simpson wholly on his own. Yet most, if not all, of Willie's zingers--the Bayard, Dr. Hall, and so on--were predictable opportunities for courteous correction. Surely the well-paid and talented defense team deserves some credit for Willie's fine performance.
10. Runyon, 70.
11. *New York Times,* November 24, 1926.
12. Rothblatt, 76.
13. *New York Times,* September 20, 1926. An unnamed source provided the *Times* with what was claimed to be the state's evolving theory of the crime. It held that Willie, frustrated at having the gun snatched from his hand, ran to the parked automobile and grabbed a pair of garden shears or clippers, which he later used to cut Eleanor Mills' throat. By the time of the trial Simpson seemed to favor a straight razor as the cutting tool. The *Times* reporter observed correctly that the state's theory "leaves Henry Carpender . . . out of the picture."
14. Runyon, 69.
15. *New York Times,* November 24, 1926.
16. Charles Boswell and Lewis Thompson, *The Girl in Lover's Lane* (1953), 18.

17. *New York Times,* November 23, 1926. The defense team put Dr. Runyon on the stand to refute the Dicksons' opening-day testimony about a stuttering epileptic whom they had misidentified as Willie Stevens. Simpson devoted much of his cross-examination to the general question of epilepsy. Case, on redirect, began to name some of the great epileptics of history, such as Napoleon and Julius Caesar. Simpson objected to this, and Judge Parker sustained the objection.

18. Dr. Richard McKeon of Newton, New Jersey, in personal communication. This is a tentative suggestion based on William Stevens' most obvious personality traits. Whatever Willie's mental disorder may have been, it did not prevent him from testifying with confidence, skill, and verbal facility. The startling contrast between the prior portrayal of him in the press as a laughable dimwit and Willie's actual showing on the witness stand made his sensible, polite responses all the more effective.

19. American Psychiatric Association, *Diagnostic and Statistical Manual of Mental Disorders, 4th* ed. (1994), 76-77.

20. Reginald Kavanaugh, "Classic in Horror Had Bloody Start Half-Century Ago," New Brunswick *Home News* (September 14, 1972). In this article about the recollections of Julius Bolyog concerning the Hall-Mills saga (forty-eight years after the murders), Kavanaugh quotes Bolyog to the effect that Willie did have a girlfriend, "a widow who lived with her teenage daughter on Somerset Street near City Alley. . . . He used to give her money, and he said he wanted to marry her and buy a farm out on 27 Highway." Bolyog's story about Willie's romance may or may not be true. What is undeniably true is that, owing to the reluctance of nearly everyone who had knowledge of the circumstances leading to the slayings (including Bolyog) to come forward at the time of the investigations, a great deal of information that would be ferreted out by the media today was successfully buried in 1922 and 1926.

21. See Chapter 5, "Willie the Fireman."

22. *New York Times,* November 23, 1926. The *Times* uses a long dash in place of the word *bitch.* Runyon, 69-70, has it as *b--h.* The exchange is mentioned in both sources, but only Runyon mentions the smile: "And Willie smiled at him from across the room as an old acquaintance."

24 The State's Case Collapses (pages 263-274)

1. *New York Times,* October 4 and 5, 1926. When the Hall-Mills case broke, the New Jersey State Police had been in existence for only a year. Dickman was a member of the first training class.
2. *Ibid.,* November 7, 1926.
3. *Ibid.,* November 20, 1926.
4. *Ibid.,* November 6 and 7, 1926. Mrs. Demarest also testified that she had once seen Minnie Clark and Ralph V. Gorsline spying on Reverend Hall and Eleanor Mills in Buccleuch Park. It was daylight at the time, and nothing improper was going on between Hall and Mills. They were sitting on a bench, Mrs. Demarest said, and the rector was showing the choir singer something in a book.
5. *Ibid.,* November 28, 1926.
6. Damon Runyon, "The Hall-Mills Case," *Trials and Other Tribulations* (1946), 83.
7. *New York Times,* November 28, 1926.
8. *Ibid.*
9. *Ibid.*
10. *Ibid.* Phillips was positive he had seen the woman in gray go into the Hall residence by herself. To the extent that anything is beyond dispute in this muddled affair, the accuracy of Phillips' objective, promptly reported observation probably is. It seems safe to assume that Mrs. Hall returned alone to 23 Nichol Avenue. Her solo arrival created a problem for both the defense (was Mrs. Hall lying about Willie having been with her, and, if so, why?) and the prosecution (what happened to Willie Stevens between the shooting and the homecoming?). Both sides dealt with the problem by ignoring it.
11. *Ibid.* For Totten's pretrial testimony on this interrogation of Mrs. Hall, see the *New York Times,* August 14, 1926.
12. *Ibid.*
13. Runyon, 77.
14. At the pretrial hearing Jim Mills testified that Mrs. Hall had said, "Oh, no [to his suggestion that their spouses had eloped], they are dead or they would come home," *New York Times,* August 17, 1926. The actual words spoken were quoted somewhat differently in different sources, but Simpson's assertion that Mrs. Hall had put the words "foul play," "together," and "dead" all in one brief, spon-

taneous sentence to Jim Mills is what Huckleberry Finn would have called "a stretcher."
15. *New York Times,* November 28, 1926.
16. *Ibid.*

25 Summations (pages 275-286)

1. *New York Times,* November 30, 1926.
2. *Ibid.* Although Van Doren signed the letter, he was not its author. Apparently it was written by Herbert B. Mayer of the New York *Daily Mirror* and Captain Harry Walsh of the Jersey City Police Department. It was typed by Mayer and delivered to Judge Cleary by George D. Totten, who at the time of the trial was employed by the *Daily Mirror.*
3. *Ibid.,* December 1, 1926.
4. Damon Runyon, "The Hall-Mills Case," *Trials and Other Tribulations* (1946), 80.
5. Runyon, 81.
6. *New York Times,* December 2, 1926.
7. Runyon, 84.
8. *New York Times,* December 2, 1926.
9. *Ibid.*
10. Runyon, 83.
11. *Ibid.*
12. *New York Times,* December 3, 1926. Gossip in New Brunswick about an intended lovers' flight to Japan or China, presumably an elopement, made the rounds early on in the 1922 investigation. No credible evidence of such a plan appears to have been uncovered. Both McCarter and Simpson mentioned a possible flight to Japan in their summations. See the *New York Times,* September 26, 1922, for some commentary on the rumored flight.
13. *Ibid.*
14. *New York Herald Tribune,* December 3, 1926. The *Herald Tribune's* coverage of the Hall-Mills case was less complete than that of the *Times,* but it was substantial. Ishbel Ross lived in a small apartment on Manhattan's East 76th Street with her husband, the brilliant *Times*man Bruce Rae, who also covered the Hall-Mills case (but without a byline). Both maintained that they never discussed

the trial while they were writing about it. See Barbara Belford, "Ishbel Ross," *Brilliant Bylines* (1986), 233.

15. *New York Times,* December 3, 1926.
16. *Ibid.*
17. Runyon, 90.
18. *New York Times,* December 3, 1926.
19. *Ibid.*
20. Runyon, 91.
21. *New York Times,* December 3, 1926. Senator Case's analysis of Mrs. Gibson's testimony and her motives for it seem basically correct. No psychologists or psychiatrists ("alienists" as they would have been called in the 1920s) appeared as expert witnesses for either side--unfortunately, because both the Pig Woman and Willie Stevens needed to have their heads examined if any kind of truth about the crime and its aftermath were to be arrived at. Although Case's summation portrayed the "untruthful" Mrs. Gibson in acerbic detail, his picture of Willie, while accurate as far as it went, avoided probing, or even mentioning, the less sunny aspects of Willie's personality. As for Simpson, he had no evident strategy toward the eccentric bachelor except to avoid "bullyragging" him.
22. *Ibid.*
23. Runyon, 92.
24. *New York Times,* December 4, 1926.
25. Runyon, 96. Jurors Nos. 2 and 6 were both named Young. Juror No. 2 was John W. Young, a sixty-year-old farmer from Middlebush. Simpson's mistrial affidavit charged him with sleeping during Jane Gibson's testimony. The affidavit is reprinted in the *New York Times,* December 1, 1926. Juror No. 6 was Raymond Young, a thirty-five-year-old farmer from Skillman. The members of the jury are identified by name, number and occupation in the *New York Times* of November 4, 1926, and again in the *Times* of December 4, 1926. In the latter listing Raymond Young's age is shown as twenty-five rather than thirty-five.
26. *New York Times,* December 4, 1926.
27. *Ibid.*
28. Runyon, 93.
29. *New York Times,* December 4, 1926. The quotation is not from Byron but from William Congreve: "Heaven has no rage like love to hatred turned,/Nor hell a fury like a woman scorned."

THE NEW YORK TIMES, SATURDAY, DECEMBER 4, 1926.

'NOT GUILTY' IS VERDICT IN HALL CASE; PLAN TO FREE PRISONERS ON BAIL TODAY AND PROBABLY QUASH ALL OTHER CHARGES

JURY OUT FOR FIVE HOURS

Mrs. Hall Calm at News, Willie Stevens Beams, Henry Near Tears.

SIMPSON FOR NEW TRIAL

But Moore Says State Has Gone Far Enough and Won't "Persecute."

THREE BALLOTS BY JURORS

Mrs. Gibson's Story Not "Real" to Them—Impressed by Widow on Stand.

Mrs. Frances Stevens Hall and her brothers, Henry Stevens and Willie Stevens, were acquitted last night of the murder of Mrs. Eleanor R. Mills. The jury rendered its verdict after five hours and eight minutes of deliberation in the court house at Somerville, N. J.

Assistant Attorney General Alexander Simpson, who had pilloried the defendants earlier in the day in his summing up, quickly announced that he would recommend to Governor A. Harry Moore that the defendants go to trial on the indictment accusing them of the slaying of the Rev. Edward W. Hall. Senator Simpson, who had not awaited the verdict, said the result had been no surprise to him. He said that it had "been evident that the State could not get a fair trial in Somerset County."

Confident that the prosecutor's plea for more court action would fail, the attorneys for the defendants applied to Supreme Court Justice Charles W.

Mrs. Hall 'Glad at Vindication in Court After Four Years of False Accusation.'

The following statement was issued last night for Mrs. Hall by Robert H. Neilson of defense counsel, who is a cousin of the widow:

My brothers and I are very glad, after four years of gossip and false accusations, to have had this opportunity to face the situation in open court, to have personally gone on the witness stand and submitted ourselves to thorough cross-examination and to have obtained complete vindication through the verdict of a Somerset County jury.

The testimony of the witnesses has been broadly distributed daily through the public prints and we believe the verdict will have full approval throughout not only New Jersey but the United States.

We shall not be able personally to acknowledge the many kind letters we have received and we shall appreciate it if the press will give this word of thanks to their writers.

Parker for a hearing on bail. They asked that Mrs. Hall, her brothers and the fourth person named in the indictment, Henry de la Bruyere Carpender, who has been scheduled to be tried on the Mills indictment later, be released under bonds. Justice Parker said he would hear the application at 10 A. M. today. He telegraphed to Senator Simpson, directing him to be present.

Simpson to Consult Moore.

The special prosecutor was obdurate on the bail plea also. He said that he would not commit himself on whether or not he would oppose bail until he had discussed that and the need for prosecution of the second indictment at a conference with Governor Moore.

Although Senator Simpson took a determined stand for future prosecution, Attorney General Edward L. Katzenbach expressed the view in Trenton last night that the bail application for the defendants should be granted and that Mr. Simpson should not oppose it. He so notified Senator Simpson in a telegram. Attorney General Katzenbach added that the remaining indictment should be disposed of "as speedily as possible." He admitted that the quickest way to dispose of them would be for the State to nolle-pros them. He will be at the bail hearing in Somerville this morning.

Governor Moore would not comment on the verdict. He was asked what his attitude was with regard to further trials.

"I think the State has gone far enough," he said. "We are prosecuting, not persecuting. However, I am to confer tomorrow morning with Senator Simpson and then I shall know better what course is to be pursued."

Mrs. Hall received the news of her vindication with the same remarkable composure that marked her demeanor

during the twenty-four days of court sessions. She had entered the court room with quick steps and settled herself in the chair to await the decision of the twelve men. Her face seemed whiter than usual, but the same faint smile played about her lips. When the verdict was given—a verdict of "Not Guilty" was given to each defendant individually—the smile spread.

Henry Stevens, the ruddy-faced man of the outdoors, had strained forward when the jury reported on him. As he heard the welcome words tears came into his eyes. He slumped in his chair and then sat erect, wiping his eyes with his handkerchief. A great smile wreathed his face, as he clasped the hand of his wife, who moved over to stand behind his chair, patting his shoulder.

Willie Stevens Beams.

It was Willie Stevens, the greatest witness of the trial, who showed the greatest delight. He had walked into court somewhat blankly as the defendants were called to hear the verdict. His large, brown eyes had fastened with intense eagerness on the jury. But when the words proclaiming him innocent were heard, Stevens's face was all abeam. He looked happily about the court and, although it had seemed an impossibility, the beam grew greater.

Subsequently, after the excitement in the court had died down and the defendants had gone back to the jail, where Mrs. Hall chatted for a few minutes before returning to her home in New Brunswick, the defense issued a statement for Mrs. Hall expressing the gratitude of Mrs. Hall and her brothers for their vindication in a court of law.

When Mrs. Hall, speeding through the snow flurries, reached her home in New Brunswick, she appeared radiant. She hurried from the auto-

Continued on Page Ten.

30. *New York Times,* December 4, 1926.
31. *Ibid.*
32. *Ibid.*

26 Money Can Buy Anything (pages 287-293)

1. *New York Herald Tribune,* December 4, 1926.
2. *New York Times,* December 4, 1926. The lead story in the *Times,* uncredited but presumably written by Bruce Rae, has a subhead reading "Three Ballots by Jurors," and the article tallies the votes on each of the three. The lead story in the *New York Herald Tribune,* credited to Ishbel Ross, Rae's wife, is headlined "Mrs. Hall and Brothers Acquitted/On Second Ballot, Jury Out Five Hours;/State Ready to Drop Whole Case." This startling discrepancy tends to support two propositions: (1) Rae and Ross, husband and wife, really did refrain from exchanging information in their reporting, as they always maintained. (2) Even good newspaper reporting must be viewed with caution unless it is corroborated by other or later accounts.
3. William M. Kunstler, *The Minister and the Choir Singer* (1964), 302.
4. *New York Herald Tribune,* December 4, 1926.
5. Kunstler, 308.
6. *New York Times,* December 4, 1926.
7. *New York Herald Tribune,* December 4, 1926. The consultation never took place. Despite Simpson's talk of getting a foreign jury to try the three defendants for Hall's murder, and his repeated promise to try Henry Carpender, Simpson had no intention of doing either.
8. *New York Times,* December 5, 1926.
9. *Ibid.,* December 4, 1926.
10. *Ibid.* Charlotte, in her role as a reporter for a news syndicate, was in the courtroom when the verdicts were announced. See *New York Herald Tribune,* December 4, 1926.
11. *Ibid.,* December 5, 1926.
12. *Ibid.*
13. *Ibid.* Mrs. Hall also thanked Dunster effusively, but according to the *Times,* it was Willie to whom the jury foreman made his self-effacing comment. See Kunstler, 307-308.

27 Stranger Than Fiction (pages 294-303)

1. William M. Kunstler, *The Minister and the Choir Singer* (1964), 331. The Ku Klux Klan of the 1920s was not the terroristic "Invisible Empire" of the post-Civil War era. Although still white-supremacist and anti-Catholic, as its predecessor had been, it became a quasi-mainstream political power throughout the United States in the 1920s. Its klaverns sometimes took extreme measures, but seldom resorted to murder. And as Kunstler implicitly acknowledges, they almost never left any doubt as to who had committed their acts. This second Klan was preoccupied with civic boosterism and self-promotion.

2. Barry A. J. Fisher *et al.*, *Techniques of Crime Scene Investigation*, 4th ed. (1987), 21.

3. Vincent Bugliosi, *Outrage* (1996). This entire book, subtitled *The Five Reasons Why O. J. Simpson Got Away with Murder*, stresses the crucial importance of the prosecutor's explaining evidence to the jury in a clear, thorough, and orderly way.

4. Gay Talese, *The Kingdom and the Power* (1969), 342.

5. James Thurber, "A Sort of Genius," *Hanging by a Thread* (1969), 451.

6. *New York Times*, October 26, 1922.

7. Paula S. Fass, *The Damned and the Beautiful* (1977), 21.

8. James Truslow Adams, "Our Dissolving Ethics" *Atlantic Monthly* (November 1926), 579.

9. Jules Abels, *In the Time of Silent Cal* (1969), 208.

10. *New York Times*, November 22, 1922.

11. *Ibid.*, November 3, 1926.

12. *Ibid.*, October 21, 1926.

13. *Ibid.*, September 18, 1922. On this second day of major press coverage it was reported that "telegrams had been received from clergymen all over the country, declaring the confidence of the senders in the slain man. Many of these telegrams, it was said, came from clergy high in the Episcopal Church who were attending the Protestant Episcopal convention in Portland, Ore., all of whom knew Dr. Hall."

14. Such fears can only be inferred, but some of the actions (and in-actions) of the doctors, undertakers, and detectives suggest that the prominence of the Halls and the nature of the rector's death made a number of people in New Brunswick and Somerville uneasy.

15. Some kind of cover-up indisputably occurred. The persons who knew the identity of the killer or killers, including the actual shooter and anyone else at the immediate crime scene, were either lying or not talking. It is impossible to know how many people had positive knowledge of the events under the crab apple tree, but over time there may have been quite a few.

16. Charges of threats and bribery were commonplace. Simpson saw the villain in this regard as Felix De Martini, the chief private detective hired by the defense. There is no question that someone or something spooked William Phillips, night watchman at the New Jersey College for Women, whose spotting of Mrs. Hall returning to her home early on the morning of September 15, 1922, created something of a hurdle for the defense. Phillips told a prompt and straightforward story in 1922. Four years later his memory failed him badly. Simpson was convinced that the two live-in Hall maids, Louise Geist and Barbara Tough, had been bribed. It was the alleged bribery of Geist, who by 1926 was Mrs. Riehl, that set off the crusade of the New York *Daily Mirror* to have the case reopened. Among the prosecution witnesses, a few--Henry L. Dickman, William Garvin, and Frank Caprio come to mind--clearly hoped to gain something from giving what appeared to be false testimony.

17. Mrs. Jane Gibson, the Pig Woman, was both a liar and a publicity seeker. So too, in all likelihood, was Paul F. B. Hamborszky, the ex-clergyman who told of his lengthy, hard-to-believe conversations with Reverend Hall. Hamborszky, who was interested in the reward money, appeared on Simpson's list of prosecution witnesses, but rather than commit perjury, or so it would seem, he disappeared on the eve of the trial.

18. Several prosecution witnesses fit this category, among them John and Charlotte Dickson, who mistakenly thought they had seen Willie Stevens in North Plainfield on the night of the murders, and Marie Demarest, who thought she had seen Henry Stevens in New Brunswick on the Saturday morning following the murders. It should be acknowledged, though, that Henry Stevens *could* have been in New Brunswick early on Saturday, September 16, and still not have participated in the crime, if Mrs. Hall had phoned him at Lavallette on Friday to tell him of the lovers' lane murders the previous evening.

19. Given the nature of the profession, it is probably unfair to call even an overzealous attorney a liar. Nevertheless, it seems fair to say

that no prudent lawyer could have believed the tales of Mrs. Gibson, Frank Caprio, William Garvin, and Henry L. Dickman; or could have believed that Case spoke with complete candor when he said he considered Mrs. Gibson to be a credible murder suspect.

20. *New York Times*, August 3, 1926.
21. *Ibid.*, December 4, 1926.
22. *Ibid.*, November 24, 1926.
23. See Simpson's cross-examination of Henry Stevens, *New York Times*, November 21, 1926.
24. *New York Times*, October 8, 1922.
25. *Ibid.*, September 12, 1926.
26. *Ibid.*, September 11, 1926. An anonymous tip may have helped to convince Simpson that Gorsline and Rastall had been near the scene of the slayings. See the *New York Times*, September 17, 1926.

28 Theories of the Crime (pages 304-315)

1. *New Yorker* (December 4, 1926), 23.
2. Morristown *Daily Record*, December 4, 1926.
3. Dorothy Dix, "A Nation of Detectives," *New York Evening Post*, November 18, 1926. Reprinted in Barbara Belford, *Brilliant Bylines* (1986), 79.
4. *Ibid.*
5. *Ibid.*
6. See McCarter's cross-examination and summation, *New York Times*, November 6, 1926, and December 2, 1926.
7. Nick Pelino, Jr. *The Final Word: The Hall-Mills Murders*. Play presented at the Somerset Valley Playhouse, Hillsborough, NJ, October 14 and 15, 1994.
8. *New York Times*, October 19, 1922.
9. Dix, 81.
10. William M. Kunstler, *The Minister and the Choir Singer* (1964), 331.
11. Dix, 81
12. Kunstler, 330.
13. Marc Mappen, "Passion in the Parish," *Rutgers University Magazine* (Winter 1992), 19.
14. Richard K. Tucker, *The Dragon and the Cross* (1991), 67, 81. For a brief history of the Klan in New Jersey, see David M. Chalmers,

Hooded Americanism: The History of the Ku Klux Klan (1965), 243-253. Chalmers portrays the New Jersey KKK as having fairly benign objectives--"'the return to the teachings of our mothers' . . . the virtues of Protestant fundamentalism, Prohibition, and opposition to the Roman Catholic Church." The Klan in the Garden State "was on the receiving end and more the object rather than the doer of violence." It was not the lynch-law Klan of the Reconstruction South.

15. Kunstler, 334. Kunstler's answer to the Klan's silence is that "the knowledge that there is no statute of limitations for murder in New Jersey would certainly curb the tongues of even the most loquacious survivors." That does not ring true. When a large number of people, or even a small number, are involved in a conspiracy, it is all but impossible to keep critical information from leaking out. The history of crime is replete with examples of conspiracies that failed because one or more participants were unable to keep from talking.

16. Dix, 81.

17. Kunstler, 318.

18. Dix, 81.

19. Variations on the blackmail theme are reported in the *New York Times* of October 15 and 16, 1922, and November 8, 1922.

20. See the New Brunswick *Home News,* September 14, 1972. It is arguable that the payoff, if there was one, was made to compensate the two men, "Ike" and "Freddie," not for committing the murders but rather to buy their silence about Willie's having approached them earlier with an offer to pay them to slay the rector. The seventy-year-old Bolyog suggested that such an offer had been made.

21. Kunstler, 321.

22. *New York Herald Tribune,* December 3, 1926.

23. Kunstler, 318.

24. *New York Times,* November 11 and 13, 1926 (Barbara Tough's testimony); November 13, 1926 (Louise Geist Riehl's testimony) Barbara Tough stated that she did not see Willie at all that day. Louise Geist Riehl testified that she went to bed "sometime between nine and ten." Mrs. Hall's testimony as to Willie's bedtime is vague, *New York Times,* November 30, 1926.

25. Willie could not drive a car, and no one saw him on the trolley that night. Nor did anyone see him walking toward the Phillips farm. Either he was in bed, as he said, or someone drove him to the lovers'

rendezvous.
26. Sir Arthur Conan Doyle, "A Scandal in Bohemia," (1887).

29 No Fierce Beast (pages 316-330)

1. New Brunswick *Daily Home News,* November 4, 1926. This article contains a partial transcript of Totten's testimony. The more detailed coverage in the *New York Times* does not contain this segment of the transcript.
2. *Newsweek* (February 24, 1964), 92. The reviewer of William M. Kunstler's book, *The Minister and the Choir Singer,* refers to the Hall-Mills case as a "perfect crime."
3. *New York Times,* August 17, 1926. Gorsline, not surprisingly, claimed that "actual wrongdoing between Dr. Hall and Mrs. Mills never was suspected" by the vestry or other members of the congregation, *New York Times,* September 14, 1926.
4. *Ibid.,* September 17 and 18, 1926. The person making this allegation was Mrs. Marie Demarest, a member of the St. John's choir who testified for the prosecution. Mrs. Demarest, who was tall, plump, and belligerent, did not prove to be an effective witness.
5. *Ibid.,* October 18, 1922.
6. As indicated in Chapter 24, "The State's Case Collapses," there is some question about this phone call having actually been made. The afternoon call formed a part of Mrs. Hall's alibi at the trial, suggesting that she knew her husband's purported reason for going out on the night he was slain but did not know his destination.
7. *New York Times,* November 13, 1926.
8. *Ibid.,* October 19, 1922.
9. Of the eleven letters from "D.T.L" (Edward Hall) that Charlotte found at 49 Carman Street after her mother's death, six of them mention "our road" and one specifies "our road beyond Parker home." All these letters appear to have been written in August at Islesford, Maine, or afterwards. Thus, anyone intercepting the Babykins-Wonder Heart correspondence would be reminded again and again of the lovers' usual meeting place. Minimal spying would be needed to locate the exact trysting spot. Transcripts of these letters are in Rutgers' Special Collections and University Archives.
10. Even though the Iver-Johnson might have been capable of firing the fatal bullets if it were in working condition--and even though its

firing pin might have been filed off *after* the shootings--it seems inconceivable that the murderer would have brought the weapon back to the Hall mansion and made it available to investigators. Very probably Mrs. Hall's story about the Iver-Johnson was true. The revolver was not in working order and had not been fired in some time.

11. Simpson's expert witness on bullets and arms, Calvin H. Goddard, was positive that the bullets were all fired from the same weapon, but he was not entirely sure it was a Colt pistol. He testified that "the markings on the bullets are distorted by impact with whatever objects they passed through. . . . However, a summary of my measurements of all the bullet markings link them up with bullets fired through the Colt pistol, rather than those fired through any other type of pistol, but I do not wish to make that statement without some qualification on account of the poor condition of the bullets," *New York Times,* November 20, 1926.

12. Willie's ability to shoot can only be inferred. He owned the .32-caliber Iver-Johnson revolver (often misreported as a .38) as well as a small-bore rifle. Beyond that, neither the prosecution nor the press seems to have pursued the matter of his gun use or his marksmanship very far.

13. *New York Times,* November 11 and 14, 1926. The witnesses who saw a Dodge parked on De Russey's Lane on the night of the murders were Charles Alpaugh, a bus driver, and William F. Randall, a rural mail carrier. They did not see the Dodge there at 10:20 p.m., however, but at about midnight (see footnote #20). No reliable eyewitness testified to having seen a Dodge sedan (or any other car except Gorsline's Apperson) at the scene of the crime at the time of the crime. This obviously does not preclude the Dodge's having been there. It means only that, three or four days after the murders, no one recalled seeing a rather ordinary car parked on a rather busy road at a specific time in the evening.

14. *Ibid.,* November 5, 1926.

15. Details of the two autopsy reports appear in the *New York Times* of September 30 and October 6, 1922, and October 29 and November 10 and 11, 1926. Dr. Otto H. Schultze's testimony on November 9, 1926, about the path of the three bullets is somewhat puzzling. One of the bullets, according to Dr. Schultze, took a downward course, one bullet went directly backward, and one took an upward course. Witnesses testified that the shots were fired in rapid succession, and,

as the autopsies indicated, any one of the three shots would have been fatal. Perhaps the impact of each bullet or the collapse of Mrs. Mills' lifeless body accounts for the differing bullet tracks.

16. *New York Times,* August 27, 1926. See also James Thurber, "A Sort of Genius," *Hanging by a Thread* (1969), 456.

17. *Ibid.,* November 4, 1922.

18. New Brunswick *Daily Home News,* September 21, 1922.

19. *New York Times,* October 26, 1922.

20. Charles Alpaugh and William F. Randall (see footnote #13) testified to having seen a Dodge sedan parked on Easton Avenue at about midnight on the night of the murders. What they saw at that hour may have been Mrs. Hall's Dodge on its *second* trip to the Phillips farm, the trip to check on Willie's efforts to tidy up the crime scene. And note: If Henry (Harry) Carpender (or even Henry Stevens) accompanied Mrs. Hall on this midnight journey to the crime scene, it is within the realm of possibility that the Pig Woman--if she returned later that night to the crab apple tree, as she maintained--actually did hear Mrs. Hall moan, "Oh, Henry" (or "Oh, Harry"), but heard it more than an hour and a half after the fatal shots were fired. Such a confluence of events seems far-fetched, but it would help to explain Mrs. Gibson's initial identification of Henry Carpender as the man she saw with something "glittering" in his hand, and it would also help to explain why she kept insisting on the "Oh, Henry" quote even as she was changing other parts of her story at will.

21. The possibility of an ordinary pocket knife as the instrument used to cut Eleanor Mills' throat was mentioned but apparently not pursued in 1922. "It is believed that the woman did it [cut Eleanor's throat] with a small pocket knife borrowed from her companion," *New York Times,* November 9, 1922. Several other possibilities were mentioned in 1922 and 1926 and seem to have been taken more seriously, including a straight razor, a keen-edged knife of an unnamed type, and even a pair of garden shears. Yet many men carried pocket knives in the 1920s, and a reasonably sharp pocket knife could have inflicted the wounds on Mrs. Mills' throat. Nor would it have had to be taken to the scene for that purpose, since Willie would have been (or could have been) carrying it with him anyway.

22. *New York Times,* November 14, 1926.

23. The wily but coincidence-plagued Ralph V. Gorsline was not driving the Apperson when it burst into flames. The driver was Alfred

Doucet, owner of the parking garage where Gorsline kept the car. See Chapter 14, "Iago in the Vestry." See also the *New York Times,* October 13, 1922.

24. *New York Times,* November 25, 1926. Agnes Blust's testimony reinforced Jim Mills' observation four years earlier that Eleanor "often copied passages from [books of romance] and that she used to carry them in a brown scarf. . . . I am certain that the letters were never mailed. They probably were in her scarf when she left here Thursday evening. . . ," *New York Times,* September 18, 1922. Mrs. Harkins' observations were reported in the *New York Times,* August 6, 1922. She did not testify at the trial. Simpson's assumption that Mrs. Hall brought the damning letters to the Phillips farm, plausible as it may appear, was probably wrong. The best bet is that Eleanor Mills carried the eleven love letters from Carman Street to the Phillips farm.

25. *New York Times,* September 18, 1922.

26. *Ibid.* Naturally, they mailed their love letters when Edward Hall was away from New Brunswick. The Islesford letters, though not the Islesford diary entries, were mailed. See the *New York Times,* October 20, 1922, and November 14, 1926.

27. Albert J. Cardinal, the New Brunswick *Daily Home News* reporter who was among the first to reach the scene of the crime after the New Brunswick police had been alerted, wrote in his first account that "several letters written in lead pencil appearing to be addressed to Rev. Mr. Hall lay about in confusion as though the bodies had been searched," *Daily Home News,* September 16, 1922. Somerset County detective George D. Totten agreed with Cardinal, *New York Times,* November 11, 1926. But the Somerset County sheriff, Bogart T. Conkling, who arrived at the crab apple tree along with Totten, disagreed. Conkling said the letters were in a neat packet between the bodies, *New York Times,* August 6, 1926. At the trial, however, Sheriff Conkling repudiated his earlier statement and agreed that the letters were strewn about, *New York Times,* August 14, 1926.

28. *New York Times,* August 4, 1926. Although Simpson's excoriation of the 1922 investigation was justified, that does not excuse his own conduct four years later. Simpson's case was probably unwinnable, but his reliance on the publicity-entranced Pig Woman and a knot of self-serving perjurers did not enhance his prospects.

30 Ever After (pages 331-342)

1. Alexander Woollcott, *Long, Long Ago* (1943), 116.
2. Frederick Lewis Allen, *Only Yesterday* (1931), 214
3. William M. Kunstler, *The Minister and the Choir Singer* (1964), 317-319.
4. Vincent Bugliosi, *Outrage* (1996), 239.
5. New Brunswick *Daily Home News*, December 20, 1942, and *New York Times*, December 20, 1942.
6. James Thurber, "A Sort of Genius," *Hanging by a Thread* (1969), 461.
7. *New York Times*, March 16, 1927.
8. *Ibid.*, August 16, 1927.
9. *Ibid.*, September 7, 8, and 13, 1927.
10. Woollcott, 116. There are a few factual errors in the Woollcott piece, and this $50,000 settlement may be one of them. The *New York Times* always reported the sum as undisclosed.
11. Charles Boswell and Lewis Thompson, *The Girl in Lover's Lane* (1953). The authors do not propose a solution to the mystery. A fictional treatment, *Murder of the Clergyman's Mistress,* by Anthony Abbott, was published in 1931. Another fictional retelling of the case, *The Crime,* by Stephen Longstreet, appeared in 1959.
12. New Brunswick *Daily Home News*, February 7, 1930. William Easton is misidentified in the headline and throughout a two-column feature article as James Easton.
13. *New York Times*, February 11, 1930.
14. *Ibid.*, January 1, 1927.
15. *Ibid.*, November 1, 1930.
16. *Ibid.*, November 3, 1930.
17. New Brunswick *Daily Home News*, July 21, 1953.
18. *New York Times*, July 21, 1953.
19. *Ibid.*, January 1, 1927.
20. *Ibid.*, January 24, 1948. Charles A. Lindbergh, Jr., was the maternal grandson of Dwight W. Morrow, the man who defeated Alexander Simpson in the U.S. Senate race of 1930. Morrow's daughter, Anne Spencer Morrow had married "Lucky Lindy" in 1929.
21. *Ibid.*, February 13, 1971. Catherine Rastall, who accompanied Ralph V. Gorsline to the Phillips farm on the night of the murders, outlived Pfeiffer by twenty years, dying in February 1991 at the age

of ninety-one. See Marc Mappen, "Passion in the Parish," *Rutgers Magazine* (Winter 1992), 21.

22. Newark *Star-Ledger,* November 14, 1995.
23. *New York Times,* September 4, 1961. In 1920 Clarence E. Case became acting governor of New Jersey for one week so as to keep patronage in Republican hands until governor-elect Edward I. Edwards, a Democrat, took office. Clarence E. Case was the uncle of Clifford Case, a four-term Republican U.S. Senator who served from 1955 to 1979.
24. *Ibid.,* November 9, 1965.
25. Jane Spangler, "Murder for the Minister," *Central Jersey Monthly* (November 1979), 6
26. *New York Times,* August 5 and 14, 1926.
27. *Ibid.,* February 4, 1952. Charlotte, Eleanor, and James and buried in Van Liew Cemetery, North Brunswick. A handsome marker, paid for by relatives, marks the spot. A woman named Charlotte Mills O'Neill, whose children grew up believing her to be *the* Charlotte Mills, died in Philadelphia in 1985, once again reviving interest in the old case and its absorbing cast of characters. See the New Brunswick *Home News,* March 2. 1986.
28. *New York Times.,* May 27, 1934.
29. *Ibid.,* December 5, 1939.
30. *Ibid.,* September 29, 1926.
31. New Brunswick *Daily Home News,* December 20, 1942.
32. *New York Times,* December 20, 1942.
33. *Ibid.,* October 29, 1922.

Mills' family gravestone in Van Liew Cemetery, North Brunswick. Three names are inscribed on the base of this granite monument: Charlotte E. (1906-1952), James F. (1878-1965), Eleanor R. (1888-1922). (photo 1997)

Stevens' family plot in Green-Wood Cemetery, Brooklyn. This plot contains the bodies of Edward W. Hall, Frances Noel Stevens Hall, and William Carpender Stevens. The slab on the underground vault is not inscribed. (photo 1998)

Bibliography

Abels, Jules. *In the Time of Silent Cal.* New York: G. P. Putnam's Sons, 1969.

Allen, Frederick Lewis. *Only Yesterday.* New York: Harper & Row, 1931.

Barrett, Eleanor. "Jury still out on events in 1922 double murder." Newark *Star-Ledger,* November 9, 1997.

Belford, Barbara. *Brilliant Bylines: A Biographical Anthology of Notable Newspaperwomen in America.* New York: Columbia University Press, 1986.

Bliven, Bruce. "The Hall-Press-Mills Case." *The New Republic,* December 1, 1926.

Boswell, Charles, and Lewis Thompson. *The Girl in Lover's Lane.* Greenwich, Conn.: Gold Medal Books, 1953.

Chalmers, David M. *Hooded Americanism: The History of the Ku Klux Klan.* Chicago: Quadrangle Paperbacks, 1968.

The City of New Brunswick. New Brunswick, N.J.: The New Brunswick Times, 1909.

Coakley, Leo J. "Trial and Error: The Early Years." *Jersey Troopers.* New Brunswick, N.J.: Rutgers University Press, 1971.

Dilworth, Donald C., ed. *Identification Wanted: Development of the American Criminal Identification System, 1893-1943.* Gaithersburg, Md.: International Association of Chiefs of Police, 1977.

Dix, Dorothy (Elizabeth Meriwether Gilmer). "A Nation of Detectives. Reprinted in *Brilliant Bylines,* Barbara Belford. New York: Columbia University Press, 1986.

Hann, Christopher. "A Dangerous Affair." *New Jersey Monthly,* September 1995.

Hartman, Mary S. "The Hall-Mills Murder Case: The Most Fascinating Unsolved Homicide in America." *The Journal of the Rutgers University Libraries,* June 1984.

Heidingsfeld's General Directory of New Brunswick, 1921-1922.

Jaffe, Jonathan. "Unsolved Hall-Mills murder is still drawing attention 70 years later." Newark *Star Ledger,* September 13, 1992.

Judd, Jennifer. "Longstreet knows whodunit: Minister's wife and relatives." New Brunswick *Home News,* April 10, 1986.

Kavanaugh, Reginald. "Classic in Horror Had Bloody Start Half-Century Ago." New Brunswick *Home News,* September 14, 1972.

Kunstler, William M. *The Minister and the Choir Singer.* New York: William Morrow & Co., 1964. Reprinted as *The Hall-Mills Murder Case* by Rutgers University Press (New Brunswick, N.J., 1980).

Legislative Manual, State of New Jersey, 1922. Trenton: Josephine A. Fitzgerald, 1922.

Mappen, Marc. "Passion in the Parish." *Rutgers University Magazine,* Winter, 1992.

Markey, Morris. "The Somerville Follies." *The New Yorker,* November 20, 1926.

New York Times, September 17, 1922 ff; July 29, 1926 ff.

Ruth Renyo. "Hall-Mills Mystery." New York *Sunday News,* September 12, 1954.

Runyon, Damon. "The Hall-Mills Case." *Trials and Other Tribulations.* New York: Dorset Press (originally published in 1946).

Spangler, Jane. "Murder for the Minister." *Central Jersey Monthly,* November 1979.

Stout, Rex. "Was the Murderer in the Jury Box?" *New York Times Book Review,* February 2, 1964.

Thurber, James. "A Sort of Genius." *My World—and Welcome to It.* New York: Harcourt Brace and World, 1942, 1963 (originally published in *The New Yorker*). Reprinted in *Hanging by a Thread,* Joan Kahn, ed. Boston: Houghton Mifflin Company, 1969.

Tomlinson, Gerald. "Under a Crab Apple Tree." *Murdered in Jersey.* New Brunswick, N.J.: Rutgers University Press, 1994, 1997.

"Under the Crab Apple Tree." *Time,* November 15, 1926.

Woollcott, Alexander. "The Hall-Mills Case." *Long, Long Ago.* New York: Viking Press, 1943.

Index

About the Author

Gerald Tomlinson's previous books include *Murdered in Jersey*, a true-crime chronicle of sixty-five highly publicized homicides in the Garden State, *The New Jersey Book of Lists* (with Ronald A. Mayer), and *On a Field of Black* a mystery novel set in the anthracite region of Pennsylvania. For many years Tomlinson's short stories have appeared in *Ellery Queen's Mystery Magazine* and *Alfred Hitchcock's Mystery Magazine.*